Global Poverty

Global Poverty

Deprivation, Distribution, and
Development since the Cold War

Andy Sumner

OXFORD
UNIVERSITY PRESS

OXFORD
UNIVERSITY PRESS

Great Clarendon Street, Oxford, OX2 6DP,
United Kingdom

Oxford University Press is a department of the University of Oxford.
It furthers the University's objective of excellence in research, scholarship,
and education by publishing worldwide. Oxford is a registered trade mark of
Oxford University Press in the UK and in certain other countries

Published in the United States of America by Oxford University Press
198 Madison Avenue, New York, NY 10016, United States of America

British Library Cataloguing in Publication Data
Data available

Library of Congress Control Number: 2015956474

ISBN 978-0-19-870352-5

Printed in Great Britain by
Clays Ltd, St Ives plc

▪ PREFACE

Why are some people poor? Why does absolute poverty persist despite substantial economic growth? What types of late economic development or late capitalism are associated with different poverty outcomes? It is these questions and the extent to which the answers may be changing that motivated this book. The book aims to be an in-depth analysis of the global poverty 'problem' and how it is framed and understood. The book seeks to question existing theories of the causes of global poverty.

The primary thesis of this book is that global poverty is becoming a question of national distribution. One might expect global poverty to be focused in the world's poorest countries, usually defined as low-income countries, or least developed countries, or 'fragile states'. However, most of the world's absolute poor by monetary or multidimensional poverty—up to a billion people—live in growing and largely stable middle-income countries. This is because the world's poor are concentrated in a relatively small number of countries that have experienced substantial economic growth and passed the threshold into middle-income country status. At the same time, poverty has not fallen as much as the substantial economic growth would warrant. As a consequence and as domestic resources have grown, much of global poverty has become less about a lack of domestic resources and more about questions of national inequality, social policy and welfare regimes, and patterns of economic development or types of late capitalism pursued.

This is a recent phenomenon. At the end of the Cold War, absolute poverty in developing countries could be explained by the fact that the world's absolute poor lived in countries where (almost) everyone was poor. The main argument of this book is that, in general, this is no longer the case; although there is still a relatively small set of countries where this holds true, such countries are now dwindling in number and are not home to most of the world's poor.

Looking ahead, it is argued that there is an emerging 'poverty paradox' of catch-up capitalism that is as follows: most developing countries have, or will have in the foreseeable future, the domestic resources to address absolute poverty and yet such poverty may well persist for some considerable time to come. Thus, this book argues that global poverty requires reframing from a question of deprivation or a lack of resources to a question of national distribution. However, thinking on global poverty to date has tended to underemphasize such questions of national inequality and has analysed poverty with little connection to the processes of late economic development under the assumption that the world's poor live in countries with insufficient resources to address poverty. The objective of this book is to revisit such a view and argue that the causes of global poverty are changing and that patterns of growth, economic development, and distribution are of greater significance than a lack of available resources.

The author is a Reader in International Development at King's College, London and Co-Director of King's International Development Institute, King's College, London. The US magazine, *Foreign Policy*, has listed him as one of the 'Top 100 Global Thinkers'.

ACKNOWLEDGEMENTS

I am grateful to those who have co-authored with me and commented and influenced my work on these issues since the publication in September 2010 of the first paper on the subject. With apologies for any omissions, I would like to thank the following people in particular (in alphabetical order): Tony Addison, Sabina Alkire, Owen Barder, Nancy Birdsall, Alex Cobham, Peter Edward, Alex Evans, Andrew Fischer, Ugo Gentilini, Jonathan Glennie, Duncan Green, Lawrence Haddad, Chris Hoy, David Hulme, Richard Jolly, Ravi Kanbur, Charles Kenny, Peter Kingstone, Tom Kirk, Stephan Klasen, Jeni Klugman, Nick Lea, Ben Leo, Jon Lomoy, Rich Mallet, Richard Manning, Simon Maxwell, Terry McKinley, Claire Melamed, Amy Pollard, Jose Roche, David Steven, John Taylor, Sergio Tezanos, Meera Tiwari, Myles Wickstead, and Joe Wong. I would also like to thank for research assistance and their comments the following (again in alphabetical order): Bastian Becker, Artur Borkowski, Henrique Conca Bussacos, Nicki Goh, Rich Mallet, Ricardo Santos, Lukas Schlögl, Dharendra Wardhana, Pui Yan Wong. I would add to the list of thanks, Adam Swallow at OUP and Dee Scholey. Finally, thanks are very much due to my family for their support and encouragement. Any errors and omissions are the responsibility of the author.

This book expands on the following: Chapter 1: Sumner (2010; 2012b); Chapter 2: Sumner and Tiwari (2009); Sumner (2012a; 2012b; 2012c; 2013c); Chapter 3: Sumner (2013d); Chapter 4: Cobham, Schlogl, and Sumner (2015; 2016); Sumner (2016); Chapter 5: Sumner (2012d; 2013a; 2013b); Sumner and Mallet (2012).

▓ CONTENTS

CONTENTS

■ LIST OF FIGURES

■ LIST OF TABLES

◼ LIST OF ABBREVIATIONS

ADB	Asian Development Bank
AfDB	African Development Bank
CAP	Common Agricultural Policy
CDI	Commitment to Development Index
CGD	Center for Global Development
CPIA	Country Policy and Institutional Assessment
CSO	Civil Society Organization
DAC	Development Assistance Committee
DHS	Demographic and Health Survey
DRC	Democratic Republic of Congo
FCAS	fragile and conflict-affected states
FGT	Foster–Greer–Thorbecke
FY	Financial Year
GDP	gross domestic product
GNI	gross national income
GPGs	global public goods
HIC	high-income country
ICP	International Comparison Program
IDA	International Development Association
IMF	International Monetary Fund
LDC	least-developed country
LIC	low-income country
LMIC	lower-middle-income country
MIC	middle-income country
MPI	Multidimensional Poverty Index
MTR	marginal tax rate
NBS	National Bureau of Statistics
ODA	official development assistance
OECD	Organisation for Economic Co-operation and Development
OPHI	Oxford Poverty and Human Development Initiative

PPP	purchasing power parity
PRSP	Poverty Reduction Strategy Paper
UMIC	upper-middle-income country
UNDP	United Nations Development Programme
UNFPA	United Nations Population Fund
UNICEF	United Nations Children's Fund
WEO	World Economic Outlook
WFP	World Food Programme

Introduction

0.1 The global poverty 'problem'

Why are some people poor? Why does poverty persist in spite of rapid economic growth? What types of late economic development or late capitalism are associated with more or less equitable socio-economic outcomes? This book is about the global poverty 'problem' and how it is framed and understood. The book seeks to question existing theories of the causes of global poverty. It is posited that explanations of poverty have tended to underemphasize questions of national distribution under the following two assumptions: much of the population of developing countries is poor and thus distribution is not a relevant variable in explaining absolute poverty in these countries and the world's poor live in countries with insufficient domestic public resources to eliminate absolute poverty. This book challenges these assumptions and in doing so existing theorizing on the causes of absolute poverty is also called into question.

The primary thesis of this book is to argue for a structural theory of global poverty. That is to say that global poverty is becoming a national distribution question. The book builds on a series of papers, a number of which have been written or co-written by the author since 2010, that have discussed the shifting location or 'geography' of global poverty (see for example, Alkire et al., 2011, 2013, 2015; Alonso et al., 2015; Edward and Sumner, 2013a, 2013b, 2014, 2015; Glassman et al., 2013; Glennie, 2011; Kanbur and Sumner, 2012; Sumner, 2010, 2012a, 2012b, 2013a, 2013b; Sumner and Tezanos, 2014; Tezanos and Sumner, 2013). In short, this body of work has posited the following: economic growth since the Cold War has expanded national resources in developing countries, and consequentially the causes of much of global poverty have become less about the lack of resources and more about questions of national inequality, and issues of social policy, patterns of economic growth and economic development and the form of late capitalism pursued.

The book seeks to question orthodox theorizing on global poverty, on the basis that the location or 'geography' of global poverty has 'shifted'. One might expect global poverty to be focused in the world's poorest countries, usually defined as low-income countries or least developed countries or 'fragile states'. However, approximately a billion people, or about 70 per cent of the world's monetary or multidimensional poor, live in middle-income countries (MICs) that may, in principle, already have the resources to eliminate poverty. The shift in global poverty is due to the fact that the world's poor are concentrated in a relatively small number of countries that have experienced substantial economic growth and passed the threshold into MIC status. At the same time, poverty, given the amount of economic growth, has not fallen to the extent one would expect. Thus as domestic resources have grown the causes of much of global poverty has become less about a lack of resources and more about questions of the distribution of expanding domestic resources and opportunities.

The fact that the world's poor now live in one category of country—MICs—could mistakenly be dismissed as simply related to economic growth in India on the basis that about a third of the world's poor live in India and India crossed the line into the MICs category. Of course, there is a framing or threshold effect at work: countries have crossed a line in per capita income and been reclassified as MICs. However, this is a reframing or reclassification of the poverty 'problem', reflecting an underlying change in concrete reality: the poor now live in countries that are substantially better-off countries than a generation ago. The majority of global poverty is now in countries that many foreign aid donors see as sufficiently well off to reduce or end development cooperation in effect divorcing much of global poverty from foreign aid. What this book argues is that the stylized fact that the world's poor live in such countries is—of course—a product of the thresholds *but* that it is also indicative of a shift in the causes of global poverty. Although there is no sudden change in a country (or a person) when a line is crossed in per capita income and a country (or a person) is reclassified, higher levels of average per capita income do imply substantially more resources and potentially more access to private capital markets to expand these resources further (albeit at commercial interest rates) to address and end absolute poverty. This is in contrast to the early 1990s when it was clear that developing countries needed external resources to end absolute poverty because domestic resources were so limited. Now the world's poor live in developing countries that are much better off, so much so that this book argues that much of global poverty could be eliminated by countries themselves with redistribution of public resources away from certain areas, such as regressive fossil-fuel subsidies which now amount to one trillion dollars in current dollars in developing countries.[1]

Regressive fossil-fuel subsidies such as those on petroleum mainly benefit the upper-middle classes and elites and those groups that consume greater amounts of those fuels. Such subsidies are larger in value than the total poverty gap—the cost of ending poverty—in most middle-income developing countries. Absolute poverty is thus no longer a question of poor people in poor

---

[1] Estimate of Clements et al. (2013). The amount is equivalent to almost two trillion dollars in 2011 PPP dollars.

countries. Absolute poverty is in fact a question of the distribution—of domestic public resources, of access to the new opportunities arising from growth and relatedly, of spatial and social inequalities—and development. In other words the context for poverty reduction efforts is now one of poverty reduction amid growth and new wealth rather than, as it was towards to the end of the Cold War, poverty reduction amid stagnation and insufficient domestic resources to address absolute poverty.

The book argues that this shift in the nature of global poverty has generated an emerging 'poverty paradox' as follows: most developing countries have (or will have in the foreseeable future) the domestic resources to address absolute poverty at a national level and yet projections suggest such poverty may well persist for some time. This is for two reasons: first, even moderate economic growth is insufficient to end absolute poverty in the foreseeable future due to the prevailing level and trends in inequality and second, fully escaping poverty could potentially take the current poor over one hundred years if left to growth alone for the same reason. The emergence of this poverty paradox of catch-up capitalism comes after a period of incredible economic expansion. The period of history since the Cold War has been one where $50 trillion in new GDP and $15 trillion in new consumption (taking survey data) has been created by economic growth, and as a result, the size of the global economy has doubled.[2]

Given the world's poor now largely live in growing middle-income developing countries, it might be posited that surely there is little need to worry about poverty because economic growth or the election of progressive governments will end poverty in the near future? The poor in MICs are likely to be relatively disconnected from a country's growth due to spatial inequality, meaning in particular the geographical distance from the economic growth poles. Social inequality is likely to mediate poverty too in fast growing MICs. The poor in MICs may be discriminated against in public services and public-spending allocations and where social and geographical inequality interact this marginalization is compounded. The MIC poor are also likely be relatively voiceless in domestic governance structures, and within-country migration may be hindered or constrained by cost and/or administrative regulations related for example to entitlements to public education or health services. All of which is consistent with estimates made in this book that the proportion of the global poverty in MICs could remain high for some years to come because although economic growth can reduce poverty, growth alone in MICs is unlikely to eradicate poverty in the foreseeable future given prevailing patterns of inequality.

The persistence of absolute poverty in better off and fast-growing developing countries points towards the fact that contemporary poverty is the

---

[2] See for discussion Edward and Sumner (2015). Unless explicitly stated all data in this book are in 2011 PPP dollars. Unless explicitly stated data is processed from World Bank (2015).

outcome of specific patterns of growth and distribution. Not only does this provide an imperative to consider redistribution policies in terms of spatial and social inequality in particular, it also re-shapes how development cooperation and aid should be pursued. Most of the world's poor live in countries where traditional aid is becoming irrelevant as domestic resources grow and access to private capital markets is gained. This book thus also argues for a new model of development cooperation. Over time, emerging MICs may not need or want development cooperation of the traditional sort (meaning resource transfers). Instead, they will likely be more concerned with genuine development-related policies such as designing favourable and coherent policies on international trade to sustain growth or technical advice on tax systems to minimise illicit and untaxed capital outflows and ensure tax revenue collection in developing countries. Nonetheless, it is possible that aid to a small number of low-income countries or least-developed countries (LDCs) will still be about old-fashioned resource transfers, especially in some of the poorest fragile and conflict/post-conflict countries (although some fragile and conflict/post-conflict countries are experiencing rapid growth too). This will, though, represent a small minority of developing countries. In addition to 'policy coherence' in external policies from the advanced or industrial countries, donors from such countries may have a role to play in MICs in the co-financing of domestic infrastructure with high upfront costs to link sub-national and social groups to growth poles. This role may extend to co-financing regional and global public goods whose benefits go beyond borders of individual countries (such as vaccination programmes). Or providing technical assistance in, for example, the negotiation of legal contracts with international companies for natural resources that extract greater benefits to the country itself. In sum, development cooperation will need to adapt to the new 'geography' of poverty outlined and to the changing developing world.

0.2 **The literature on global poverty and the structure of this book**

The intended intellectual contribution of the book is to assess the extent to which the observed shift in global poverty away from the poorest countries towards the MICs represents a substantive change and what the implications are for theories of poverty.[3]

---

[3] A caveat not to forget is that the severity of poverty is typically higher in the world's very poorest countries though this is not always the case.

There are, of course, numerous contemporary books and articles on global poverty and its various aspects. One could note the literature on the meaning and measurement of poverty or that on theories of poverty from various traditions or that on development cooperation and poverty (e.g. to name but a few: Alkire et al., 2015; Anand et al., 2010; Banerjee and Duflo, 2012; Hulme, 2015; Mavrotas, 2010; Sen, 1999; Stewart et al., 2007). However, none of these deal with the changing patterns of global poverty with regard to emerging MICs because the history is relatively recent. In this sense, this book's focus is a new area of exploration. Much writing on global poverty has been, not surprisingly, focused on the world's very poorest countries or 'bottom billion' countries (meaning here the total population of those poorest countries) (e.g. Collier, 2007, 2009). Additionally, most scholarly writing on the emerging economies is focused on their impact on the global economy or economic growth in emerging economies (e.g. Dadush and Shaw, 2011). Further, the focus has been on the small group of emerging economies known as the BRICS countries in particular—Brazil, Russia, India, China, and South Africa—or other similar small groups of emerging economies (see Beausang, 2012 or de Mello, 2010) rather than the group of emerging MICs beyond the BRICS. The BRICS as new donors have garnered much interest (e.g. Mawdsley, 2012) though poverty in MICs, with a few exceptions (e.g. Alonso, 2007; Sumner and Mallet, 2012), has received less attention.

The discussion of this book seeks to remedy this situation and is framed by a set of questions about deprivation, distribution, and development and their changing nature since the end of the Cold War: What is poverty? Who are the poor? Where do the poor live? Is global poverty really concentrated in countries that have the domestic resources available to end poverty? Is insufficient economic growth the main cause of poverty or the distribution of resources and opportunities generated by that substantial growth? Is the persistence of poverty an outcome of specific patterns of growth and distribution?

The book is structured as follows: Chapters 1 and 2 discuss global poverty and economic growth since the Cold War with an emphasis on the empirical side of matters relating to contemporary patterns of development and absolute poverty. Chapter 3, 4, and 5 then have a stronger emphasis on the theoretical side albeit with an empirical basis wherever possible and consider the implications for thinking about the relationship between poverty, inequality, and late economic development. The book expands the discussion from one of absolute poverty to include the burgeoning insecure or 'precariat' group (a label drawn from Standing, 2011), which is the substantial proportion of the population living above absolute poverty but at risk of falling back into poverty during economic slowdowns or other stressors or shocks such as ill-health. The precariat is what the absolute poor will become in the future if they escape absolute poverty. As the absolute poor move into this insecure group poverty is potentially perpetuated in a different way, which is likely to lead to slower growth and slower governance reform in a self-reinforcing mechanism or a new kind of poverty trap for MICs. In short, the cost of rising inequality during late economic development is the delayed elimination of absolute poverty and the delayed emergence of a consuming class. This book outlines such a theory as its culmination.

The starting point for this book is the end of the Cold War and the contemporary era of globalization or catch-up capitalism meaning aspirations for the convergence of developing countries with the industrial or advanced nations of the OECD. The era is one that has been fundamentally shaped by a resurgence of economic liberalization even in state-led models of development. In short, rather than there being no alternative to capitalism, what has happened is that the forms or varieties of capitalism or what could be called growth regimes have taken different forms, and with regard to poverty the case is the same as differentiated welfare regimes across the developing world have emerged. In light of this, the point of departure in Chapter 1, is titled 'Catch-up Capitalism'. This chapter asks the question: How has the developing world changed since 1990? The chapter discusses the emergence of new MICs. In such countries, attainment of higher per capita incomes sits uncomfortably with structural economics characteristics that are still a considerable distance from those of advanced or OECD countries. Chapter 2, 'The Geography of Poverty' then asks the question: How has global poverty changed since 1990? The chapter is concerned with the shifting pattern of global poverty or the new 'geography' or location of poverty. In short, where do the poor live? The chapter discusses data related to changes in the distribution of global poverty towards MICs.

The emphasis of the book then, as noted above, shifts focus towards more theoretical discussions as far as is possible with an empirical basis. Chapter 3, 'Kuznets' Revenge', focuses on the relationship between poverty, inequality, economic growth, and structural change. Economic growth and economic development can be accompanied by rising inequality where the distribution of benefits are skewed away from the poorest, especially so if the poor remain in marginalized provinces or marginalized social groups. In the countries where the world's poor are concentrated, growth has been accompanied by structural change and rising inequality. Such rises in national inequality are counter to in orthodox economic theory regarding comparative advantage. Indeed, it has been thought that economic liberalization would lead to falling national inequality (see for discussion, Maskin, 2015). The rise in inequality in new MICs is of yet more significance as the Kuznets hypothesis that inequality rises during development has been largely dismissed in recent years.

Chapter 4, 'The Poverty Paradox', builds on the above and poses the central question of the book: Why are some people still poor (in spite of substantial growth)? The chapter seeks to revisits thinking on the causes of global poverty, and notes how many existing theories of absolute poverty are unsatisfactory: the poor are poor because they do not have something, whether that is assets or appropriate values that they need to be non-poor. In doing so the chapter seeks to reconnect poverty analysis with the broader processes of late economic development. Finally, Chapter 5, 'Slowdown Capitalism', looks ahead and asks: Is there a new middle-income poverty trap? The chapter presents theory on this 'trap', drawing on the discussions of preceding chapters. This middle-income poverty trap, it is argued, may form the basis for continued development cooperation with MICs. In short, rapid economic development may be accompanied by persistently high and/or rising inequality and this has the potential to hamper future growth, governance, and poverty reduction. The trap is that countries can get 'stuck' in middle-income as rising inequality slows the expansion of a genuinely secure consuming class and this in turn slows growth, political change, and poverty reduction. The trap is, though, neither inevitable nor unavoidable. If spatial and social inequalities are attended to, and sub-national geographies and marginalized social groups are better connected to growth poles, and the emerging 'middle' groups in society made more secure, then countries may circumnavigate the trap. Finally, a short 'Conclusions' chapter summarizes the key arguments that the book makes.

The intention of this book is to trigger discussion on global poverty in terms of the framing of the global poverty 'problem'. One perspective on the data is that global poverty is—or at least in the foreseeable future will be—turning into a national distribution question; and that the form of catch-up capitalism pursued—is becoming more important than 'traditional' aid or resource transfers. In short, global poverty is turning from a question of poor people in absolute poor countries to poor people in countries that, in principle, may have the resources to eliminate absolute poverty now or in the near future. Thus, the causes of poverty are no longer simply about a lack of resources and opportunities but about the distribution of those resources and opportunities during the process of late economic development.

1 Catch-up capitalism

How has the developing world changed since the end of the Cold War?

1.1 Introduction

The argument of this chapter is threefold: first, that there has been a substantial amount of economic growth in the pursuit of catch-up capitalism in developing countries since the end of the Cold War leading to a large number of countries crossing the per capita income line into the category of middle-income country (MIC) though the actual catch-up in purchasing power parity terms with advanced nations has been limited to relatively few developing countries. Second, that in spite of that growth, economic development—meaning structural change away from an agrarian economy—is also only evident in a relatively small number of those developing countries who attained middle-income status in the last generation. Third, although many new MICs have not experienced more significant structural change, in average terms, MICs are much better off than those countries left behind, the remaining low-income countries (LICs). At the same time MICs are still a considerable distance away from the structural characteristics of advanced or OECD countries. In short, MICs are (as the label implies), in between the world's poorest countries and advanced countries. MICs may no longer be absolutely poor countries by various development indicators but may still be relatively poor countries compared to OECD countries.

The chapter is structured as follows: Section 1.2 asks how the developing world has changed overall since the Cold War. Section 1.3 then outlines the emergence of a greater number of MICs within this context. Section 1.4 then explores what being a MIC means. Section 1.5 concludes.

1.2 The developing world since 1990

As a result of considerable growth in income per capita there has been an increase in the number of MICs in the twenty-five years since the end of the

Cold War and the last decade in particular.[1] Whether such growth illustrates a major change in the developing world since the end of the Cold War is a question worth posing. Certainly, such changes represent substantial rises in average income per capita. However, the changes in the developing world are, in some ways, far smaller than one might expect given the amount of economic growth. There are relatively few new MICs with clear evidence of structural change for example, suggesting that for some new MICs average income growth has been, at least to a considerable extent, commodity-led growth. This has implications: the future sustainability of that growth is vulnerable to global commodity prices. Even where there is evidence of some structural change, commodities, notably fuel exports have played a major role in growth.

Figures 1.1 to 1.5 give an overview of changes in the developing world since the Cold War. Countries are plotted in ascending order and on a linear scale. Where appropriate, the data is presented henceforth in GDP PPP per capita with LICs, LMICs, and UMICs shaded differently rather than by GNI Atlas per capita (that is the basis of the income classification of countries).[2] The five populous new MICs of China, India, Indonesia, Nigeria, and Pakistan are identified because much of global poverty is in these countries (see discussion in Chapter 2).

Collectively, the data show changes in some ways but little change in other ways.[3] First, economic growth: Figure 1.1 shows GDP PPP per capita (constant 2011 PPP$), 1990–5 versus 2010–12. The overall shift of the curve of countries upwards from the 1990–5 data (shown in circles for LICs, LMICs, and UMICs) to the 2010–12 data (shown in diamonds for LICs, LMICs, and UMICs) is pronounced and widespread. At the lower end, there are a relatively small set of countries stuck at the bottom—with low and barely growing GDP PPP per capita—but overall the curve of developing countries has shifted upward. Mean GDP PPP per capita in 1990 across all developing countries

---

[1] Such countries are currently defined by the World Bank as countries with GNI Atlas per capita (an exchange rate conversion) as follows: Lower Middle Income Countries (LMICs) are those with GNI Atlas per capita of approximately $1,000 to $4,000 and Upper Middle Income Countries (UMICs) are those with GNI per capita of approximately $4,000 to $12,500 per capita (see later discussion for further details).

[2] This is for three reasons: First, because GNI (Atlas) per capita is largely based on exchange rate conversion and PPP comparisons are superior for comparing countries (although not without contention—see Chapter 2) especially so over time. Second, a number of developing countries do not have GNI PPP per capita data for the early 1990s to make a comparison but all have GDP PPP per capita data. Third, GDP is used in preference to GNI because it is a measure of production and further GDP is used in preference to GNI as it is—arguably—more reliable for cross-country comparisons given that the difference between GDP and GNI is that the latter adjusts GDP for factor incomes earned by foreign residents minus factor incomes earned by non-residents and the inclusion of this cross-border aspect means the comparability of GNI across countries is subject to a number of contentions. Of course there are various questions about GDP and any national account measures too (see for discussion Jerven, 2013).

[3] Unless stated all data are processed from World Bank (2015) and are in 2011 PPP.

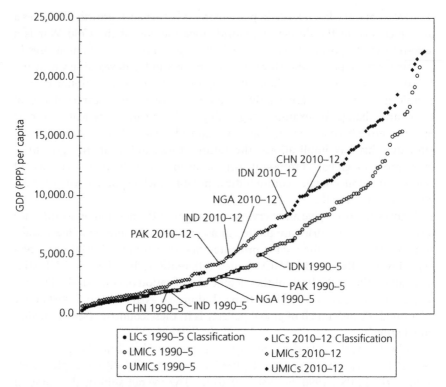

Figure 1.1 All developing countries (ascending order): GDP PPP per capita (2011 PPP), 1990–5 versus 2010–12

Source: Data processed from World Bank (2015).

was approximately $3,500. In 2012 it just under $8,000. Mean GDP PPP per capita for all countries (developing and advanced nations) was $9,000 in 1990 and just under $14,000 in 2012.

In contrast to Figure 1.1, Figure 1.2 shows convergence or catch-up with the richer nations, the OECD countries, in terms of GDP PPP per capita where OECD GDP PPP per capita is set at 100.0 in both 1990–5 and 2010–12. Figure 1.2 shows there has actually been little shift in this curve of developing countries overall, despite the increase in GDP PPP per capita evident in Figure 1.1. That said, there are some developing countries that have achieved some catch-up in GDP PPP per capita with OECD nations.[4] However, overall, the developing world is not that much closer to the OECD GDP PPP per capita but specific countries have moved closer and up

---

[4] There could be a 'dynamic Penn effect' whereby economic growth comes with higher prices (see Ravallion, 2010b).

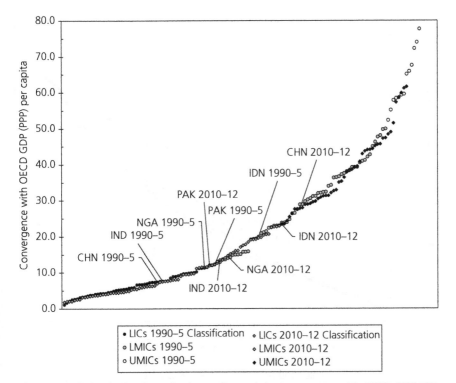

Figure 1.2 All developing countries (ascending order): convergence with OECD GDP PPP per capita (2011 PPP), 1990–5 and 2010–12 (OECD = 100.0)

Source: Data processed from World Bank (2015).

the chain of developing countries. China, as is well known, has experienced a large jump up the chain of developing countries. India's movement is significant too. Other very populous new MICs, such as Indonesia and Nigeria have moved up the chain of developing countries but much less so than China and India. Pakistan has moved down the chain. For comparison the mean for developing countries has moved slightly from 18.4 per cent of OECD in 1990–5 to 20.2 per cent of OECD in 2010–12.

Second, structural characteristics: although there has been substantial economic growth in average per capita incomes in the developing world, there has been far less structural change away from agriculture overall since the end of the Cold War but substantial urbanization is evident as is a decline in aid dependency: Figures 1.3 and 1.4 and 1.5 respectively show agriculture as a proportion of output, urbanization, and aid dependency. It is worth viewing these figures together because they illustrate some differences: Figure 1.3 shows relatively little shift in the developing world overall in

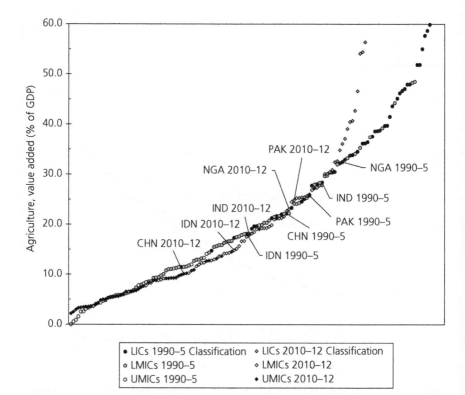

Figure 1.3 All developing countries (ascending order): agriculture, value added (as % of GDP), 1990–5 versus 2010–12

Source: Data processed from World Bank (2015).

terms of movement away from the proportion of agriculture in GDP. The five populous MICs have all moved down the chain of countries as agriculture as a proportion of GDP has fallen, although Pakistan's shift is small.[5] Figure 1.4 shows a major shift in the developing world in terms of urbanization, meaning the proportion of the population living in urban areas, clear in the shift of the curve overall for developing countries. Three of the five populous new MICs have experienced notable urbanization. The urbanization of India and Pakistan since 1990 is less pronounced. Urbanization without structural change away from GDP in agriculture sit uneasily together as one would expect a shift away from agriculture as a proportion of GDP (in short, economic development) to be associated with urbanization in general (see discussion of Chapter 4). Figure 1.5 shows the developing world by aid dependency (ODA/GNI) in 1990–5 versus

---

[5] Unfortunately, the data set on labour force in agriculture is too limited for LICs, meaning insufficient plots to consider the change across all developing countries.

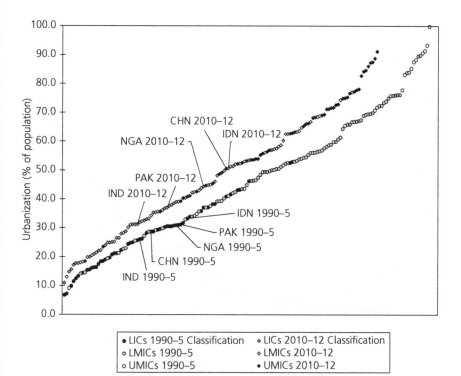

Figure 1.4 All developing countries (ascending order): urbanization (% population), 1990–5 versus 2010–12

Source: Data processed from World Bank (2015).

2010–12. One measure of whether a country is 'poor' is the extent to which it is absolutely or relatively dependent on foreign aid, measured as net ODA/GNI at above 9 per cent, taking the traditional donors' definition from OECD-DAC (2003).[6] There has been a tangible shift of the curve overall showing an overall decline in aid dependency. In this instance, the five big new MICs noted were already relatively low in aid dependency in the early 1990s and since then have moved down the chain of countries to a very low ratio of ODA-to-GNI. In the early 1990s, about a third of developing countries had ODA-to-GNI ratio below 3 per cent, about a third of developing countries had a ratio above 9 per cent and the remaining countries were in between. Looking at the 2010–12 data, what is evident is the decline of the number of highly aid-dependent

---

[6] The thresholds for medium and high aid dependency at 3 per cent and 9 per cent ODA-to-GNI ratio are drawn from the OECD-DAC (2003). In reality, such thresholds are more complex: the best indicator of aid dependency would be official development assistance (ODA)/final absorption, where final absorption equals household consumption plus investment spending plus government consumption, which shows the share of total spending on final goods and services effectively 'financed' by ODA. However, the readily available data is ODA/GNI.

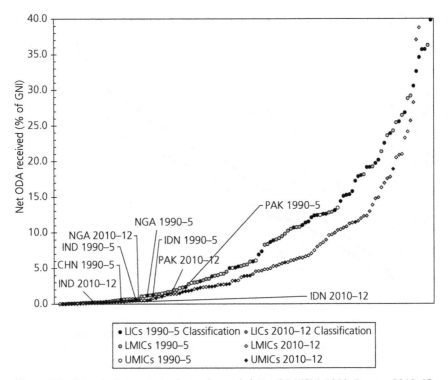

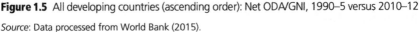

Figure 1.5 All developing countries (ascending order): Net ODA/GNI, 1990–5 versus 2010–12

Source: Data processed from World Bank (2015).

countries taking the OECD-DAC thresholds. In fact, half of all developing countries are below the 3 per cent ODA-to-GNI threshold and only about twenty-five countries and a set of islands are above the 9 per cent threshold. In short, the number of highly aid-dependent countries has virtually halved.

Taken together, these figures show that there has been a drastic increase in GDP PPP per capita and an accompanying decline in aid dependency in the developing world overall. This is evident in the shifts in the curve of plots. However, convergence with OECD countries in GDP PPP per person and a structural shift away from agriculture as a proportion of output is much less evident across the developing world since 1990 although some countries have moved along the chain of developing countries.

In section 1.3 we focus on those developing countries which have experienced rapid economic growth in average incomes, and where income per capita has risen sufficiently to cross the income threshold, taking the country from low- to middle-income country status. Thirty-six such countries have crossed the threshold since the end of the Cold War.

1.3 **The expanding middle in the developing world**

Since 1990, and since 2000 in particular there has been a decline in the number of countries classified as LICs as countries have grown into MICs. Table 1.1 shows the number of countries in each group and threshold ceilings for the groups since the Cold War. The three thresholds that separate low-income, lower-middle-income, upper-middle-income, and high-income countries were, respectively, approximately $1,000, $4,000, and $12,500 GNI per capita in the 2010–13 period. In the early to mid 1990s, after the end of the Cold War, the number of LICs increased, partly due to the break-up of the Soviet bloc to just over sixty countries. By 2013, that had fallen to closer to thirty remaining LICs with a total population of about 850 million people. In short, almost a 'bottom billion' in total population (drawing upon the label of Collier, 2007). The most populous remaining LICs are Bangladesh (with a population in 2013 of 160 million), Ethiopia (95 million), the Democratic Republic of Congo (70 million), Myanmar (55 million), Tanzania (50 million), Kenya (45 million), and Uganda (40 million). However, Kenya will be classified as a new MIC due to a statistical revision—an updating—of its national accounts, and Bangladesh and Myanmar will also 'graduate' to MIC status as their income per capita is close to the threshold.

Once these three countries leave the LIC group that collection of countries will be home to just 600 million people, which will be split between the remaining four populous LICs above and a set of small or very small countries (meaning respectively less than ten million people or less than one million people).

The extent to which MICs reflect the broad characteristics of advanced or developed countries, typically identified as OECD countries is an important issue. In the following, it is argued that, at least in general terms, although

Table 1.1 Number of countries classified as LIC, LMIC, and UMIC and thresholds used (upper ceiling), 1990–2013

Year	1992	1997	2002	2007	2012	2015
Year of data	1990	1995	2000	2005	2010	2013
Number of countries						
LICs	51	62	62	54	35	34
LMICs	56	64	54	58	56	50
UMICs	33	29	38	40	51	55
Thresholds (upper ceiling)						
LIC	610	765	755	875	1,005	1,045
LMIC	2,465	3,035	2,995	3,465	3,975	4,125
UMIC	7,620	9,385	9,265	10,725	12,275	12,745

Note: Data include countries which are no longer in existence; data also include countries whose status is politically contested; data are based on classifications two years after GNI per capita (e.g. 2013 data = 2015 classification).
Source: World Bank (2015).

MICs are really quite different from the world's very poorest countries, at the same time, MICs are also a considerable distance from the structural characteristics of OECD countries.

A useful point of departure is to revisit Seers' characterization of developing and developed countries. In a seminal paper, Dudley Seers (1963) argued that developed countries look different. One might even say that developed countries represent a 'special case' as Seers (1963) did in his discussion of the characteristics of developed nations, and their divergence from the characteristics of developing countries.[7] The developed or industrialized nations, he argued, represented 'a few countries with highly unusual, not to say peculiar, characteristics' (p. 80). This is in contrast to developing countries, for whom:

The typical case is a largely unindustrialised economy, the foreign trade of which consists essentially in selling primary products for manufactures. There are about 100 identifiable economies of this sort, covering the great majority of the world's population. (p. 80)

This was written fifty years ago. Since then there has been industrialization and manufacturing export-led growth notably across East and Southeast Asia though the causes and consequences remain contentious (see for discussion, Wade, 1990; World Bank, 1993). The characteristic set out by Seers as the 'special case' does, though, represent an important set of features as to what defines an advanced economy. Seers (1963, pp. 81–3) identified the following list to demonstrate how one might differentiate developed nations from developing nations: by sectors of the economy (e.g. manufacturing much larger than either agriculture or mining), by public finance (e.g. reliance on direct taxes), by household consumption (e.g. very few people below subsistence level and a moderately equal distribution of income), by savings and investment (e.g. well-developed financial intermediaries), and by 'dynamic influences' (e.g. slow population growth and high urbanization). Drawing upon the thinking of Seers one could conceptualize contemporary developing and developed countries in various ways. In absolute terms, one might conceptualize 'poor' countries in terms of absolute poverty, relative poverty, or a non-poor country by mean (or median) income/consumption compared to an international (PPP) poverty line.[8] An alternative would be in terms of the overall 'burden' of absolute poverty, meaning the total poverty gap as a percentage of GDP, or by structural indicators as per Seers, such as the proportion of agriculture in economic output, employment, or exports. In relative terms, one could think of 'poor' countries relative to other countries,

---

[7] Seers (1972) was also influential in the critique of income or output per capita as a measure of development which is of relevance to the debate of this book.

[8] Strictly speaking one would want to compare like with like (meaning average per capita consumption and a consumption poverty line).

be that relative to the OECD countries or to the poorest countries such as the LICs or the UN classification of least-developed countries (LDCs) or the classification of fragile and conflict-affected states (FCAS) (see later discussion on these classifications).[9] For example, by per capita income relative to per capita income in the OECD countries or low-income, least-developed, or fragile states; or by overall levels of absolute poverty (proportion of the population) compared to the OECD countries or low-income, least-developed, or fragile states; or by various structural indicators (e.g. aid dependency, the proportion of GDP in agriculture, exports, or employment), again relative to the OECD countries or low-income, least-developed, or fragile states.

Taking such characteristics as those outlined it is clear in the data that MICs are—on average at least—much better off than the world's poorest countries defined as low-income, least-developed, or fragile states group averages (see Figure 1.6). The LDCs and FCAS in general have indicators comparable to LICs with the exception of GDP PPP per capita and the significance of fuel exports.[10] This is not surprising given the overlap between the low-income, least-developed or fragile-state country groups (see later discussion).

In section 1.4 we consider heterogeneity among MICs themselves beyond simply the difference between LMICs and UMICs. For the moment, if the income categories are considered by group averages, average (mean) GDP PPP per capita for the LIC group of countries is $1,500 per year (or about $4/day per person) but for LMICs it is almost $5,000 (approximately $15/day) and $13,000 (approximately $35/day) for UMICs.

In terms of economic development indicators there are some very large differences, even when large countries such as India and China are removed from LMICs and UMICs mean aggregates respectively. For example, take agriculture value-added as a proportion of GDP, and agricultural raw materials, ores, and metals as a proportion of merchandise exports: the data for LICs are, respectively, 33 per cent and 28 per cent, while for LMICs the corresponding data is 17 per cent and 14 per cent, and for UMICs the corresponding data are much lower at 8 per cent and 9 per cent. Furthermore, LICs have much lower levels of urbanization on average (31 per cent versus 45 per cent in LMICs and 63 per cent in UMICs) while average aid levels are much higher (14 per cent in LICs compared to 8 per cent in LMICs and 4 per cent in UMICs).

---

[9] The label used by the World Bank for this list is Fragile and Conflict-Affected Situations. In the text reference is made to fragile states as the commonly used label.

[10] Of course, all aggregate groups are sensitive to outliers. In the case of GDP PPP per capita for example, the LDC outlier is Equatorial Guinea which is a high-income country and for FCAS, there are several outliers, specifically, Bosnia and Herzegovina, Iraq, Kosovo, and Libya.

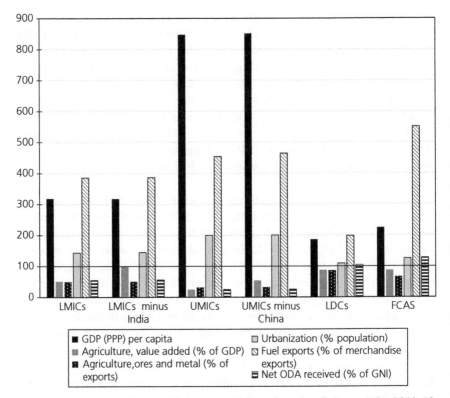

Figure 1.6 Structural indicators of country groupings (mean), relative to LICs, 2010–12 (LICs = 100.0)

Note: Insufficient data coverage for employment in agriculture (% of total employment) in LICs, LDCs, and FCAS.
Source: Data processed from World Bank (2015).

MICs are still, though, some considerable distance from OECD countries. Figure 1.7 shows data for aggregate country groups relative to OECD countries in 2010–12. Although much better off than LICs, LDCs, and FCAS on average, MICs do not compare well with the OECD countries' mean. For example, GDP PPP per capita in LMICs and UMICs is respectively just 14 per cent and 36 per cent of the OECD mean. The data for economic development by agriculture value-added as a proportion of GDP, employment, and exports show too that LMICs and UMICs have a considerable distance to go to reach advanced nations' averages. Agriculture value-added as a proportion of GDP and employment in LMICs are, respectively, 670 per cent and 600 per cent of the OECD mean and even for UMICs are 300 per cent and 300 per cent respectively of the OECD mean. Urbanization levels are closer, respectively about 60 per cent and 80 per cent of the OECD mean for the LMIC and UMIC groups. Interestingly, the proportion of exports in agriculture, ores, and metals

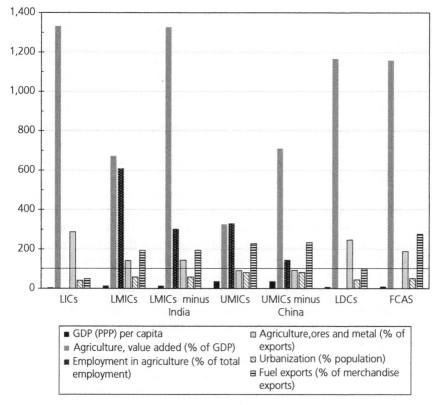

Figure 1.7 Structural indicators of country groupings (mean), relative to OECD, 2010–12 (OECD = 100.0)

Note: Insufficient data coverage for employment in agriculture (% of total employment) in LICs, LDCs, and FCAS thus no data is presented for these indicators in the figure.
Source: Data processed from World Bank (2015).

in MICs is closer to the OECD mean suggesting some convergence. That said, fuel exports are about 200 per cent of the OECD mean in both the LMIC and UMIC groups, suggesting that MICs may be less reliant on agriculture and mining for exports, although fuel exports remain important.

In sum, MICs are substantially better off than low-income or least-developed countries or fragile states when one considers group averages. At the same time, MICs are a considerable distance from OECD countries in terms of structural characteristics. Of course, within all these aggregate data is considerable variance between countries within each group. Thus one needs to consider the 'new' or emerging MICs that have become MICs since the end of the Cold War in greater detail.

The new MIC set of countries is heterogeneous. The group of thirty-six new MICs includes former Soviet or former Communist countries such as

Ukraine and Albania and a number of small-island developing states such as the Maldives and the Solomon Islands and a set of other countries with populations of less than a million such as Bhutan and Guyana. If one removes former Soviet and Communist economies and small islands and countries the list of countries attaining middle-income status since 1990 falls to just twenty countries. One could argue that former command economies of the USSR and Eastern Europe are a special group themselves. Indeed, many of these countries are re-emerging, meaning that they were MICs then dropped back to LICs after the end of the Cold War due to the economic collapse and then in time grew again.[11] Many of these countries also have an industrial base to some degree. Further, one could also argue that small-island states or countries with small populations are a special group. Small-island developing countries have their own UN grouping in part due to a recognition of the shared concerns such as the typically volatile nature of small economies.[12]

The twenty new MICs remaining of the original thirty-six countries are listed in Table 1.2 together with various economic development indicators as follows: GDP PPP per capita and convergence with OECD GDP PPP per capita, as well as structural change indicators of agriculture as a proportion of GDP, and urbanization as a proportion of population.[13] Some of these twenty new MICs have attained economic growth with structural change away from agriculture. Other new MICs have not. Indeed, a number of issues arise in the data. First, there are some pseudo MICs: some of the new MICs are actually not much better off in GDP PPP per capita terms now than in the early 1990s (e.g. Cameroon, Senegal, Zambia, and Yemen are only slightly better off, and Côte d'Ivoire is actually worse off in GDP PPP per capita than in 1990–5). Most of these countries have not experienced substantial economic development, which would suggest growth has been commodity-price-driven and is, in part, due to exchange rate movements, given the basis of GNI Atlas per capita in exchange rate conversion. If we remove from the set of twenty countries those countries not substantially better off in GDP PPP per capita terms we lose six countries.[14] Then if we remove countries with a population of less than ten million (Laos, Lesotho, Mongolia, and Nicaragua) on the basis

---

[11] In the group of thirty-six new MICs there are eight former Soviet or former Communist countries (Albania, Armenia, Azerbaijan, Georgia, Kyrgyz Republic, Moldova, Ukraine, Uzbekistan).

[12] In the group of thirty-six new MICs there are seven countries that are small-island developing states (Maldives, São Tomé and Príncipe, and Solomon Islands) or populations of less than one million people (Equatorial Guinea, Bhutan, Guyana, and Mauritania).

[13] GNI PPP per capita is not used for the reasons previously outlined. In the set of countries listed the differences between the GNI PPP per capita and GDP PPP per capita are relatively minimal in general although the Republic of Congo is one exception to this. In all the countries listed here GNI PPP per capita follows the pattern noted in GDP PPP per capita: that the 'genuine' MICs have experienced substantial increases in GDP PPP per capita and GNI PPP per capita and the pseudo MICs have not.

[14] These countries are: Cameroon, Republic of Congo, Côte d'Ivoire, Senegal, Yemen, and Zambia.

Table 1.2 Selected new MICs, 1990–5 versus 2010–12

	Changes in output per capita				Structural change			
	GDP per capita PPP (constant 2011 international $)		Convergence with OECD GDP PPP per capita (OECD = 100.0)		Agriculture value-added (% of GDP)		Urbanization (% of population)	
	1990–5	2010–12	1990–5	2010–12	1990–5	2010–12	1990–5	2010–12
Genuine new MICs								
Angola	3,355.8	7,124.6	12.9	19.8	15.9	8.8	27.2	40.9
China	1,905.0	10,009.2	7.3	27.8	21.8	9.6	28.7	50.6
Ghana	1,970.3	3,392.9	7.6	9.4	43.6	26.8	38.3	51.4
India	1,913.9	4,857.1	7.4	13.5	28.4	18.2	26.1	31.3
Indonesia	5,005.3	8,439.8	19.3	23.4	18.1	13.9	33.3	50.7
Nigeria	2,895.9	5,275.7	11.1	14.6	32.5	22.7	30.9	44.4
Pakistan	3,124.7	4,281.2	12.1	11.9	25.8	25.0	31.2	37.0
Sri Lanka	3,682.0	8,179.7	14.2	22.7	25.1	12.0	18.5	18.3
Sudan	1,981.8	3,465.3	7.6	9.6	39.7	26.3	31.0	33.2
Vietnam	1,739.4	4,705.2	6.7	13.1	32.9	19.5	21.2	31.0
Pseudo new MICs								
Cameroon	2,298.4	2,506.2	8.9	7.0	24.1	23.4	41.1	52.1
Congo, Rep.	5,032.6	5,577.7	19.4	15.5	11.3	3.6	55.4	63.7
Côte d'Ivoire	2,887.2	2,689.0	11.1	7.5	29.7	26.9	40.3	51.3
Senegal	1,800.3	2,172.8	6.9	6.0	19.9	16.7	39.3	42.5
Yemen	3,546.7	4,020.0	13.7	11.2	23.3	10.1	22.3	32.3
Zambia	2,362.4	2,882.7	9.1	8.0	21.6	19.9	38.3	39.2
Small new MICs (1–10 million population)								
Lao PDR	1,737.2	4,140.7	6.7	11.5	58.7	30.1	16.3	34.2
Lesotho	1,400.2	2,295.8	5.4	6.4	19.1	8.9	15.4	25.3
Mongolia	3,652.9	7,422.5	14.1	20.6	24.1	15.7	56.9	68.5
Nicaragua	2,915.1	4,163.5	11.2	11.6	21.2	19.3	52.9	57.5

Source: Data processed from World Bank (2015).

that these countries do not make a significant difference to global poverty, which is the primary discussion of this book, this leaves a set of ten new MICs on which to base discussions. This set of ten 'genuine' new MICs have all experienced substantial GDP PPP per capita growth and have populations of over ten million people.[15] That set of ten new MICs includes three countries from East Asia (China, Indonesia, Vietnam), three from South Asia (India, Pakistan, and Sri Lanka) and, perhaps surprisingly, four from Africa (Ghana, Sudan, Angola, Nigeria).[16] It is this set of new MIC countries that are home to most of the world's absolute poor.

[15] Even within this set of 'genuine' new MICs some have achieved MIC status previously then fallen back to LIC and then attained MIC status again (for example, Indonesia).

[16] There is some overlap which the *Commission on Growth and Development* identified, taking a longer perspective of change:

Since 1950, 13 economies have grown at an average rate of 7 percent a year or more for 25 years or longer. At that pace of expansion, an economy almost doubles in size every decade.... Thirteen economies qualify: Botswana; Brazil; China; Hong Kong, China; Indonesia; Japan; the Republic of

In these ten more populous new MICs, there are many unequivocal and dramatic increases in GDP PPP per capita and some catch-up or convergence with the OECD countries. For example, as is well known, China, Vietnam, India, and Indonesia have experienced drastic increases in GDP PPP per capita and notable convergence with OECD GDP PPP per capita. Surprisingly perhaps, there have been substantial increases in output per capita in a set of countries that one might not consider to be 'emerging economies' at least not in the high profile BRICS sense; that is, Angola, Ghana, Sri Lanka, and Sudan who have experienced large increases in GDP per capita in PPP terms. The remaining countries, Nigeria and Pakistan, have increased GDP PPP per capita also by substantial amounts.

Most of the set of ten new MICs have experienced structural change in the sense of a reduction of agriculture as a proportion of output and a significant increase in the proportion of the population urbanized. However, for one of the ten—Pakistan—the change in agriculture as a proportion of GDP is minimal over the course of the post-Cold War period. Furthermore, the extent of urbanization is much more evident in East Asia—in China, Indonesia, and Vietnam—and in the sub-Saharan Africa countries in the set of ten new MICs (with the exception of Sudan) but limited in South Asia—in India, Pakistan, and Sri Lanka.

One could say there are three stylized types of new MICs: first, ten genuine new MICs with populations of more than ten million people. These countries have a GDP PPP per capita that has substantially increased since the end of the Cold War and for the most part, structural change (though in Pakistan the structural change of output away from agriculture has been minimal over the period). Second, a set of pseudo new MICs: these are countries achieving MIC status in GNI per capita but progressing little in GDP PPP per capita. Third, small new MICs— meaning populations of less than ten million people. In this book it is the group of ten genuine new MICs with populations of more than ten million people that are the focus henceforth because most of the world's poor live in these countries.

One could further say there have been three types of economic development: first, a Polanyian 'great transformation' (see Polanyi, 1957), meaning an unambiguous shift from a low-income, subsistence-sector-dom-inated, high-absolute-poverty country to a middle-income, modern-sector-dominated, country as per the Lewis model of economic development. This is only evident in a small number of new MICs (e.g. the East Asian

Korea; Malaysia; Malta; Oman; Singapore; Taiwan, China; and Thailand. Two other countries, India and Vietnam, may be on their way to joining this group. (World Bank, 2008, pp. 1, 13)

new MICs of China, Indonesia, and Vietnam). Second, 'incomplete transformations', meaning undeniable change but the retaining of structural characteristics common in the world's poorer nations as per some new MICs (e.g. the South Asian and sub-Saharan African new MICs of Angola, Ghana, India, Nigeria, and Sudan). We could add a third: 'pseudo transformations'. These are countries with higher GNI (Atlas) per capita, driven by commodity-led growth resulting in relatively low GDP PPP per capita growth, remaining mass poverty and insecurity, as well as the same structural problems that poorer nations which would include the countries referred to as pseudo MICs in Chapter 1 (e.g. Senegal, and Zambia).

In sum, a transformation across the developing world is clear in output per capita, aid dependency, and urbanization. However, the thirty-six new MICs can be whittled down to as few as ten countries once one focuses on countries with unequivocal increases in GDP PPP per capita and population of over ten million people and thus of significance to global poverty analysis. Indeed, it is in this set of ten countries, and five of these new MICs in particular, where much of global poverty is situated.

1.4 The meaning of middle income

In the discussion so far this book has made use of the dominant classification of countries by income per capita into low- and middle-income countries. Judging by media reports and the national development plans that often set escaping LIC status as a goal in itself, national policymakers in developing countries typically view the attainment of MIC status, as an important line to cross.[17] This is because the attainment of MIC status has the symbolic value of a country departing from the group of the world's poorest countries. The attainment of MIC status is also generally associated with the attainment of private credit rating and thus access to non-aid finance in capital markets. This may be appealing to national leaders given that it does not carry the kind of conditionalities that aid does. Further, from the donor point of view, the status as an MIC itself has become viewed as some kind of departure from the world's unequivocally poor countries. Some aid donors view the crossing of the line in per capita income to MIC as sufficient cause to reduce, end, or at least change the terms of engagement and aid allocations.[18]

---

[17] For example, Ethiopia's national development plan aims to attain MIC status by 2025 (See World Bank, 2013a).

[18] Take for example, UK aid and the debate surrounding DFID's withdrawal from India (in spite of working in low-income states within India), or the European Commission's decision in May 2012 to

There is a sense that the income classifications are significant, and they are indeed the 'root' of many other classifications and are embedded in the international system in various ways. As noted, the income classifications inform private credit rating agencies' decisions on country ratings that in turn are likely to play a role in determining the rate of interest a country will pay when issuing treasury bonds (by determining a country's level of credit-worthiness). It is for these reasons that this book, while taking into account the weakness of the classifications and comparing income grouping with other groupings such as the UN LDCs and the World Bank's FCAS, focuses largely on the income classifications. Furthermore, in order to assess the nature of the change in the developing world since the end of the Cold War, some form of country classification is useful to see how countries have changed or moved between groups. Where appropriate data is presented on a continuous scale so the impact of the cut-offs is clear.

The income thresholds, though in need of updating and review, do have reasonable supporting logic in differentiating countries that are stuck at the bottom, poor and aid-dependent, for the foreseeable future from countries that are not. Almost all of the remaining LICs are likely to remain LICs in 2020 and the vast majority may remain LICs even in 2030 if one takes economic growth of the last five years as a guide.[19] In short, the income thresholds matter because they are embedded in many international agencies, their allocation models, in private credit-rating agencies and, in the mindsets of national policymakers and donors alike but also because they do separate those countries stuck at the bottom for the foreseeable future from those who are not.

It is worthwhile at this point setting out the methodology used to generate the thresholds in order to assess in more depth what it means to be a MIC and how well this dominant classification by income per capita differentiates the developing world. The World Bank's classification of countries by income has several underlying layers of historical oddity, obscurity, and complexity. The classifications of LIC, LMIC, and UMIC are based on the Bank's operational lending categories. The classifications were established by the World Bank in the late 1980s. The thresholds are based on gross national income (GNI) per capita produced using the 'Atlas method'. The Atlas method takes GNI in national currency and converts it to US dollars using the three-year average of

withdraw bilateral development cooperation programmes from 19 MICs including India and Indonesia, both home to large numbers of poor people. For a detailed discussion of how the thresholds are used by UNICEF, UNDP, UNFPA, WFP, and the Global Fund to Fight AIDS, TB and Malaria see UNICEF (2007, pp. 76–80). For discussion of aid allocations and income classifications see, with reference to health aid allocations specifically, Ottersen et al. (2014).

[19] These projections of LICs in 2020 and 2030 are based on a simple model of linear extrapolation of the LIC/MIC threshold for 2015–30 based on thresholds for 2009–14 and the average GNI (Atlas) per capita growth rate for each country.

exchange rates. It takes the average of a country's exchange rate for that year and its exchange rates for the two preceding years, adjusted for the difference between national inflation and that of 'international inflation' (the weighted average of inflation in the eurozone, Japan, the UK, and the US as measured by the change in the International Monetary Fund's Special Drawing Rights deflator). The classification is connected to World Bank 'civil works prefer-ences' and International Development Association (IDA) eligibility categories, that seek to give better conditions to poorer countries based on economic capacity as measured by GNI Atlas per capita. In this sense, the categories are a framing that has a real life impact on resources potentially available to developing countries.[20]

The thresholds for LIC/LMIC/UMIC are recalibrated annually in line with international inflation. This means that the lines are effectively held constant in real terms at least in the sense of being based on inflation rates in developed countries (which is itself contentious). So any country growing for sufficient time at a rate faster than 'international inflation' will cross the threshold eventually.

According to the short history of the Bank's classifications (World Bank, 2015), the basis for the original setting of the thresholds in income per capita was as follows:

The process of setting per capita income thresholds started with finding a stable relationship between a summary measure of wellbeing such as poverty incidence... and economic variables including per capita GNI estimated based on the Bank's Atlas method on the other. Based on such a relationship and the annual availability of Bank's resources, the original per capita income thresholds were established.

The exact basis of how the thresholds were originally empirically established by the World Bank, however, is less clear. The documentation containing the original formulae are identifiable by their World Bank document numbers in

[20] Low-income countries are those with a GNI (Atlas) per capita of less than $1,045 in 2013 which tallies with the Bank's operational 'civil works preference' lending category (civil works can be awarded to eligible domestic contractors for bids procured under a competitive, international bidding process). However, the thresholds for IDA eligibility and IDA allocation represent an additional layer of complexity due to resource constraints on the World Bank. In addition to the LIC to LMIC threshold there are two different thresholds for countries to access the World Bank's concessionary lending via the IDA. First, there is the IDA eligibility threshold (the ceiling for eligibility), which is no longer applied due to insufficient resources. Second, there is the IDA allocation threshold, which is an operational cut-off currently used, and has become the actual or effective operational cut-off for IDA eligibility. The IDA allocation threshold has evolved to be slightly higher than the $ LIC/MIC threshold and it stood at $1,215 GNI (Atlas) per capita in 2013. The result of this is that some countries that are MICs may be still under the IDA allocation threshold and are thus still eligible to receive concessionary resources. In short, in operational terms even the World Bank, who established and revises the income classifications each year, uses a higher threshold for its own concessionary lending. Countries that are both MIC and still have access to IDA are labelled 'blend' countries by the World Bank but the available financing terms from IDA become less favourable compared to other IDA-only countries. Countries continue to access IDA resources on regular terms until Atlas GNI per capita exceeds the cut-off for three consecutive years, with exceptions being made for small and vulnerable economies.

World Bank (2015b), but these are World Bank board documents and not publicly available. Other relevant sources such Kapur, Lewis, and Webb (1997) in particular do have some relevant information about the period and discussions around the IDA charter and lending. However, Kapur et al. (1997) does not contain the exact formulae of the thresholds (IDA or LIC/MIC) as they have not been published. Indeed, the World Bank's Public Information Centre notes in personal correspondence that:

> There is no official document that we can find that ever specified an exact formula for setting the original income thresholds...When IDA was established in 1960, member countries were classified as Part 1 or Part 2 countries, *based more on a general understanding and agreement by the executive directors of each country rather than strict income guidelines* [emphasis added]—though, for the most part, the classifications were in line with per capita income levels. Part 1 countries were more developed countries that were expected to contribute financially to IDA; and Part 2 countries were less developed countries of which only a subset could be expected to draw on IDA's concessional resources.

World Bank (1989, pp. 8–13) does explain the background and the logic of the MIC-to-HIC original threshold setting and the correlations between GNI per capita and various other development indicators are noted. The MIC to HIC threshold was set at $6,000 per capita in 1987 prices which separated countries listed before that time as 'industrial' which then became categorized as 'high-income countries' (see World Bank, 1989).

In fact, if one plots GNI (Atlas) per capita against poverty, taking the incidence of monetary poverty (at $2.50 per capita at 2011 PPP) and multidimensional poverty (a combined measure of a range of poverty indicators including health, nutrition, and education—see discussion in Chapter 2) (see Figures 1.8 and 1.9), there is considerable dispersal and the correlation between GNI (Atlas) per capita and poverty, although strong in LICs, weakens notably in MICs as income per capita rises.[21] The graphs are not presented here using a linear scale, but rather a lognormal distribution.

One could argue though that it makes more sense to take a whole-of-society indicator, to consider poor countries by their entire population and not just by the poorest population (which may be a minority of the population), as one is seeking to consider the status of a whole country rather than a proportion of the population. An indicator such as average life expectancy would do this. Such a relationship—that between life expectancy and income per capita—is known as the Preston curve after the demographer Samuel H. Preston, who first identified a relationship between average life expectancy and average income per capita. The basic idea is this: average life expectancy rises as

---

[21] These figures should be interpreted as descriptive. The use of scatter plots should not be interpreted as implying causation.

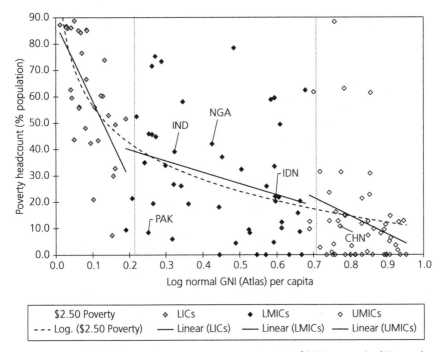

Figure 1.8 GNI (Atlas) per capita versus monetary poverty at $2.50 per capita (% population), 2010–12

Source: Data from Edward and Sumner (2015) and World Bank (2015).

average income rises, but that rise levels out at a fairly moderate level of income per capita. Where that level of income stops contributing to higher life expectancy, or at least, where its contribution slows down considerably, might be a reasonable place to set thresholds between types of countries (for further discussion, and application as a poverty line for individuals, see Edward, 2006). A caveat to this is that life expectancy is, of course, distributed unevenly *within* countries. Therefore, one would really need to get the distribution of life expectancy across the entire expenditure distribution and find the median but such data are not easily available.[22]

Globally, mean life expectancy is about seventy years and ranges from forty-five years in Sierra Leone to more than eighty years in France, Switzerland, Iceland, Italy, Japan, and Hong Kong. The current mean life expectancy across the world's richest countries, the OECD countries, is also about eighty years (in 2013). The lowest life expectancy in an OECD country is currently

---

[22] One would need comparable surveys that asked what a household consumed and in the same household, whether any household members had died during the last month.

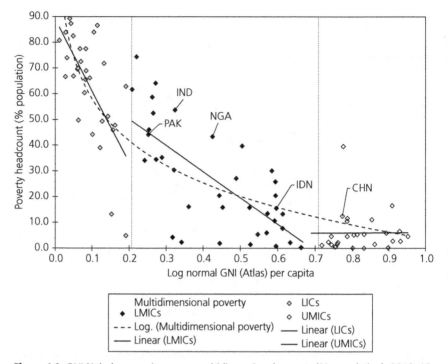

Figure 1.9 GNI (Atlas) per capita versus multidimensional poverty (% population), 2010–12

Source: Data from OPHI (2014) and World Bank (2015).

seventy-five years in Turkey (in 2013). One new MIC, Vietnam, did achieve a life expectancy similar to that of Turkey, seventy-five years, at just $1,000 GNI (Atlas) per capita in 2008 as it crossed the threshold into MIC status (and GDP PPP per capita was $4,000). In contrast, Turkey with the same life expectancy had a GNI (Atlas) per capita of almost $11,000, close to the HIC threshold (and $19,000 in GDP PPP per capita). However, when another new MIC, Nigeria, crossed the LIC–MIC threshold of $1,000 in 2008 it had life expectancy of just fifty years. In 2013, Nigeria and Vietnam, had virtually the same income or output per capita (in GNI and GDP PPP) but life expectancy remains fifty years in the former and seventy-five years in the latter. In short, life expectancy close to the lowest in the OECD has been reached at about $1,000 GNI per capita per year (or $4,000 GDP PPP per capita) but this is by no means guaranteed.

If one plots developing countries by GDP PPP per capita against average life expectancy (see Figure 1.10) one finds the correlation weakens as GDP PPP per capita rises. The logic here is that underlying the classification of countries is a relationship with life expectancy that is better assessed in PPP$ because, as noted, PPP dollars are superior for cross-country comparisons.

In plotting average life expectancy against GDP PPP per capita, what is evident is that the crossover points of the linear curves for LICs, LMICs and UMICs are in general in keeping with the country groupings although there are a few countries the 'wrong' side of the intersect and a number of outliers. One finds that Vietnam is quite exceptional in the sense that the linear curves dissect at just over 60 years and at 70 years life expectancy meaning in general the LIC/LMIC threshold is associated with about 60 years and the LMIC/UMIC threshold with about 70 years life expectancy.

In sum, plotting life expectancy versus GDP PPP per capita lends qualified support to the current country groupings. Although unusual, life expectancy close to an OECD country can be reached at $1,000 GNI (Atlas) per capita, as was done by Vietnam. This would suggest that the LIC/LMIC threshold would best be considered as a minimum threshold for a country to be considered not among the world's very poorest countries. More importantly, if almost all of the remaining LICs are likely to be under that $1,000 threshold for some considerable time to come, the thresholds may separate the countries likely to be stuck at the bottom from the countries that are progressing.

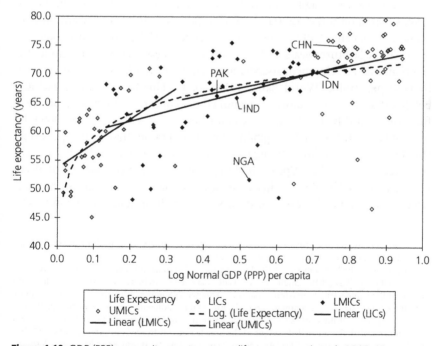

Figure 1.10 GDP (PPP) per capita versus average life expectancy (years), 2010–12

Source: Data processed from World Bank (2015).

How well does the income classification tally with other classifications that go beyond solely income per capita? As used earlier in this chapter, two other classifications are the UN's Least Developed Countries (LDC) group and the World Bank's Fragile and Conflict-Affected States (FCAS). Both classifications incorporate income per capita and add other variables.

The UN LDC is based on a methodology that combines human assets (including nutrition, child mortality, school enrolment, and adult literacy), economic vulnerability (measures of the instability of agricultural production, population displaced by natural disasters, instability in exports, and the share of agriculture in GDP, and exports), proxies for economic 'smallness', 'remoteness', and *GNI (Atlas) per capita*. The main problem of the LDC category is that it is somewhat static. Guillaumont (2009), among others, has argued that the graduation criteria make it very difficult for countries to 'graduate' as the conditions for exit are difficult to meet.[23] Furthermore, some of LDCs are actually MICs which somewhat undermines the sense of the LDCs being the poorest countries across a set of dimensions if some are, at least in income per capita terms, not among the poorest. However, most LDCs that are MICs are small population or small-island developing states which as noted ought to be considered separately due to the specific macroeconomic vulnerabilities of such economies.

In contrast, the 'fragile and conflict-affected states' category of the World Bank is based on three criteria: the World Bank's Country Policy and Institutional Assessment (CPIA) score; the presence of UN or other peacekeeping forces in the last three years and eligibility for concessionary lending under the International Development Association (IDA), of the World Bank as assessed by GNI per capita (World Bank, 2013b, p. 1). This last condition excludes better-off developing countries, meaning those countries who have 'graduated' from the World Bank's IDA. These countries will be MICs above $1,985 GNI per capita in 2013 (the IDA eligibility thresholds) rather than $1,045 per capita (the LIC/LMIC threshold) though such countries can be included if there is a peacekeeping or political/peace-building mission.[24] Many countries that are not defined as 'fragile' by this classification may have fragile or conflict-affected sub-national areas (e.g. India's Naxalite insurgency) and conversely,

[23] Not only do countries have to meet a set of technical conditions, it is also necessary for the government to express a wish to leave the classification.

[24] In contrast, the 'non-official' OECD-DAC fragile and conflict-affected states list has evolved in two stages: first, OECD (2010) combined the lists of fragile states produced by Brookings, Carlton, and the World Bank into a list of forty-three countries. As noted in Sumner (2010), only seventeen of those forty-three fragile states were common across the lists, and the differences in the countries listed mean that the proportion of the world's poor in fragile states in 2007 ranged from 6 per cent to 25 per cent (see Sumner, 2010). For a detailed critique of the 'fragile states' lists, see Harttgen and Klasen (2010). OECD (2013) revisited the OECD-DAC category and one list, the World Bank list of conflict/post-conflict countries, was merged with a further source, the Failed States Index of the US think tank, the Fund for Peace, which had the effect of producing forty-seven countries. The result was that a third of

Table 1.3 Number of countries by income classification, least developed countries and fragile and conflict-affected states (FCAS), based on GNI per capita in 2013

	LICs	LMICs	UMICs	HICs	Total
Total	34	50	55	76	215
Total excluding countries of less than 1m	33	40	40	46	159
Total excluding countries of less than 10m	25	22	21	20	88
Least developed countries (LDC)	30	15	2	1	48
LDC excluding countries of less than 1m	29	8	1	0	38
LDC excluding countries of less than 10m	22	4	1	0	27
Fragile and conflict-affected states (FCAS)	19	12	5	0	36
FCAS excluding countries of less than 1m	18	9	3	0	30
FCAS excluding countries of less than 10m	12	5	1	0	18

Note: FCAS = World Bank definition (Harmonized List of Financial Year 2013).
Source: Author.

those countries defined as fragile states may have large areas of territory that are not fragile or conflict-affected.

If we consider how LICs, LMICs, and UMICs are distributed across the classifications of LDC and FCAS (see Table 1.3), we can make two pertinent points: first, if one considers LDCs to be unequivocally poor countries, there is a close association between countries that are LDCs and LICs: thirty of the thirty-four LICs are also LDCs. Most MICs are not LDCs if one pulls out small countries with less than a million in population and if one pulls out small countries with less than ten million in population just five of the MICs are LDCs.

Second, there is some overlap between MICs and FCAS, taking the World Bank's definition. About half of all FCAS are MICs, although many of these are small islands or small countries.[25] This would suggest fragility and conflict are not synonymous with the poorest countries by income per capita.[26] It also points towards the fact that a number of fragile states are bunched in between the LIC and IDA eligibility thresholds currently (meaning in between approximately $1,000 and $2,000 GNI Atlas per capita).

In conclusion, the use of the LIC/MIC threshold has some logic on the basis of average life expectancy. Further, the MIC group does tally somewhat with the non-LDCs suggesting that the MICs are different from the world's very poorest countries. That said, there are good reasons for the thresholds to be

all developing countries fall under the OECD-DAC definition and fragile states range from $300 per capita to $12,000 per capita. This book has used the World Bank's definition on the basis that it has a consistent analytical basis across countries rather than an amalgamation of countries from different sources.

[25] Those 17 fragile MICs (or HICs) are: Bosnia and Herzegovina, Republic of Congo, Cote d'Ivoire, Iraq, Libya, Kiribati, Kosovo, Marshall Islands, Micronesia, Solomon Islands, South Sudan, Sudan, Syria, Timor-Leste, Tuvalu, West Bank and Gaza, and Yemen.

[26] For reference, use of the longer OECD-DAC FCAS list would lead one to find that two thirds of LICs are fragile states as are one third of LMICs. This point demonstrates that even better-off developing countries such as MICs may have fragile and conflict-affected characteristics.

updated given that the detailed methodology for original threshold setting has never been published but also because some twenty five years of new data have become available since the thresholds were originally established (the thresholds would presumably have been based on correlations using data from the 1970s and 1980s). Further, there are questions over whether 'international inflation' ought now to include China and other large emerging economies in its calculation. Or whether the use of 'international inflation' rates for the world's richest countries is an appropriate way to assess the thresholds over time for the world's poorer countries, which may have had inflation rates above the 'international inflation' rate. Also, the graduation of countries may reflect higher per capita income in exchange-rate conversions, but it would make more sense to use PPP conversion. Finally, the thresholds have been fixed in real terms over time but could alternatively be linked to world income or output per capita.

In spite of the limitations of the income classifications and the need to update them, the classifications, as noted, are embedded in the international system and in the minds of policymakers in developing countries and donors alike as the dominant analytical frames. For these reasons, and because of the reasonable correlation with life expectancy, the income categories are used in this book and compared to LDCs and FCAS in discussion throughout.

1.5 **Conclusions**

This chapter has sought to address the following question: how has the developing world changed since the end of the Cold War? This chapter has presented three arguments related to late or catch-up capitalism in the developing world. First, economic growth in developing countries since the early 1990s has been significant and many countries have crossed the line into the category of middle income. Second, those new MICs are very much better off, by a range of indicators, than the countries left behind but still far short of the OECD countries and their structural characteristics. Third, economic growth has been accompanied by structural change in relatively few new MICs and the group of thirty-six new MICs emerging since the Cold War can be quickly whittled down to just ten with a substantial increase in output per capita and more than ten million people in population size. As we shall see in Chapter 2, these ten countries, and five countries in particular, are central to global poverty.

The chapter has also argued that the income classifications are far from perfect and in need of review and update, but are difficult to dismiss, given their embedded nature in the minds of developing-country policymakers and donors and even credit-rating agencies. There is some reasonable logic with reference to average life expectancy to suggest that the income classifications, as crude as they are, do differentiate countries, and do differentiate countries 'stuck' at the bottom from those countries growing fast and pulling away from the bottom.

In sum, there has been a substantial amount of economic growth in developing countries since the end of the Cold War leading to a large number of countries crossing the line into the category of middle income. In fact, only thirty or so LICs remain. The increase in the number of MICs should be placed in a broader context of changes in the developing world since 1990. Since the end of the Cold War, there has been rapid growth in average incomes in a number of countries and a consequential decline in countries that are aid-dependent. There have been some 'great transformations' in the developing world, meaning unequivocal economic development away from agrarian societies and attainment of unambiguous middle-income levels of per capita income, though these are relatively few. Indeed, there have also been a number of pseudo-MICs, meaning some countries attaining middle-income status are barely better off in PPP terms than in the early 1990s. As we discuss in Chapter 2, poverty rates remain higher than one might expect in many MICs despite average incomes increasing substantially since the Cold War. Although many new MICs have attained drastically higher average per capita incomes poverty or insecurity remain widespread.

2 The geography of poverty

How has global poverty changed since the end of the Cold War?

2.1 Introduction

The argument of this chapter is threefold: first, that the 'geography' or location of global poverty has largely shifted from LICs to MICs because a relatively small set of populous countries were reclassified from LICs to MICs following substantial economic growth. Second, as a result of this about a billion poor people now live in MICs. Third, that the world's poor have, of course, not moved; rather, as noted, the countries that account for a large proportion of global poverty have experienced rises in average incomes, passing the threshold into middle income, and poverty in absolute numbers has not fallen as much as one might have thought the growth would warrant.[1]

The chapter is structured as follows: section 2.2 discusses the conceptual point of departure—global poverty—and contentions in estimating levels of and trends in global poverty. It is posited that both monetary and multidimensional poverty should be considered side by side wherever possible to ensure the analysis of poverty be considered by monetary dimensions or standards of living, as well as health, nutrition, and education or the various dimensions of poverty. Sections 2.3 and 2.4 respectively discuss the 'geography' or location and composition of global poverty. The arguments here are that the poor now live in MICs and that spatial and social inequalities are important aspects of the composition of contemporary poverty. Section 2.5 concludes.

---

[1] One would expect poverty to fall with economic growth at any given poverty line because as average income/consumption rises with economic growth, the income/consumption of the poorest in society, tend, judging by the largest empirical studies, that provide generalization across a large sample of countries, to rise in line with that average income/consumption (e.g. Kraay, 2006; Dollar et al., 2013). The main contention with such studies is there is a large variation across countries hidden in global averages (see Chapter 3 for discussion).

2.2 **Defining global poverty**

2.2.1 THE EMERGENCE OF POVERTY WITHIN DEVELOPMENT DISCOURSE

In order to discuss how global poverty has changed since the Cold War one first needs to define poverty. In discussions of global poverty, both the monetary and non-monetary or multidimensional aspects of global poverty need to be considered. Indeed, monetary and multidimensional poverty are inseparable although the exact monetary income or consumption needed to escape multidimensional poverty could differ by country because different countries have different policies (and thus costs) for public health and education. In short, income is instrumental in addressing non-monetary or multidimensional poverty but the extent to which it is depends on the prevailing configuration of public (and private) health and education and the broader 'welfare regime' (see Chapter 3). Further, given the weaknesses of monetary poverty, such as questions over comparisons across and within countries in purchasing power parity (PPP) dollars and the volatility of household income/expenditure, the inclusion of non-monetary or multidimensional poverty becomes ever more essential.

A useful point of departure is to consider how the conceptual and empirical investigation of global poverty emerged in the development literature in the late 1960s and 1970s. A series of seminal works argued that economic development was failing to raise living standards at the lower end of the distribution. For example, Chenery et al. (1974, p. xiii) posited that a decade of growth had passed with 'little or no benefit' to a third of the population in developing countries and Adelman and Morris (1973) wrote of hundreds of millions 'hurt' by economic development. In the background to this was the Kuznets hypothesis: if economic development, in the early stages at least, leads to an inevitable increase in inequality as Kuznets suggested then the implication was that poverty may take many years to fall, as the benefits of growth to the poor are curtailed by the increase in inequality.

Discussion and critiques of the Kuznets hypothesis can be said to have played a role in increased interest in the relationship between poverty, inequality, and rising income per capita. In particular, the importance of considering variables beyond income per capita in assessing progress became recognized because rising average income per capita is not necessarily synonymous with falling poverty (and inequality). Here we return again to Dudley Seers. Seers (1969) in *The Meaning of Development* was instrumental in re-orienting the debate in the literature away from relying solely on income per capita growth and towards asking deeper questions about trends in poverty and inequality and employment:

The questions to ask about a country's development are therefore: What has been happening to poverty? What has been happening to unemployment? What has been happening to inequality?... If one or two of these central problems have been growing worse... it would be strange to call the result 'development', even if per capita income has soared. (Seers, 1969, p. 24)

Seers's paper signalled something of a challenge to the literature in terms of promoting a broader understanding of development as including a set of 'basic needs'.[2] Indeed, such thinking is the basis for setting any poverty line. There is a normative judgement on what constitutes a minimum or basic set of needs and it follows that potentially moral and/or legal obligations of the state follow to those below the line. However, in most contexts that legal, let alone moral, obligation is fuzzy. Entitlements to state support are often related to that line although who exactly receives such benefits may not match well the official poverty line and there may be little difference between the poor and the non-poor if the latter are barely above the poverty line. At a global level, one might argue the UN and the international aid system has some kind of obligation to those below whatever global poverty line taken in the form of development assistance and aid. This would include a sufficient or minimum income (i.e. monetary poverty) and employment but also the physical necessities or 'basic needs' for a minimum standard of living such as food, shelter, and public goods (i.e. the non-monetary dimensions of poverty) (see discussion in Hicks and Streeten, 1979; Streeten, 1984). The research of ILO (1976, 1977), Morris (1979), as well Baster (1979), McGranahan et al. (1985), and UNRISD (1970) set the foundations for Sen (1981, 1983, 1992, 1997, 1999), and UNDP (1990–present) thinking on the concepts of human development and human poverty, the latter of which was broadened into a measure of multidimensional poverty by Alkire and Santos (2010, 2014), Alkire and Foster (2011), and UNDP (2010).

In the same year as the launch of the UNDP Human Development Report in 1990, the global monetary poverty line of a dollar-a-day emerged in World Bank (1990) and monetary poverty later took a prominent role as the first goal in the UN poverty goals, the Millennium Development Goals in the 2000s though with considerable contention (see later discussion and Chen and Ravallion, 2012; Pogge, 2013; UN, 2014).

Global monetary poverty, however, was first estimated by Ahluwalia et al. (1979), using the 45th percentile in India as a poverty line and converting this into other currencies in PPP dollars and then calculating the number of people under that line by applying the Gini coefficient to GDP per capita in each country. World Bank (1990) then took poverty lines from a range of the poorest countries and developed a dollar-a-day which was adjusted to $1.08

---

[2] Unemployment data for developing countries remains highly problematic and for this reason is little discussed.

in 2000 and \$1.25 in 2005 (see Ravallion et al., 2008). The US\$1.25 iteration was based on the average value of the national poverty lines of the fifteen poorest countries in the world at that time.[3] However, many of the world's poor live in populous countries which are not the poorest in the world and thus not part of the poverty line construction, such as the populous MICs, China, India, Indonesia, Nigeria, and Pakistan or the populous LICs, Bangladesh and DRC.

Conceptual debates over whether monetary or multidimensional poverty (however each are defined in the detail) better capture the nature of poverty have continued unabated since the 1990s, fuelled by the annual UNDP Human Development Report, the impact of the various PPP revisions, and the 2010 launch of the new UNDP and Oxford Poverty and Human Development Initiative (OPHI) multidimensional poverty measure noted previously (see Alkire and Foster, 2011).[4] Much debate in the 1990s centred around human development or human poverty as an alternative to income or money-metric assessments of progress. Sen (see, in particular, 1999), Nussbaum (see, in particular, 2000), and UNDP (1990–present) argued that attention should be to the capabilities—means, opportunities, or substantive freedoms—which permit the achievement of a set of 'functionings'—things which human beings value in terms of 'being' and 'doing'. Echoing Seers, development is not, as previously conceived, based on desire fulfilment (utility or consumption measured by a proxy of income per capita) as this does not take sufficient evaluative account of the physical condition of the individual and of a person's capabilities. Income is *only* an instrumental freedom—it helps to achieve other constitutive freedoms. Like Seers, Sen does not ignore income; rather, he argues that too much emphasis can be placed on this dimension of development. Sen argued that a broad set of conditions or 'functionings' (including being well fed, healthy, clothed, and educated) together constitute well-being. Although Sen has refused to name the actual functionings or accompanying capabilities or opportunities as these ought to emerge from a societal deliberative process of some kind, he did identify a set of basic freedoms.[5] In the case of absolute poverty he noted that:

---

[3] Those 15 countries were as follows: Chad, Ethiopia, Gambia, Ghana, Guinea-Bissau, Malawi, Mali, Mozambique, Nepal, Niger, Rwanda, Sierra Leone, Tajikistan, Tanzania, and Uganda (for detailed discussion, see Ravallion et al., 2008).

[4] There is no reason why monetary poverty and human or multidimensional poverty cannot be considered together (as this book does). The former has the advantage of a time series data set since 1990 (or before for some countries). In contrast, multidimensional poverty has only data for recent years which is aggregated here to make estimates for 2010 (by using population data for that year and applying headcount estimates from the most recent survey).

[5] Sen (1999, p. 38) identifies: political/participative freedoms/civil rights (e.g. freedom of speech, free elections); economic facilities (e.g. opportunities to participate in trade and production and to sell one's labour and product on fair, competitive terms); social opportunities (e.g. adequate education and health facilities); transparency guarantees (e.g. openness in government and business and social trust); and protective security (e.g. law and order, social safety nets for the unemployed).

[w]e may be able to go a fairly long distance in terms of a relatively small number of centrally important functionings (and the corresponding basic capabilities, e.g. the ability to be well nourished and well sheltered, the capability of escaping avoidable morbidity and premature mortality, and so forth). (Sen, 1992, pp. 44–5)

Making estimates of such poverty was made possible in a more systematic way by the UNDP/OPHI multidimensional poverty measure. This has gone some way to making for a plausible consensus based on the data that is available for a large set of countries (108 countries in OPHI, 2014). The multidimensional poverty headcount measure is based on the following ten component indicators in three poverty dimensions (see Table 2.1) echoing the domains of human development indicators preceding the multidimensional poverty measure in the UNDP Human Development Reports: health (nutrition and mortality), education (years of schooling and child school attendance), and living standard (access to electricity, sanitation, safe drinking water, good house flooring, cooking fuel, and household assets).

The multidimensional poverty measure, like any poverty measure, is not without its critics, notably that data are taken from different years and not interpolated/extrapolated as there is no accepted way to do this. Further, the choice of components themselves, the weighting and the cut-offs have been subject to heated debate (see, for details, Alkire, 2011).

Table 2.1 Dimensions, indicators, deprivation cut-offs, and weights used in the estimation of multidimensional poverty

Dimension (weight)	Indicator	Deprivation cut-off	Weight
Health (1/3)	Nutrition	Any adult or child in the household with nutritional information is undernourished	1/6
	Mortality	Any child has died in the household	1/6
Education (1/3)	Schooling	No household member has completed five years of schooling	1/6
	Attendance	Any school-aged child in the household is not attending school up to class 8	1/6
Standard of living (1/3)	Electricity	The household has no electricity	1/18
	Sanitation	The household's sanitation facility is not improved or it is shared with other households	1/18
	Water	The household does not have access to safe drinking water or safe water is more than a 30-minute walk, round trip	1/18
	Floor	The household has a dirt, sand, or dung floor	1/18
	Cooking fuel	The household cooks with dung, wood, or charcoal	1/18
	Assets	The household does not own more than one of the following: radio, TV, telephone, bike, motorbike, or refrigerator, and does not own a car or truck	1/18

Source: Adapted from Alkire et al. (2015).

In spite of such contentions, the multidimensional nature of poverty and well-being more broadly has become well established in the development discourse. For example, the Stiglitz-Sen-Fitoussi Commission noted:

The following key dimensions that should be taken into account... [are] (a) Material living standards (income, consumption and wealth); (b) Health; (c) Education; (d) Personal activities including work; (e) Political voice and governance; (f) Social connections and relationships; (g) Environment (present and future conditions); and (h) Insecurity, of an economic as well as a physical nature. (Stiglitz et al., 2009, p. 10, 14–15)

This concurs with global attempts to codify the multidimensionality of poverty such as those at the milestone UN Social Development Summit in 1995 that noted:

Poverty has various manifestations, including lack of income and productive resources sufficient to ensure sustainable livelihoods; hunger and malnutrition; ill health; limited or lack of access to education and other basic services; increased morbidity and mortality from illness; homelessness and inadequate housing; unsafe environments; and social discrimination and exclusion. It is also characterized by a lack of participation in decision-making and in civil, social and cultural life. (UN, 1995, p. 1)

Such an approach to poverty, ill-being, and well-being as multidimensional was further validated across sixty countries in the participatory poverty assessment of Narayan et al. (1999) that concluded that poor people define poverty as multidimensional, with an emphasis on hunger in particular, as well as subjective or psychological dimensions and poor infrastructure and ill health:

Poverty is multidimensional... poverty consists of many interlocked dimensions. Although poverty is rarely about the lack of only one thing, the bottom line is always hunger—the lack of food... poverty has important psychological dimensions, such as powerlessness, voicelessness, dependency, shame, and humiliation... poor people lack access to basic infrastructure—roads (particularly in rural areas), transportation, and clean water... poor health and illness are dreaded almost everywhere as a source of destitution. (Narayan et al., pp. 4–5)

In sum, although the UNDP/OPHI multidimensional poverty measure does not cover all the dimensions listed by Narayan et al. (1999) or Stiglitz et al. (2009) or UN (1995) largely due to data availability, it does provide a more nuanced picture of poverty than relying on estimates of monetary poverty alone. While there is no global consensus on the list of the core set of capabilities or functionings (see discussion on various sets in Alkire, 2005), the multidimensional poverty measure could be said to represent a minimum set of international comparable standards based on what data is available for a large set of countries. Importantly, multidimensional poverty does not face the same need for price data across countries that has caused considerable revision of, and contention for, global monetary poverty. We turn to this next.

2.2.2 GLOBAL MONETARY POVERTY: CONTENTIONS

As posited above, focusing solely on monetary poverty is insufficient to capture the multidimensional nature of poverty. Further, there are some important conceptual and empirical issues that place a question mark over the precision of assessing global poverty solely by monetary measures.

A number of critiques have been levelled at monetary poverty, not least is whether the achievement of functionings such as being healthy and educated or the escaping of multidimensional poverty can be achieved at a dollar-a-day or its iterations or (see Alkire, 2011; Ravallion, 2002, 2008; Reddy and Pogge, 2002, 2005; Pogge, 2013). A further issue is the volatility of household income/expenditure over time results in people moving in and out of poverty, sometimes frequently, because of the clustering of the global poor around one to two dollars per day. This clustering issue also makes estimates of global poverty sensitive to where the consumption line is drawn. Although there is a range of issues in global monetary poverty measurement, one might say that it is the use of PPP data to estimate global poverty that has been a primary source of contention.[6]

Market exchange rates are thought to be misleading for comparisons between countries, since the price of rice in China is very different to the USA. PPPs attempt to deal with this problem by comparing prices across countries for similar items in order to estimate what could be bought in the US with a country's currency. The PPP numbers matter for various reasons, not least because they are central to estimates of global monetary poverty.[7]

In 2014, the International Comparison Program (ICP), responsible for the production of PPP data released the latest round of price data (collected in 2011).[8] The PPP revision had two impacts on global poverty: first, many of the countries where global poverty is concentrated were the subject of substantial

---

[6] There is also a set of issues about the raw data (some of which apply to other poverty data beyond monetary poverty data): there is the comparison cross-country of different surveys (individual versus household); different types of data collection (consumption expenditure, net income, or gross income) and the fact that data from national accounts (GDP data) may not match survey data (where poverty data typically comes from), not to mention missing people in the sample frame (e.g. the homeless or migrants) and missing countries. There are also, of course, a range of further methodological questions about the construction of monetary poverty lines (what to include in the basket of consumption of a poor person, for example), and the international poverty lines in particular (health and education are free in some countries and paid for in others, for example).

[7] There is a question as to whether national average consumption-based PPPs can be used to estimate global poverty given how consumption patterns differ between and within countries between the rich and the poorer populations (see Deaton, 2005, 2010a; 2010b; Deaton and Dupriez, 2011; Deaton and Heston, 2010; Klasen, 2010a). However, when Deaton and Dupriez (2011) constructed new PPPs for consumption near the poverty line using 2005 PPPs, they found there was little difference between PPPs for the consumption of the poor and PPPs based on national accounts using the ICP 2005.

[8] The ICP was established in the late 1960s on the recommendation of the UN Statistical Commission. Both the 2005 and 2011 data collection rounds were housed by the World Bank Global Office with regional offices around the world. ICP 2005 covered 146 countries. ICP 2011 covered 199 countries.

PPP revisions meaning that, as with previous PPP revisions, all estimates of global monetary poverty require revising at whatever poverty line taken. Second, specifically the revisions also mean the established monetary global poverty line of a dollar-a-day and its iterations ($1.25 per day in 2005 PPP) require re-basing.

Such debates are not purely academic. The use of the ICP (2014a) data is endemic in the development community from the UNDP estimation of the Human Development Index (of which GDP PPP per capita is a component), to the World Bank's global poverty estimates, to the International Monetary Fund's (IMF) economic growth projections, the Penn World Table, a range of data in the World Bank's World Development Indicators, and the World Health Organization (WHO) estimates of health spending to name but a few of the uses. Indeed, given that the UN aspires to end poverty by 2030, a measure of monetary absolute poverty is needed.

Prior to the release of the latest data, the PPPs have been subject to considerable contention (see, for example, Anand and Segal, 2008; Chen and Ravallion, 2010; Deaton, 2010a, 2010b; Deaton and Heston, 2010; Edward and Sumner, 2014, 2015; Klasen, 2010a; Milanovic, 2012, and on the ICP 2011 round specifically, see Deaton and Aten, 2014; Inklaar and Rao, 2014; Ravallion, 2014a, 2014b; Ravallion and Chen, 2015). Deaton and Heston (2010), for example, note four issues relating to the construction of the 2005 PPPs though the points raised are generic to all PPPs: how to address international differences in quality of products; the treatment of urban and rural areas of large countries; how to estimate prices for 'comparison resistant items' (e.g. government services, health, and education); and the effects of the regional structure of the ICP. They argue that some international comparisons are close to impossible, even in theory, and that practical difficulties arising from the above make comparisons 'hazardous'.[9]

Deaton and Aten (2014) however describe new 2011 PPP data as 'superior' to the 2005 PPP data and that 'there is no reason to doubt it'. Thus it is reasonable to assume that Deaton's (2010b, p. 31) comment on the 2005 PPPs holds for 2011 PPPs:

PPPs for the poorer countries in Africa or in Asia may be good enough to support global poverty counts, at least provided the uncertainties are recognized. Probably the

---

[9] Deaton (2010b) contributes some further and related points on the 2005 PPPs. He notes that the absence of weights within basic headings may result in basic headings being priced using high-priced, unrepresentative goods that are rarely consumed in some countries; and that urban bias in price collection in some countries, especially China may make the data misleading. Not surprisingly, ICP (2014a, pp. 21–3, 2014b, pp. 167–70) notes many if not all of the issues raised by Deaton. It further highlights that PPPs are statistical constructs not precise estimates; that the margins of error on PPPs are the result of sampling and non-sampling errors and variability in price and economic structures between economies. They also note that national average prices may be problematic in the analysis of large economies with large rural areas and/or rural populations.

most urgent area for the poverty counts is not the ICP, but the improvement in the consistency and timeliness of household surveys, and the upgrading of national accounts. We have come a long way since Simon Kuznets (1955) apologized in his Presidential Address to the Association for 'the meagreness of reliable information presented', but there is still much to be done.

The availability and quality of household surveys has improved drastically over the last decade and continues to do so. Furthermore, the PPPs *have* been used for global poverty estimates for twenty-five years since at least the late 1980s. Under what conditions might it be reasonable to use the PPP data for global poverty analysis? As Deaton's citation above proposed: when estimates of global poverty are presented the inherent uncertainties are clearly recognized and discussed at the outset, as this book has done here.

2.2.3 CONTEMPORARY ESTIMATES OF GLOBAL MONETARY POVERTY

With the previously stated caveats in mind, several contemporary estimates of global monetary poverty are possible. The most contentious issue is how to adjust the established global poverty line of $1.25 (in 2005 PPP) per person per day in light of the new price data. Table 2.2 shows various approaches to setting a new global poverty line. Estimates of global poverty headcount and gap are made for 2012 (based on data from Edward and Sumner, 2015). The use of a consistent methodology across poverty lines and the making of estimates for 2012 (rather than 2010) means that estimates in the table differ slightly to other authors' original estimates.

First, let us consider poverty lines proposed by others: Chandy and Kharas (2014), closely following the World Bank's method of calculating the $1.25

Table 2.2 Global poverty headcount and gap estimates, 2012, at various poverty lines

Global poverty line (2011 PPP)	Method and logic	Number of poor, million	% world population	Poverty gap ($bn)	Poverty gap (% GDP)
$2	Median of low-income country poverty lines ($1.92) (Jolliffe and Prydz, 2015) or 'Same number of poor' poverty line (same number of poor as per $1.25 in 2010 in 2005 PPP)	963.3	13.9	205.4	0.2
$2.50	Monetary poverty line equivalent which produces for 2010 the same count as multidimensional poverty	1,447.4	21.0	426.3	0.5
$10	A 'security from poverty' line (Lopez-Calva and Ortiz-Juarez, 2014)	4,694.8	68.0	10,065.1	10.7

Note: Estimates use consistent data set and thus differ slightly from authors listed in terms of method.
Source: Data from Edward and Sumner (2015).

(2005 PPP) global poverty line (which to recap, was the national poverty line in the world's fifteen poorest countries), and recalibrate the $1.25 poverty line to $1.78 in 2011 PPP. These estimates take the average increase in the fifteen national poverty lines in 2005 used by the World Bank for the poorest countries, and then look at the average increase in the national poverty lines for the current poorest fifteen countries. They then take an average of the two averages to adjust the global poverty line. This method generates an estimate of 750 million poor (using consistent estimates of Edward and Sumner, 2015). Jolliffe and Prydz (2015) estimate a new poverty line close to this too at $1.82 based on the poverty line of the same set of the world's poorest fifteen countries or $1.92 based on the median poverty line of the LICs which has become the new 'official' global poverty line, rounded down to $1.90 (see Ferreira et al., 2015). Another alternative approach is to say that there were a billion poor using the $1.25 threshold in 2005 PPP, so where would the poverty line be set to produce the same number of poor in 2011 PPP? That level would also be approximately $2 per day.

The poverty headcount for multidimensional poverty was higher than this, at an estimated 1.6 billion people in 2010 (OPHI, 2014). On this basis, one might draw a global monetary poverty line for that same year, 2010, at the level of consumption at which there are 1.6 billion people. This would be $2.50 per capita. If one then applies this daily consumption line to estimate global poverty in 2012, one finds that 1.4 billion people would be counted as poor. One limitation of this approach is that it may be the case that the multidimensional poor and the monetary poor are not necessarily the same 1.6 billion people. Alkire et al. (2014) review numerous studies and argue that the monetary poor and the multidimensional poor are not synonymous. That said, at a global level, if one accepts the logic that one is going to set a line somewhere as an *indicative* line then this is not an unreasonable approach to take and—importantly—one can compare global monetary poverty alongside global multidimensional poverty. Further, a line drawn anywhere is a poverty line of some kind and $2.50 per day per capita is still a frugal poverty line. It represented the poorest consumption quintile of the world population in 2012 (see Table 2.2) and approximately half of global median income, making it a poverty line relative to global consumption too. Most importantly perhaps, the correlation between $2.50 (2011 PPP) and multidimensional poverty headcounts at national level is closer than correlations to lower poverty lines.

It is sobering just how sensitive the global poverty numbers are to small changes in the value of the line taken. There are 500 million people *between* the $2 and $2.50 poverty line (2011 PPP). In short, fifty cents on the global poverty line adds 500 million people. On average every dime (10 cents) adds 100 million people. There are also perhaps 250 million people who may well be poor but are not included in the data such as homeless people and other groups often missed in data collection sample frames (as estimated by

Carr-Hill, 2013). This brings to the fore again the importance of considering estimates of monetary global poverty alongside multidimensional global poverty whenever possible. The revisions in the price data did not change multidimensional poverty estimates because education, health, and nutrition poverty data did not change with the price revisions.

In the forthcoming discussion this book takes the $2.50 poverty line (in 2011 PPP) outlined above for analysis and compares estimates with multidimensional poverty. This is not to argue that the $2.50 threshold should be seen as the global poverty line; rather, that the $2.50 line captures the poorest quintile of world population, which would seem a reasonable level to focus on, and $2.50 is well below the median consumption per capita for developing countries which is approximately $4 per day and, as noted, half of the value of the global median consumption which is approximately $5 per day (in 2012). The correlation between the poverty headcounts by $2.50 monetary poverty line and multidimensional poverty is stronger than the correlation between multidimensional poverty and the lower monetary poverty lines.[10] Furthermore, the structure of global poverty by $2.50 and multidimensional poverty is surprisingly similar when plotted as cumulative poverty versus GDP PPP per capita in 2010–12 (see Figures 2.1 and 2.2).

Such estimates of monetary poverty should, though, be viewed as very low standards of living and it makes more sense to view such lines as a consumption line not a precise poverty line. In short, any global poverty estimates come with large caveats. Not least because if we take a $10 poverty line—a line associated with security from poverty using the national poverty lines in Mexico, Chile, Brazil, and Indonesia too—we find that 4.7 billion people or two-thirds of the world's population would live in poverty.[11] This kind of picture is also true at country level. For example, the poverty headcount is one in ten of the population in China at $2.50 per day in 2012 but seven in ten at $10 per day. Similarly, in Indonesia, two in ten people live under $2.50 in 2012 but nine in ten people live under $10 a day. A higher poverty line would be much less sensitive to future PPP revisions and given $10 per day is the consumption at the upper limit of the poorest decile in OECD countries in 2012 (2011 PPP)

---

[10] The correlation of poverty headcounts in 2010–12 by $2.50 monetary poverty line and multidimensional poverty is 0.816 and this correlation is significant at the 0.01 level (2-tailed). In contrast, the correlation at $1.78, and $2 are weaker, respectively, 0.733 and 0.765, all of which are significant at the 0.01 level (2-tailed).

[11] The $10 poverty line is a proposal for a 'security from poverty' consumption line developed and used by López-Calva and Ortiz-Juarez (2014) based on the 10% probability of falling back below national poverty lines (which are $4–$5/day in 2005 PPP) in the near future in Mexico, Brazil, and Chile. The 10% probability line is actually $8.50–$9.70 depending on whether Brazil, Mexico, or Chile are used (and comparable estimates for Indonesia are $8.37 for a $4 national poverty line and $13.03 at $5, in 2005 PPP—see Sumner et al., 2014). Thus, the mean is $9.27 and if the mean is inflated to 2011 prices it is $10.47. However, given that this is not intended to be a precise estimate—rather a rough proxy used for illustration purposes here—$10 per capita is used here in 2011 PPP.

this would mean it might in future qualify as a genuinely *global* poverty line for all countries as well as a line representing security from future poverty. (see later discussion).

2.3 The 'geography' or location of global poverty

If we take the $2.50 poverty and multidimensional poverty estimates we find a consistent picture of where the world's poor are located. This was first noted for a range of poverty measures in Sumner (2010, 2012b). Most may have assumed that the world's poor live in the poorest countries such as LICs or LDCs or fragile states. In this section data is presented that shows much of global poverty, however defined, has shifted away from the poorest countries. Instead, most global poverty is now in countries officially classified as MICs. This pattern holds for both monetary and multidimensional poverty (and is consistent with earlier estimates of Alkire et al., 2013, 2015; Kanbur and Sumner, 2012; Sumner, 2010, 2012b). That said, it should not be forgotten that LICs, LDCs, and FCASs typically though not always have higher rates of headcount poverty and a larger total poverty gap.

As previously noted, the transfer of global poverty from LICs to MICs is in part a product of the reclassification—following economic growth—of a set of former LICs. In particular, within the set of new MICs, there are a small number of populous countries where most of the world's poor live: China and India alone represent half of the world's poor (as noted earlier in Kanbur and Sumner, 2012; Sumner, 2010, 2012b). Indeed, global poverty overall is concentrated in approximately ten or so countries, some of which are LICs and some of which are MICs. LICs of significance are the populous, soon-to-be-MIC, Bangladesh, as well as Ethiopia, and the DRC. MICs of significance in addition to China and India are the populous Indonesia, Nigeria, and Pakistan (although the last of these has lower $2.50 poverty than multidimensional poverty). Further, a number of other new MICs contribute notably to global poverty counts such as Angola, Ghana, Sudan, and Vietnam as do several longstanding MICs such as Brazil, Colombia, the Philippines, and South Africa.

It is surprising that the substantial economic growth that took some LICs to MIC status did not do more to reduce poverty headcounts in countries beyond China. In China the fall in poverty is breathtaking at $2.50 over the period since the Cold War and yet a third of the population continue to live under $5 per day per capita (as noted, the global median consumption in 2012). While the fall in India at $2.50 is 100 million people, 84 per cent of the population remained under $5 per day line in 2012. There are plausible reasons, discussed in Chapter 3, for expecting a greater drop in poverty given the large increases in output and consumption per capita over the period since 1990. However, as noted in Chapter 1, correlations between poverty as this growth weaken during middle-income, especially so if inequality rises as this weakens the efficiency of growth in reducing poverty.

What is important to reiterate in this debate is that the poor have not moved. It is the case that the countries the poor live in (a few populous ones in particular) have had substantial growth in average income per capita and poverty has not fallen as much as one would have expected. As populous countries, first China around the millennium, and then India, 'graduated' to MIC status in the late 2000s the proportion of global poverty in MICs substantially increased.

The billion poor people that live in the world's MICs largely reside in five MICs which have grown from LIC status since the end of the Cold War, specifically, China, India, Indonesia, Nigeria, and Pakistan. Table 2.3 shows the global distribution of monetary and multidimensional poverty by country income groups (LICs, LMICs, and UMICs) and for comparison, the LDCs and FCASs. In Table 2.3 data is presented for monetary poverty for 1990 and 2012 and multidimensional poverty for 2010.

The total number of $2.50 poor fell from 2.4 billion to 1.4 billion from 1990 to 2012 or from almost a half to approximately a fifth of the world population. However, most of this decline is accounted for by one country, China, where poverty fell from 860 million to 150 million. Global poverty excluding China at $2.50 was 1.5 billion in 1990 and 1.3 billion in 2012.

Countries that contributed 5–10 million or more poor people in either period are relatively few in number, as noted, and only in a small

Table 2.3 The distribution of global poverty, $2.50/day (2011 PPP) poverty and multidimensional poverty, 1990 and 2010–12

| | $2.50/day poverty (2011 PPPs) | | | | Multidimensional poverty | | | |
| | Millions | | Headcount (% pop'n) | | Millions | | Headcount (% pop'n) | |
	1990	2012	1990	2012	1990	2010	1990	2010
Global	2,381.4	1,447.4	45.3	21.0	–	1581.9	–	22.8
LICs	2,087.6	446.3	67.9	53.8	–	449.9	–	56.6
LMICs	176.2	750.7	19.6	29.7	–	935.2	–	38.2
UMICs	110.3	235.7	23.7	9.9	–	194.2	–	8.2
LDCs	–	464.1	–	53.5	–	460.7	–	55.6
Fragile and conflict-affected states	–	198.8	–	41.1	–	191.1	–	41.3
China	859.7	145.3	75.7	10.8	–	160.5	–	12.5
India	600.0	483.6	69.0	39.1	–	648.0	–	53.7

Note: Historical country classification taken for LICs, LMICs, and UMICs. Fragile and conflict-affected states = World Bank definition; 14.8m of global $2.50 poverty was in high-income countries (in 2012), whilst this may seem surprising, Gentilini (2013) estimated at least 60m people or 7.2 per cent of population in HICs used food banks in 2009–11.
Source: Estimates based on data from Edward and Sumner (2015) and OPHI (2014).

number of countries did poverty actually fall drastically, in terms of a decline in the absolute number of poor people, between 1990 and 2012. In most countries $2.50 poverty stayed about the same number of people or even rose slightly even if poverty fell as a proportion of population.[12]

The result of the above is that although in 1990, 90 per cent of global $2.50 poverty was accounted for by LICs, by 2012 MICs accounted for around seventy per cent, or about a billion people, of global monetary and of multidimensional poverty. The contribution of different countries to the MIC poor is similar in monetary and multidimensional poverty. Beyond the five populous new MICs, a range of other countries cover the remainder of poverty in MICs such as Angola, Brazil, Cameroon, Columbia, Ghana, Mexico, Pakistan, the Philippines, Senegal, South Africa, Uzbekistan, Vietnam, and Zambia. One will notice that many of these listed here are also new MICs.

In contrast to MICs, the total number of poor people in LICs is about 450 million or about 30 per cent of global poverty. There is a similar amount—450 million poor—in the LDCs. Fragile states accounted for just 200 million or just under 15 per cent of global poverty (which is much less than half of the number of poor people in India). These numbers are similar whether monetary or multidimensional poverty are taken. It is important to reiterate too that, in spite of the global distribution of poverty shifting towards MICs, average poverty incidence as a proportion of population in LICs or LDCs or FCASs is typically substantially higher as is the total poverty gap. The poverty headcount is about 50 per cent of the population in LICs or LDCs and about 40 per cent of the population in fragile states. However, poverty in MICs still affects one in three people in LMICs and one in ten people in UMICs.

One question is how sensitive the shift in global poverty is to the LIC/MIC thresholds themselves and whether moving the thresholds would make much difference. Figures 2.1 and 2.2 show in a more detailed way how global poverty is distributed and how global poverty has shifted by considering cumulative global poverty by $2.50/day (2011 PPP), and by multidimensional poverty (for 2010 only) by GNI per capita (Atlas), and thus the thresholds, and then by GDP PPP per capita. In terms of the structure of global poverty, Figure 2.1 shows that there is considerable similarity between monetary and multidimensional poverty headcount with the slightly higher poverty count for multidimensional poverty in India pushing the multidimensional poverty curve upwards when India is added. Whether revising or updating the LIC/MIC threshold would make a difference would depend on how much it was revised by. India is not too far over the line taking the 2010–12 data. However, India's economic growth continues as does other new MICs thus the line is

---

[12] Alvaredo and Gasparini (2015, p. 67) concur on the point that falls in poverty look much less significant when one focuses on actual numbers of poor people (using 2005 PPP poverty rates).

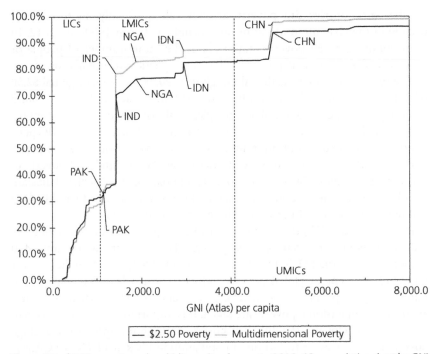

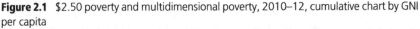

Figure 2.1 $2.50 poverty and multidimensional poverty, 2010–12, cumulative chart by GNI per capita

Source: Data from Edward and Sumner (2015), OPHI (2014), and World Bank (2015).

moving to the right over time. Nigeria, India, and Pakistan had experienced their GNI per capita rise by 2013 to $2,700 and $1,600 and $1,400 GNI per capita respectively (and $5,400 and $5,200 and $4,500 in GDP PPP per capita) which is substantially above the $1,045 GNI per capita threshold. It should be noted that Pakistan is important for global multidimensional poverty counts but less so for monetary poverty at $2.50 though there are some substantial questions about the quality of monetary poverty data in Pakistan (see Khan et al., 2015 for discussion). Pakistan accounts for 21 million (just 1 per cent) of global poverty by $2.50/day poverty but almost 80 million (or 5 per cent) of global multidimensional poverty. The other populous new MICs are much more advanced in income per capita: China has GNI Atlas per capita of $6,500 (and GDP PPP per capita of $11,500); Indonesia has GNI per capita of $3,600 (and GDP PPP per capita of $9,250). Furthermore, when Bangladesh crosses the low- to middle-income country line, it will transfer about a further 5 per cent of global poverty or 90 million $2.50 poor and 80 million multidimensional poor to the MIC group. Kenya's upgrade to MIC status (GDP PPP per capita of $2,700) brings a further 20 million $2.50 poor and/or 20 million multidimensional poor to the MIC group. There are,

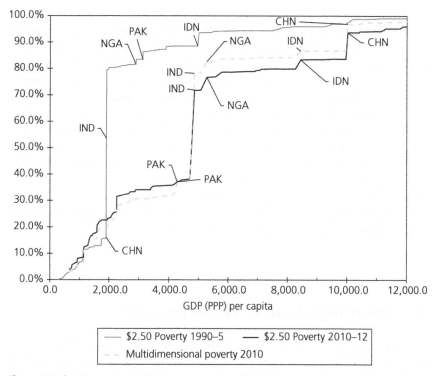

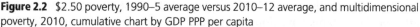

Figure 2.2 $2.50 poverty, 1990–5 average versus 2010–12 average, and multidimensional poverty, 2010, cumulative chart by GDP PPP per capita

Source: Data from Edward and Sumner (2015), OPHI (2014), and World Bank (2015).

however, a set of post-1990 MICs which are not significant to global poverty but are close to the $1,045 GNI per capita LIC/MIC threshold. These are as follows (and in parenthesis are their GDP PPP per capita for reference): Senegal ($2,200), Cameroon ($2,750), and since 2014, Kyrgyz Republic ($3,100) and South Sudan ($2,000).

In sum, the shift in the global distribution of poverty from LICs to MICs is a function of the thresholds themselves, but the bulk of global poverty is gradually moving further away from the current LIC threshold. The shift is not a product of the world's poor living in countries who have only just crossed the threshold in average income per capita into the MIC group. One would need to at least double (or triple) the LIC/MIC threshold to make much of a difference, as that would push India and Nigeria back under the threshold. One would need to increase by fourfold or sixfold the threshold to bring Indonesia and China respectively back into the LIC group of countries.

A better approach is to compare PPP poverty numbers with GDP PPP per capita by considering the cumulative global poverty by GDP PPP per capita (see Figure 2.2). Most of global poverty is either in countries that have a GDP PPP per capita above $10/day or will soon if growth continues. Figure 2.2 shows the shift in global poverty between 1990–5 and 2010–12 for $2.50 poverty by GDP PPP per capita: as countries became better off in average income per capita the curve moves rightwards, illustrating that absolute poverty numbers did not fall drastically but average income rose considerably.

The shift of global poverty towards MICs is thus due to economic growth in a relatively small group of populous countries where most of the world's poor live, where the absolute numbers of poor people did not fall as much as one might expect during the transition to MIC. In section 2.4 this book argues that the composition of remaining poverty in MICs shows a pattern of spatial and social inequality and marginalization that suggests certain sub-national regions and social groups are relatively disconnected from the growth poles that have produced MIC status at a country level.

2.4 **The composition of global poverty**

The fact that most of the world's poor now live in MICs (and could well remain in MICs in the future—see discussion in Chapter 4) raises a set of questions about those 'left behind', given that those countries who have attained MIC status have done so through sustained economic growth. Two questions are thus: To what extent do the MIC poor reside in rural or remote provinces or low-income provinces or 'LICs within MICs' that are poorly connected to rapid economic growth? And/or do the MIC poor belong to specific social groups who are to some extent marginalized from the benefits of rapid economic growth? The main argument of this section is that to a considerable extent global poverty is becoming characterized by spatial and social inequalities. The poor live in certain sub-national geographies and social groups that are marginalized from the opportunities and new resources generated by growth.

Addressing questions of sub-national poverty rates and poverty rates by social groups is not easy in a comparable and consistent way. Theoretically, it is possible to use monetary poverty but the extent of work entailed is not justified by the number of leaps of faith necessary. Fortunately, it is possible to pursue such questions with non-monetary poverty indicators such as undernutrition. One can explore the composition of undernutrition poverty and ask questions about the characteristics of poor households in terms of the spatial and social characteristics of household heads using the Demographic and Health Survey (DHS) data sets which are internationally comparable, standardized, nationally representative household surveys.[13] Analysis for sub-national geographical areas is also possible using multidimensional poverty data.

The approach operationalized next is based on a taking child undernutrition as a poverty indicator, specifically, the proportion of children under five years who are two standard deviations or more below WHO standard weight-for-age (a value commonly taken to indicate undernutrition), as a percentage of all children under five years. Then, as is common practice one assigns 'poverty' status to the whole household based on the nutrition data for children under five in the household, with weighting for incidence. The approach taken does not purely assess deprivation in a dichotomous way but considers intensity too. If one of three children in the household is undernourished, this is recorded as a 33.3 per cent deprivation in that case rather than full—meaning 100 per cent—deprivation.[14]

The justification for, and assumption of a focus on child undernutrition is that the ill-being of children is likely to reflect the poverty of the household. Childhood poverty also has significant and lasting consequences into adulthood (Bird, 2007; Corak, 2006; Smith and Moore, 2006). Furthermore, the undernutrition global data show similar patterns to the monetary and multidimensional poverty patterns already noted: in 2012, three-quarters or more of child stunting and wasting is in MICs: 73 per cent of the world's stunting and 80 per cent of the world's wasting is in MICs. Although one country, India, that moved from LIC to MIC accounts for about a third of the total of stunting and wasting, a range of other fast-growing emerging economies or new MICs account for substantial proportions of the totals of stunting and wasting, notably the populous other new MICs of China, Indonesia, Nigeria, and Pakistan and a number of older MICs such as Brazil, Egypt, Mexico, the Philippines, and South Africa.[15]

---

[13] The DHS can generate most data for all household members though the DHS are based on interviewing households with a woman of reproductive age (defined as 15–49 years). The DHS have been conducted since the 1980s in a range of developing countries, typically those receiving US foreign aid as the DHS is a USAID-funded project implemented by the company ICFI (formerly known as Macro International). For further details, see in particular, Rutstein and Rojas (2006). See for the DHS model questionnaire, survey organization and other technical matters, DHS/ICFI (2011, 2012a, 2012b). Disparities by gender have been very well documented by DHS data and for this reason are not included in the estimates here (see UNICEF, 2011).

[14] See for full details Sumner (2012a; 2013c). Indicators are constructed at a household level as this is the unit DHS is randomized over. Household data are used, then weights applied according to household size. Aggregates are presented for covariates that are standardized in the DHS. The sample of countries used here are equal to 80 per cent of the total population of low and lower middle-income countries in the 2005–10 period.

[15] Thirty-two countries have more than a million stunted children. The largest are, surprisingly perhaps, many of the MICs. For example, as noted, India (60m), and also Nigeria (10m), Pakistan (10m), Indonesia (9m), China (8m), Philippines (3.4m), Egypt (3m), Mexico (1.5m), South Africa (1.3m), and Brazil (1m). Fourteen countries have more than 500,000 wasted children. The largest numbers again include some of the MICs. India (25m), Nigeria (5m), Indonesia (3m), Bangladesh (2m), Pakistan (2m), China (2m), Philippines (1m), and Egypt (0.7m). Data from World Bank (2015).

The data from the DHS can be used to make estimates of the likely composition of global poverty more generally based on the use of child undernutrition. What does that data say? First, the composition of global poverty can be described as follows:

- Spatial aspects: More than three quarters of undernutrition-related poverty is to be found in rural areas.
- Social aspects: More than a third of undernutrition-related poverty is concentrated among those in households where the head is 'not in work' and a further third where the household head is working in agriculture; 60 per cent of undernutrition-related poverty is concentrated in those households where the head has no education or incomplete primary education; and more than two thirds of undernutrition-related poverty is to be found among those households where the head is the member of an 'ethnic minority group' (meaning an ethnic group which is not the largest ethnic group in that country though this finding should be viewed as tentative).[16]

The composition of undernutrition-related poverty can be estimated in MICs alone (see Table 2.4). In MICs, the composition of undernutrition-related poverty is highly rural and similar in other aspects to global poverty described above. In sum, one could say that by the indicator used—the poor in MICs are likely to geographically and socially marginalized.

Such issues can be considered in more detail at country level. For example, in two post-1990 MICs, India and Nigeria, spatial and social marginalization are evident (see Figure 2.3). The data suggest that poverty is very much spatially concentrated in rural areas (75–80 per cent of all undernutrition-related poverty).[17] In both India and Nigeria certain groups are over represented as a proportion of the poor (relative to their proportion of the general

Table 2.4 The composition of undernutrition (% total poverty by groups), 2005–10

% of total poor who have	All developing countries	MICs
	100.0	100.0
Rural residence	82.1	80.9
A household head with no education or incomplete primary	62.5	59.1
A household head who is working in agriculture	35.1	33.1
A household head who is not in work	41.9	44.3
A household head who is a member of ethnic minority group	72.3	72.7

Source: Estimates processed from DHS data sets in Sumner (2012a, 2013c).

---

[16] See for detailed discussion Sumner (2012a, 2013c).

[17] The urbanization rate for India for the same year as the DHS data is 29.5 per cent urbanized population and Nigeria, for the same year as DHS data is 47.7 per cent urbanized population (World Bank, 2015).

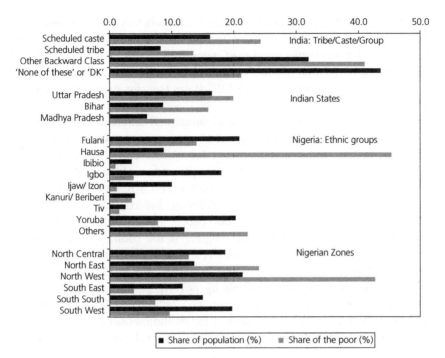

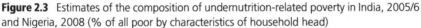

Figure 2.3 Estimates of the composition of undernutrition-related poverty in India, 2005/6 and Nigeria, 2008 (% of all poor by characteristics of household head)

Source: Data processed from DHS data sets for India and Nigeria in Sumner, 2012a, 2013c.

population). For example, India's scheduled caste, scheduled tribes, and other 'backward' classes account for approximately three quarters of undernutrition-related poverty in these estimates. Further, three populous states within India account for almost a half of undernutrition-related poverty (Uttar Pradesh, Bihar, and Madhya Pradesh) although they make up a third of the total population. In contrast, in Nigeria, there is a concentration of the poor in the Hausa ethnic group. Between a third and half of the undernutrition-related poor are accounted for by this group despite being an estimated tenth of the total population. There is also an interaction of social and spatial inequality—the Hausa ethnic group are the largest ethnic group in north-west Nigeria and parts of the north east and it is these two areas which account for half of all undernutrition-related poverty, despite only being a third of the total population. In contrast, the Yoruba ethnic group account for more than a fifth of the population but only 8 per cent of poverty and are the largest ethnic group in the south west that accounts for a fifth of population but contributes just 10 per cent of all undernutrition-related poverty.

If one considers India further, one finds more support for the hypothesis that new MICs are a collection of LIC units with a small number of MIC units that produce national per capita income levels sufficient to be classified as a MIC country. One finds that if one applied the LIC–MIC threshold at sub-national level, a substantial number of states in India would likely be LICs and an estimated two-thirds of India's poor would live in those LIC states and a third of India's poor would live in MIC states (see, for discussion, Sumner, 2012c).

Such patterns of poverty, in terms of substantial differences in urban and rural poverty rates and sub-national poverty rates are corroborated if one takes estimates of multidimensional poverty too. Alkire et al. (2011, 2015) and Alkire and Aguilar (2015) find that a large proportion of the world's multidimensional poor live in sub-national regions within MICs, notably the populous countries of India, Nigeria, and Pakistan. Indeed, Alkire and Aguilar (2015) find that there are more poor people in India than in all LDCs combined and that middle-income Nigeria is the country with the most pronounced regional differences. Alkire et al. (2015) find that, across a variety of approaches—including the poorest countries, the poorest sub-national regions, and the poorest individuals by poverty profile—the majority (61 to 68 per cent) of the world's poorest one billion people live in regions within MICs. Figure 2.4 shows the data for multidimensional poverty in the populous new MICs (sub-national multidimensional poverty data are not

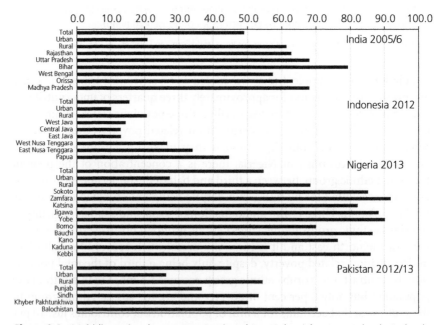

Figure 2.4 Multidimensional poverty rates in urban and rural areas and selected sub-national areas of India, Indonesia, Nigeria, and Pakistan

Source: Data from OPHI (2014).

available for China). The data show that in the four countries, there are drastic differences in poverty rates between urban and rural areas. In India, the proportion of rural population in poverty is triple that of urban areas and in Indonesia, Nigeria, and Pakistan, rural rates are double that of urban areas.

The poverty rates in sub-national regions vary much more. In India, the highest poverty rate is in Bihar state where 80 per cent of the population were multidimensionally poor, compared to Delhi's poverty rate of just over 10 per cent. Five other populous states in addition to Bihar—Rajasthan, Uttar Pradesh, West Bengal, Orissa, and Madhya Pradesh—that are home to almost half of India's population, have multidimensional poverty rates of 55 to 80 per cent. In Nigeria, half of the population of Nigeria live in ten sub-national areas that have poverty rates of 55 to 90 per cent (Sokoto, Zamfara, Katsina, Jigawa, Yobe, Borno, Bauchi, Kano, Kaduna, and Kebbi) while the poverty rate in Lagos is under 10 per cent. In Pakistan poverty rates of 70 per cent in Balochistan sit alongside poverty rates of 10 per cent in Islamabad. In Indonesia, East Nusa Tenggara and Papua have poverty rates of 30 to 40 per cent compared to Yogyakarta's rate of under 10 per cent. In the case of Indonesia, such areas are less populated but in other new MICs, some of the sub-national areas noted are highly populous, which with high poverty rates produces large numbers of poor people. For example, Bihar is home to almost 75 million multidimensionally poor people and Uttar Pradesh to 135 million, while Rajasthan, West Bengal, and Madhya Pradesh are home to about 50 million poor each. Kano in Nigeria is home to 10 million poor, Sindh to 20 million poor, and Punjab, Pakistan to 36 million. In short, most of these sub-national areas within new MICs are more significant to global poverty counts than entire countries elsewhere in the world such as some LICs and LDCs and FCASs.

It is thus a plausible theory that spatial and social inequalities reflect a marginalization of certain groups and sub-national geographies from the growth process in new MICs. One might even go as far as to hypothesize that rising spatial and social inequality and marginalization during periods of rapid growth will diminish prospects for sustaining growth and structural change unless the linking of sub-national geographies and social groups to growth poles is strengthened (e.g. by infrastructure development). In Chapter 3 we discuss the relationship between growth, inequality, and poverty with reference to new MICs.

2.5 **Conclusions**

Chapter 1 discussed the changes in the developing world since the early 1990s. This chapter has sought to address the following related question: how has global poverty changed since the end of the Cold War? This chapter has presented three arguments. First, that there has been a shift in the geography or location of global poverty from countries classified as low-income to countries classified as middle-income. This is due to rising average incomes in a relatively small group of populous countries that grew sufficiently to be reclassified from LICs to MICs. Second, that as those countries grew and were reclassified, about a billion people or approaching 70 per cent of the world's poor 'moved' from residing in LICs to residing in MICs. Finally, that the world's poor have not physically moved but the countries they live in have experienced rapid rises in average incomes and crossed the threshold into the MIC classification while poverty has not fallen to the extent that the amount of growth would warrant given the large increase in national income, output and consumption.

The chapter has discussed the conceptual point of departure, meaning the defining and measuring of global poverty and significant contentions that remain in estimating levels, trends, and the location of global poverty. Most importantly, there are questions about the PPPs that support the argument that one should consider monetary and multidimensional poverty side by side. The chapter has also considered the location or the 'geography' and composition of global poverty. The discussion outlined how and why the poor live in MICs and several populous countries in particular, not least China and India. Furthermore, the hypothesis was put forward that the data support the idea that remaining poverty in MICs is characterized by spatial and social inequalities, meaning that certain sub-national geographies and social groups have much higher poverty rates than national averages.

In sum, this chapter has argued that global poverty has changed from a low-income country phenomenon to a middle-income country phenomenon because most of the world's poor live in a set of populous LICs that grew fast and were subsequently reclassified as MICs, and the reduction in poverty has been less than warranted by the extent of the economic growth. As a result, about a billion poor people now live in MICs. A plausible theory is that much of this remaining poverty is concentrated in sub-national geographies and in certain social groups. This would be consistent with the hypothesis that some of the poor have been bypassed by growth due to certain areas and certain groups being marginalized or relatively disconnected from the growth process.

This changing distribution of global poverty challenges the orthodox view that most of the world's absolute poor live in the world's poorest countries. Research has, to date, rarely tended to present poverty as a structural outcome of specific patterns of growth and distribution, and their interaction with sub-national/spatial inequalities and social inequalities. One take on the data is that global poverty is turning gradually from a question of poor people in absolute poor countries to poor people in countries with potentially the resources to address absolute poverty. In Chapter 3 this book considers in greater detail why poverty has not fallen as much as one might expect, given the extent of economic growth in the new MICs.

3 Kuznets' revenge

Poverty, inequality, growth, and structural change

3.1 Introduction

In Chapters 1 and 2 it was noted that there has been a substantial amount of economic growth in many developing countries since the end of the Cold War and this has resulted in a number of countries, where global poverty is concentrated, becoming MICs. This transfer of global poverty from LICs to MICs occurred because poverty did not fall as much as expected during the transition. The fact that much of global poverty is situated not in the poorest countries but in MICs raises various questions about the future of aid which we turn to later on in this book. Yet, perhaps overshadowing these important debates is that the concentration of the world's poor in fast growing countries raises questions about why poverty levels are not falling faster and how different modes of late capitalism are associated with different poverty outcomes.

The argument of this chapter is threefold and builds upon Sumner (2013d): first, that the substantial economic growth since the end of the Cold War has not reduced poverty as much as it could have. There has been a relative weakness of the responsiveness of poverty to growth in many fast-growing countries. In short, growth has not been as efficient in reducing poverty as it could have been expected to be. Second, that this weak efficiency of growth in reducing poverty is due to the reappearance of the Kuznets curve and rising inequality during economic development. In the countries where the poor are concentrated growth has been accompanied by structural change and dramatically rising inequality even after tax and transfers. Third, that the weaker than might be expected responsiveness of poverty to economic growth is less due to the initial levels of inequality as the research literature would tend to suggest, and rather due to rising inequality *during* economic growth which has skewed the benefits of growth further away from the poorest than might have been the case.

The chapter is structured as follows: Section 3.2 considers conceptual and empirical debates on the relationship between poverty and economic growth. Section 3.3 then discusses the factors potentially contributing to an explanation of the weaker than could have been reasonably expected responsiveness of poverty to growth in the new MICs. The thesis of this section is that poverty has been less responsive to growth in the ten new MICs identified previously where much of global poverty is concentrated not only because of rising inequality, but limited structural change in employment, and because commitments to welfare regimes including the characteristics of social policy and social spending, to date, have not been more significant. In light of the experience of new MICs, Section 3.4 revisits the seminal work of Simon Kuznets. It is argued that while there is no universal empirically founded law that inequality will rise during economic development, the Kuznets hypothesis and underlying logic although largely dismissed has reappeared in the post Cold War era in the countries that have experienced growth with structural change and it is in those countries where most of the world's poor live. Finally, Section 3.5 concludes.

3.2 **Poverty and growth**

In order to address the question as to why poverty has fallen more in some countries than in others, it is useful to consider the literature on the responsiveness of poverty to growth. In general, economic growth is good for the poor in the sense that the incomes of the poor rise in line with average income (see Kraay, 2006; Dollar et al., 2013). However, the extent that the poor benefit can differ considerably across countries, within countries over time, and by the poverty line (or definition of poverty) taken. In general, it is important to note that if inequality is rising during growth the benefits of growth to the poor will be weaker than if inequality is static, at any given poverty line. Further, high and rising inequality can hamper not only poverty reduction but also future growth prospects and thus future poverty reduction too.

A useful point of departure is to consider the evolution of literature on what determines the relationship between economic growth and poverty. This is not a new debate. Discussion can be traced back conceptually, as well as empirically, to at least the previously noted work of Adelman and Morris (1973) and Chenery et al. (1974). Distributional patterns of growth are determined by the starting point—initial inequality—and what subsequently happens to distribution during growth, and thus the distribution of the growth increment. The literature has tended to highlight the former, though attempts to characterize what kind of growth pattern is more desirable have received considerable attention too. There is a wealth of literature on 'pro–poor' growth and its genealogy from earlier conceptualizations of 'growth with equity', 'growth with redistribution', and other iterations. 'Pro–poor growth' has been defined in numerous ways but has particularly been shaped by the works of Kakwani and Pernia (2000) and Ravallion (2004). Two types of definition can be outlined by the outcomes of growth: those definitions that are based on whether the poor have benefited in an absolute way—the absolute poverty headcount rate falls at a given poverty line and/or the incomes of the poor rise taking, for example, the poorest 40 per cent of the population; and those definitions based on the poor benefiting in a relative sense vis-à-vis the non-poor, that implicitly entails reductions in inequality.

There is a substantial empirical literature in this area of poverty, inequality, and growth which is reviewed in Sumner (2013d) and Sumner and Tiwari (2009) (See also: Adams, 2003; Bourguignon, 2003; Dollar et al., 2013; Fosu, 2011; Eastwood and Lipton, 2001; Fields, 2001; Kalwij and Verschoor, 2007; Kraay, 2006; Loayza and Raddatz, 2010; Ravallion and Chen, 1997). Monetary or income/consumption poverty is directly related to average income/consumption and inequality in income/consumption as a mathematical relationship (Bourguignon, 2003; Datt and Ravallion, 1992; Misselhorn and Klasen, 2006). The relationship between multidimensional poverty and growth is more complex. Rising incomes among the monetary or multidimensional poor can lead to improved nutrition intake and outcomes or improved access to education and health and education and health outcomes but public spending is important in terms of the provision of free or subsidized public education and health. Social policy such as redistributive transfers can further support the reduction of both monetary and multidimensional poverty (see, for discussion of countries with multidimensional poverty data over time, Alkire et al., 2014 and for a review of the effectiveness of cash transfers and other social policy and social protection measures Kabeer et al., 2012).

Earlier debates on poverty and growth sought to estimate the value of the relationship between growth and monetary poverty in the growth elasticity of poverty, and explore its determinants across countries. This, not surprisingly, had a large variance. Numerous estimates of the global average were made (e.g. Ravallion, 1995, 2001, 2005a). Estimates ranged substantially depending on the poverty line taken, the initial level of inequality, and the initial poverty rate. Studies sought to do decomposition analysis to assess the relative importance of growth in incomes and changes in distribution on poverty. A number of studies separated the poverty reduction due to the 'growth effect' (the change in average income) and the 'distribution effect' (the shift in the Lorenz curve holding average income constant) using Datt and Ravallion's (1992) methodology. Bourguignon (2003) argued that overall, half of poverty reduction was due to growth effects and half to distribution. White and Anderson (2001) found that, in a quarter of 143 growth 'episodes', the distribution effect was stronger than the growth effect. Some studies have focused on specific countries (see, for example, on India, Ravallion and Datt, 1999 and on China, Ravallion and Chen, 1996). Studies such as Kraay (2006) and Dollar et al. (2013) were interpreted as 'growth is all' but did find distributional changes to be important. For example, Kraay (2006) provided a decomposition analysis of the change in poverty between household surveys. It found, using data for forty-one countries with data for long-run growth spells, that 80 per cent of poverty reduction, taking the poverty headcount, was due to changes in average income. However, for the poverty gap and the poverty headcount times the poverty gap, respectively, 70 per cent and 60 per cent of the changes were due to changes in average income, suggesting that changes in distribution do matter. Further, findings, based on the 185 country growth spells, many of which are shorter than ten years, gave a contribution of growth to poverty reduction of between 43 per cent to 70 per cent, again suggesting changes in inequality should not be dismissed. Even if one accepts growth is important in reducing poverty, changes in distribution still matter, possibly even as much as growth in some cases.

In contrast to decompositions and elasticities, semi-elasticities, as Misselhorn and Klasen (2006) have argued, capture the *absolute change* in poverty as some countries have higher poverty heacounts at the outset. In the case of two data points available per variable, a simple arc elasticity makes sense: the ratio of percentage change over percentage change. However, the problem with this measure is twofold: first, percentage changes in poverty headcounts are (arithmetically) easier to accomplish at low levels of poverty (e.g. a drop from a headcount of 2 per cent to 1 per cent equals a 50 per cent drop while a drop from 80 per cent to 40 per cent is also 50 per cent drop). A problem of distortion also exists for gross domestic product (GDP) changes (a higher growth is arithmetically 'easier' at lower GDP levels). Semi-elasticities are a way to correct for one of the two problems above but not both simultaneously. How the semi-elasticity is calculated depends on whether you want to correct for the former, poverty, or the latter, GDP.[1] Misselhorn and Klasen (2006) propose one should calculate the percentage *point* change of the headcount over the percentage change in GDP. It is worth reiterating, not only is there a wide variation across countries for elasticities and semi-elasticities and decompositions, all estimates can change over time within the same country and with reference to the specific poverty line taken even within the same country.

Since the late 2000s, conceptual debates have widened to a new concept of 'inclusive growth', to consider more than the outcomes of economic growth on monetary and non-monetary poverty (see, for discussion, McKinley, 2010; Rauniyar and Kanbur, 2010; Ranieri and Ramos, 2013). Studies have considered participation in the growth process itself, either by increased employment opportunities created during or by growth, and/or the reallocation of public spending or additional resources, created from growth. The fault-line in 'inclusive growth' debates is, as in earlier debates, between the necessity or not of falling inequality and additionally a focus on inequality of opportunities. For example:

---

[1] One method, which corrects for the GDP issue would be to calculate the semi-elasticity as a unit change of the independent variable (GDP) over the percentage change of the dependent variable (poverty headcount). This would give the change in the headcount ratio per dollar change. An alternative is that proposed by Misselhorn and Klasen (2006).

Growth is inclusive when it allows all members of a society to participate in and contribute to the growth process on an equal basis regardless of their individual circumstances. (Ali and Zhang 2007, p. 10)

Klasen (2010b, p. 3) similarly defines an inclusive growth episode as one that requires:

The participation by all members of society; meaning that it is nondiscriminatory . . . A declining inequality in non-income dimensions of well-being, such as health, nutrition and education; meaning that the episode of growth is disadvantage-reducing.

In short, although pro-poor growth has been generally defined as poverty-reducing growth and/or inequality-reducing growth, and thus by outcomes and typically by monetary poverty, inclusive growth, in contrast, expands the lens to include the process of inclusion or participation in growth processes themselves in terms of employment and access to public goods and thus inherently multidimensional poverty too.

What unites the strands of the historical debate is an interest in why incomes of the poor or other aspects of poverty may or may not have been responsive to economic growth or to what extent they are responsive. If we take cross-sectional data for the most recent time period, 2010–12: Figures 3.1 and 3.2 show how correlations between poverty and growth are indeed very strong in countries where per capita income is at low-income levels then may become weaker in countries at lower-middle-income and in upper-middle-income levels.[2] One possible reason for this is that there may be diminishing returns to rising incomes (as per life expectancy and the Preston Curve) because the remaining poor are further from the poverty line, and/or that rising inequality during periods of growth in some counties dampens the rate of poverty reduction. In the process of development, as mean income rises, one might expect it to be easier to reduce poverty (meaning people close to the poverty line move across it) and that it would gradually get harder to improve as the average distance of the remaining poor under the poverty line increases. However, there is also a counter or distributional argument that fewer poor people and greater numbers of non-poor people would generate higher tax revenues (from those now non-poor) and give the state fiscal space to target redistributive spending towards the remaining poor. Figures 3.1 and 3.2 show $2.50 poverty and multidimensional poverty have somewhat similar patterns in the sense that the fall in poverty is substantial in LICs as average GDP PPP per capita rises. Then the decline is slower in MICs so additional income rises make less difference to the poverty headcount than in LICs.

---

[2] The relationship is similar and even stronger if one takes survey means as opposed to national accounts data.

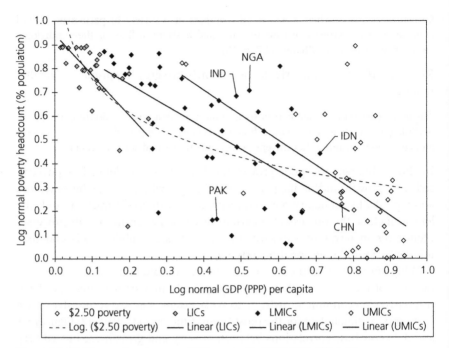

Figure 3.1 $2.50 poverty rate versus GDP per capita (2011 PPP), 2010–12

Source: Data processed from Edward and Sumner (2015) and World Bank (2015).

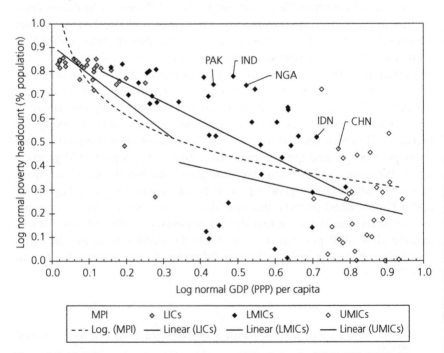

Figure 3.2 Multidimensional poverty rate versus GDP per capita (2011 PPP), 2010–12

Source: Data processed from OPHI (2014) and World Bank (2015).

Such patterns of the responsiveness of poverty to economic growth and economic development have been linked to a set of factors such as initial conditions, the sources of growth, and the nature of the welfare regime including social policy and social spending. Before moving on to these discussions we consider growth–poverty patterns with time–series data, for the set of ten new MICs identified in Chapter 1 that have experienced substantial growth in GDP PPP per capita since the Cold War.

3.3 Poverty, growth, and welfare regimes in the new MICs

In this section it is argued that the disappointing responsiveness of poverty to growth in many new MICs is due to rising inequality during growth that has been accompanied by structural change, and a relatively weak public or state commitment to a welfare regime vis-à-vis developing country averages for social spending or the types of social policy. Table 3.1 presents estimates on the responsiveness of poverty to growth in the set of ten new MICs identified previously in this book. Surprisingly, perhaps, Pakistan had the best responsiveness of $2.50 poverty and multidimensional poverty to growth in this group of ten new MICs. This is, in part, because Pakistan experienced a smaller increase in GDP PPP per capita than other new MICs listed and had a large population just below the $2.50 who moved above the line. The result is that in 2012 Pakistan had a poverty headcount of just 8.5 per cent at $2.50 a day but three-quarters of the population live on between $2.50 and $10 per day who in all likelihood may be at risk of falling back into poverty during growth slowdowns or other stressors and shocks.

Across the entire sample of 109 developing countries, 1 per cent growth in GDP PPP per capita is associated on average (median) with a decrease in poverty at $2.50 of just 0.6 per cent. In the set of ten new MICs, only Angola, Indonesia, and Pakistan were above even this rather weak average and the remaining new MICs were actually below this average for all developing countries. A 1 per cent growth in GDP PPP per capita is associated with a 1.9 per cent reduction in the monetary poverty headcount in Pakistan. In contrast, Ghana, Sri Lanka, and Sudan achieved just a 0.3–0.6 per cent reduction in the poverty headcount for the same amount of growth. India, and—surprisingly, China, achieved only a –0.2 fall in monetary poverty for the same growth, while Nigeria achieved no fall in monetary poverty headcount for the same amount of growth. This is sobering given half of the world's absolute poor live in China and India. And Nigeria adds substantially more poor people. In fact it implies that ending poverty in these countries, with large numbers of the

Table 3.1 Growth elasticity and semi-elasticity of $2.50 and multidimensional poverty in selected new MICs, 1990–2010 (or nearest available data)

	Growth elasticity of poverty		Growth semi-elasticity of poverty	
	(The % change in the poverty headcount ratio that a 1% growth in GDP PPP per capita is associated with over time period)		(The % point change in the poverty headcount ratio that a 1% growth in GDP PPP per capita is associated with over time period)	
	$2.50 poverty	Multidimensional poverty	$2.50 poverty	Multidimensional poverty
East Asia and the Pacific				
China	−0.2	–	−11.9	–
Indonesia	−0.9	−1.0	−57.2	−21.4
Vietnam	−0.4	–	−35.0	–
South Asia				
India	−0.2	−0.4	−17.0	−20.6
Pakistan	−1.9	−1.8	−110.4	−87.5
Sri Lanka	−0.6	–	−15.5	–
Sub-Saharan Africa				
Angola	−0.7	–	−48.6	–
Ghana	−0.5	−1.4	−22.8	−81.3
Nigeria	0.0	−0.3	0.2	−18.0
Sudan	−0.3	–	−16.3	–
Aggregates (median)				
East Asia and Pacific	−0.5	−0.9	−27.3	−34.1
South Asia	−0.5	−1.2	−21.8	−65.7
Sub-Saharan Africa	−0.4	−0.6	−26.6	−34.4
All developing countries	−0.6	−1.0	−15.4	−31.7

Source: Based on data from Edward and Sumner (2015), OPHI (2014), and World Bank (2015).

Note: Aggregates based on 109 countries for $2.50 and 34 countries for multidimensional poverty. Means are not presented due to a high standard deviation generated by outliers in the data with extreme and positive values.

world's poor, will entail a lot of growth to end poverty. In short, only Pakistan was substantially above the median for developing countries. This means that the responsiveness of poverty to growth—the efficiency of growth in reducing poverty—in new MICs, in general, was not much better than a weak global average.

Pakistan also had the most efficient growth for the reduction of multidimensional poverty in the set of ten new MICs over the period. A 1 per cent growth in GDP PPP per capita is associated with a 1.8 per cent reduction in the multidimensional poverty headcount. Indonesia and Ghana also had reasonable success with multidimensional poverty. However, Nigeria and India, for the same rate of increase of GDP PPP per capita achieved just a 0.3 or 0.4 per cent reduction in the poverty headcount respectively. The remaining new MICs—Angola, China, Sri Lanka, Sudan, and Vietnam—do not have two multidimensional poverty data points.

Table 3.1 shows that the findings of semi-elasticities mirror the relative positions of countries by elasticities. To recall from earlier, semi-elasticities seek to account for the difference in starting points in terms of the differing levels of initial poverty. Semi-elasticities consider the per cent *point* change rather than the per cent change. If one analyses the semi-elasticties, one finds that Angola, Indonesia, and Vietnam had a moderate responsiveness of $2.50 poverty to growth. Only Pakistan and Ghana had a stronger responsiveness of multidimensional poverty to growth. India, Indonesia, and Nigeria had much lower responsiveness of multidimensional poverty to growth. The relative weakness of elasticities and semi-elasticities in India, China, and Nigeria, where much of global poverty is focused, is again sobering because, all else being equal, it means very large increases in GDP PPP per capita will be required to reduce poverty in these countries.

An alternative comparison would be to assess the new MICs relative to the countries similar enough for there to be a possibiity of the new MICs achieving such elasticities. Comparing the new MICs to their respective regional averages (medians) and focusing on semi-elasticities for $2.50, we find that Angola is the only country in sub-Saharan Africa to do better than the regional average. Ghana is close. Nigeria and Sudan are some distance from the regional average. In East Asia and the Pacific, Vietnam and Indonesia are notably above the regional average. China, surprisingly is not. Finally, in South Asia, Pakistan is above, and by a considerable distance, the regional average. In sum, use of regional comparisons does not greatly change the earlier conclusion.[3]

What variables are thought in the literature to explain such cross-country variations? In terms of conditions, the role of initial inequality is most often cited in determining the responsiveness of poverty to growth.[4] Specifically, that the extent of poverty reduction depends on prevailing inequality levels and that a higher level of initial inequality leads to less poverty reduction at any given level of growth which is the mathematical relationship earlier noted (see Adams, 2003; Deininger and Squire, 1998; Fosu, 2011; Hanmer and Naschold, 2001; Kalwij and Verschoor, 2007; Misselhorn and Klasen, 2006; Ravallion, 1995, 1997, 2001, 2004, 2005a, 2005b; Son and Kakwani, 2003; Stewart, 2000). If we return to the set of ten new MICs again, Tables 3.2 and 3.3 lists the same set of ten new MICs and data for pre and post-tax and transfers or market and net Gini using the Solt (2014) data set and shares of GNI to the poorest, the richest, and the 'middle'. We find that in the set of ten new MICs, inequality as measured by the pre-tax *or* after-tax Gini was not high relative to the average (mean or median) of developing countries in 1990. In fact, most of the group of ten were close to or under this level with the exception of India whose pre and post-tax Gini were the highest in the group at 44.5 and 45.2, respectively. What is evident is that most of this

---

[3] Means are not presented due to a number of outliers with extreme and positive values.

[4] Other initial conditions identified include the literacy rate, urbanization levels, morbidity, and mortality rates (see review in Sumner and Tiwari, 2009).

Table 3.2 Selected new MICs: market and net Gini, 1990 versus 2010 (or nearest available years)

Region and country (actual survey years that estimates are interpolated from)	Market Gini		Net Gini		Market Gini—Net Gini	
	1990	2010	1990	2010	1990	2010
East Asia and the Pacific						
China (1990; 2010)	35.4	50.1	33.5	53.6	−1.9	3.5
Indonesia (1990; 2010)	34.4	41.9	32.0	39.2	−2.4	−2.7
Vietnam (1992; 2010)	37.3	41.8	36.2	39.0	−1.2	−2.8
South Asia						
India (1988; 1994; 2010)	44.5	51.9	45.2	51.4	0.6	−0.5
Pakistan (1987; 1991; 2011)	34.3	39.8	32.5	36.7	−1.9	−3.1
Sri Lanka (1985; 1991; 2010)	36.3	44.1	34.0	40.9	−2.3	−3.2
Sub-Saharan Africa						
Angola (2009)	–	51.7	–	43.6	–	–
Ghana (1989; 1992; 2006)	37.8	43.3	35.8	40.7	−2.0	−2.6
Nigeria (1986; 1993; 2010)	45.5	46.9	43.2	44.9	−2.3	−1.9
Sudan (2009)	–	37.1	–	35.6	–	−1.6
Aggregates (mean)						
East Asia and Pacific	41.2	42.1	38.9	40.3	−2.3	−1.8
South Asia	44.6	43.7	43.1	41.8	−1.5	−2.0
Sub-Saharan Africa	48.0	45.2	45.0	42.5	−3.0	−2.7
All developing countries	43.9	43.6	41.3	41.1	−2.6	−2.6
Aggregates (median)						
East Asia and Pacific	41.7	41.8	39.7	39.1	−2.4	−2.3
South Asia	42.0	41.0	39.4	39.5	−2.3	−1.9
Sub-Saharan Africa	44.1	43.7	40.7	40.9	−2.7	−2.1
All developing countries	43.9	42.9	40.7	40.3	−2.6	−2.4

Source: Solt (2014).

Note: Data for all individual countries listed are based on consumption surveys. Estimates for Gini coefficients are based on a regression which incorporates the maximum amount of information from proximate years by fitting a smooth curve point-by-point through the available data. This method results in 100 values for each variable, and the above are the average values for these estimates. The closest years to 1990 and 2010 are presented here. For greater detail see Solt (2014).

set of new MICs saw notable and sometimes drastic increases in inequality in both pre- and after-tax measures over the period of 1990–2010. This is in contrast to the developing country averages that fell slightly for both pre- and post-tax Gini (by mean and median).

The increases in pre-tax Gini in the new MICs are striking. For example, China's Gini rose from 35.4 to 50.1, India from 44.5 to 51.9, Indonesia from 34.4 to 41.9, and Pakistan from 34.3 to 39.8. Some of these increases were tempered by tax and transfers but not by a great deal in the populous new MICs: China's post-tax Gini rose from 33.5 to 53.6 and India's rose from 45.2 to 51.4, Indonesia's from 32.0 to 39.2, and Pakistan's from 32.5 to 36.7.[5] In

---

[5] In Solt (2014) only China and Bulgaria have a positive difference between market and net Gini in the 2010 period. A positive difference in the 1990 period can be found for India, Macedonia, Peru, and Ukraine. For most countries the difference between pre- and post-tax Gini is very small. The estimate that the net Gini is worse than the market Gini for China is corroborated by Cevik and Correa-Caro

Table 3.3 Selected new MICs: shares of GNI, 1990 versus 2010 (or nearest available years)

Share of GNI (% of total)	Richest 10%		'Middle' 50%		Poorest 40%	
Region and country (actual survey years of estimates cited in table)	1990	2010	1990	2010	1990	2010
East Asia and the Pacific						
China (1990; 2010)	25.3	30.0	54.5	55.6	20.2	14.4
Indonesia (1990; 2010)	24.7	28.2	52.7	52.9	22.6	19.0
Vietnam (1992; 2010)	29.0	31.1	51.8	51.7	19.2	17.2
South Asia						
India (1994; 2010)	26.0	28.8	52.1	50.5	21.9	20.7
Pakistan (1991; 2011)	27.1	25.6	52.6	51.7	20.3	22.7
Sri Lanka (1991; 2010)	27.4	30.0	51.4	50.9	21.2	19.1
Sub-Saharan Africa						
Angola (2009)	–	32.4	–	52.6	–	15.0
Ghana (1992; 2006)	30.0	32.8	52.4	52.2	17.6	15.1
Nigeria (1993; 2010)	31.5	32.9	55.7	52.1	12.8	15.0
Sudan (2009)	–	26.7	–	54.8	–	18.5
Aggregates (mean)						
East Asia and Pacific	29.2	30.0	51.7	52.1	19.1	17.9
South Asia	26.7	27.4	52.1	51.9	21.2	20.7
Sub-Saharan Africa	37.0	35.3	49.2	49.4	13.7	15.3
All developing countries	33.5	31.1	50.3	51.3	16.1	17.6
Aggregates (median)						
East Asia and Pacific	27.4	29.8	52.0	51.7	19.3	17.8
South Asia	27.1	27.0	51.6	51.7	21.2	20.7
Sub-Saharan Africa	33.8	32.9	48.7	51.2	13.0	15.5
All developing countries	32.8	29.7	51.5	52.1	16.0	18.3

Source: World Bank (2015).

Note: Data for all individual countries listed are based on consumption surveys. Regional means may not add up to 100.0 due to rounding and medians may not add up to 100.0 as medians of subpopulations need not do so.

short, even after taxes and transfers there were unequivocal increases in inequality in these new MICs. These rises in post-tax or net Gini also sit uneasily against regional averages which show that inequality was more or less static when the median is taken. The market Gini across all developing countries for within-country inequality even fell slightly overall (by both median and mean).

Palma (2011) argues empirically that there is a stability of gross national income (GNI) capture of those in between the richest and the poorest or the 'middle' (deciles 5 to 9) and changes in inequality are—in general—a contest between the richest 10 per cent of the population and poorest 40 per cent (see for more discussion in Chapter 4). One can see that the changes in the Gini have been driven by increases in the capture of the richest decile in most of the countries with data (see Table 3.3). Only in Pakistan was the

(2015) who note that whilst taxation in China makes the income distribution more equal, government spending in China has the impact of making the income distribution less equal.

change in inequality driven by a fall in share of the richest decile and a rise in the share of GNI to the poorest 40 per cent (and this sits uneasily with a rise in the Gini noted). The share of the richest and the poorest rose in Nigeria at the expense of the middle making Nigeria an exception to the stable 'middle' thesis.

In China, Ghana, India, Indonesia, Nigeria, Sri Lanka, and Vietnam the rise in GNI capture to the richest decile of the population between 1990 and 2010 was of the order of 1–5 percentage points (see Table 3.3). In contrast, the average (median) GNI share to the richest decile, for developing countries actually fell and the share to the poorest four deciles rose. In the new MICs, the opposite is the case: The GNI share to the poorest fell (with the exception of Pakistan and Nigeria) over the period, by 1–6 percentage points and on average about 2 percentage points. This is a substantial fall given the capture of GNI of the poorest four deciles was typically only about 20 per cent or less in 1990 and given too that in developing countries as a whole the share of the poorest 40 per cent actually rose.

The changes in inequality in new MICs are counter to orthodox economic theory regarding comparative advantage. The theory of comparative advantage that David Ricardo originally developed and Heckscher and Ohlin formulated further, upon which the present era of globalization and economic liberalization is logically predicated on, argues that within country inequality in developing countries will fall. Maskin (2015) notes that in previous eras of globalization inequality has declined citing the fall in national inequality in Europe and the US in the nineteenth century. The inverse has in fact as happened in the most recent period of economic liberalization. Focusing on labour (and thus wage inequality) Maskin outlines how the comparative advantage of emerging economies should be for producing goods for which skills do not really matter as much (vis-à-vis rich countries whose comparative advantage is in high-skilled labour). With globalization low-skill-worker production as a comparative advantage should cause inequality to fall. An alternative theory as to why inequality has not fallen in developing countries is that of Kremer-Maskin (in Maskin, 2015) who argues that the current wave of globalization has been distinct from earlier phases due to the internationalization of production. This has made labour markets more global due to a drastic fall in communication costs. Globalization has amplified the differences between those with better skills from low skill workers in developing countries. The only way to address this rise in inequality is for better training and education.

The rise in inequality in new MICs is of yet more significance as the Kuznets hypothesis that inequality rises during development has been largely dismissed in recent years. All of the set of ten new MICs have experienced structural change of varying degrees over the period in terms of agriculture as a proportion of GDP (with the exception of Pakistan where the rise in the post-tax Gini was due to changes in inequality outside the top decile) and urbanization of population. This would suggest that although there is no universal Kuznets law, countries experiencing not only rapid growth in GDP PPP per capita but also substantial structural change since the Cold War have experienced increases in inequality and a upward redistribution or 'trickle up' from the poorest to the richest given the preceding data.[6]

The level of heterogeneity of country experience in the efficiency of growth in reducing poverty and the differing extent of the rise in inequality points towards the role not only of those factors already discussed, but also of public policy and social policy in particular in influencing the responsiveness of poverty to growth and addressing rising inequality via the broader welfare regime including social policy and social spending. This is certainly true with reference to multidimensional poverty that entails public goods and to monetary poverty too via policies to influence the sectoral and geographical pattern of economic growth and the composition of public expenditure, as well as labour market policies (see, for discussion, Eastwood and Lipton, 2001; Epaulard, 2003; Fields, 2001; Fosu, 2011; Kalwij and Verschoor, 2007; Mosley, 2004; Mosley et al., 2004; Ravallion, 1995, 2001; Ravallion and Chen, 1997).

The welfare regimes literature focuses on these aforementioned aspects of late capitalism and their socio-economic outcomes such as poverty. Wood and Gough (2004, see also Gough, 2000; Gough and Wood, 2006), present an empirically grounded theoretical framework for the comparative analysis of 'meta-welfare regimes' and in doing so develop a taxonomy of welfare regime types to compare social policy that is of relevance to new MICs. Welfare regimes seek to insulate the population from market volatility and pursue security via collective, public insurance mechanisms. Wood and Gough (2006) argue that problems of legitimacy and poor functioning labour and financial markets limit the capacity of the state to act in a compensatory way for outcomes of the market in highly unequal societies such as those in developing countries. They modify Esping-Andersen's (1990, 1999) concept of 'welfare state regimes' and types of welfare capitalism which is based on OECD countries. Esping-Andersen (1990) identified three factors necessary to understanding differences between welfare regimes: class mobilization, political coalitions, and regime institutionalization by history.[7] One needs to consider the 'welfare mix', meaning the relationship between state, market, and family in welfare security provision; the extent of commodification, meaning the linking of welfare security to formal employment and protection from

---

[6] In order to check if there is a more general pattern to the inequality increase related to economic growth and structural change we could consider the data of earlier 'new MICs' (which are now UMICs or HICs). However, data availability for inequality prior to 1990 is too limited to do so. Another issue is that all of the new MICs here are Asian and African. There are no countries from Latin America where stronger redistributive systems were put in place in the 2000s (see for details Lustig, 2012; Lustig et al., 2012).

[7] A similar argument regarding history and path dependency is made by Haggard and Kaufman (2008).

market insecurities; and finally the extent of stratification or how the welfare regime generates social order by social policy (and this is effectively the 'political settlement' between elites and the rest of the population in the shape of the welfare regime). Esping-Anderson argued that these factors distinguish regimes and generate three types of specific regimes: liberal, corporatist–statist, and social democratic welfare regimes. In the first regime, the poorest received modest benefits (e.g. US) through targeted programmes and cash benefits as a minimal security provision. In the second regime, corporatist–statist, rights to welfare are institutionalized as part of state–citizen relationship in terms of employment protection and corporatism. Benefits are linked to employment and dependent on previous income or tax contributions and different groups receive different benefits. In the third regime, social democrat, it is organized labour that is integrated into a social security regime. Benefits are universalistic and financed by higher taxes and not linked to employment.[8]

The taxonomy of Esping-Andersen's is hard to apply to new MICs and developing countries more broadly given they do not have fully developed welfare states nor indeed fully developed capitalism in terms of employment in the formal sector (and thus a greater likelihood of a guarantee of welfare or employment security). In fact, ILO (2015) estimates of employment insecurity, based on data from ninety countries representing 84 per cent of total employment (thirteen LICs, forty-two MICs, and thirty-five HICs), estimated that in MICs 84.1 per cent of employment is insecure employment status compared to 19.9 per cent in HICs.[9]

In contrast to OECD nations, in developing countries, Wood and Gough argue that the welfare outcomes of the population are shaped by the basic institutional conditions such as the nature of markets in a given context, the legitimacy of the state, the extent of societal integration, and the nature of integration into the world economy; by the institutional responsibilities for welfare of state, market, household, and community; by the stratification system or the existing distribution of power and various assets. They note three types of meta-regime in developing countries. First, actual or potential welfare state regimes as those with high state commitment and relatively high welfare outcomes. In the developing world they argue empirically this covers the southern cone of Latin America—Argentina, Brazil, and Chile—and in East Asia, Thailand, and in Africa, Algeria and Kenya. Fairly few if any new MICs would find themselves in such a group other than possibly China or Vietnam who may be on the boundaries.

---

[8] A further type of regime, a Mediterranean model, was proposed Ferrera (1996) characterized by fragmentation in contributions and gaps in provision.
[9] 'Insecure' is defined those without permanent employment contracts such as own-account/unpaid family workers and or temporary/no-contract employees (in contrast to those who are permanent employees or employers).

Wood and Gough add two other meta-welfare regimes: *informal security regimes* and *insecurity regimes*. The first, *informal security regimes* are potentially more representative of new MICs, these are contexts whereby people reply on non-state relationships to meet security needs. In such situations poorer people often trade informal security for longer-term vulnerability and dependence. Examples, they argue, are what they call *more effective informal security regimes* or those with good outcomes at below average state spending (this group includes parts of South Asia, such as Sri Lanka, and other countries of Latin America) and *less effective informal security regimes* with weak welfare outcomes and low public spending (this includes South Asia excluding Sri Lanka and parts of sub-Saharan Africa). In contrast, *insecurity* regimes are contexts whereby there are gross insecurities, conflict, and political instability. Some new MICs, such as Nigeria or Sudan or parts of those countries may be best seen as in such groups. Unpredictability in such regimes undermines even informal rights and coping mechanisms.[10]

In keeping with Wood and Gough, Table 3.5 shows data for the set of ten new MICs, for social spending on public provision of education and health, for the country's social policies taking the World Bank's 'social inclusion' and 'equitable use of public resources' and 'social protection policies' assessments, and for social outcomes using monetary and multidimensional poverty headcount.[11] What is of interest is the relative levels vis-à-vis developing country averages. Social spending and the social policy or welfare regime in the new MICs listed here has been weaker or not much better (yet) than developing-country averages despite new resources generated by growth. Given that the group of ten developing countries here have drastically increased GDP PPP per capita and most now have reasonable levels of average incomes this may go some way to explaining weak growth elasticities of poverty. Notable exceptions are Vietnam and Ghana that had more progressive social spending and social policy or welfare regimes according to the data.

On public education and public health spending: although the public education data are patchy, it is clear that Vietnam and Ghana spend significant proportions on public education and health (combined, around 10 per cent of GDP in 2010–12) compared to developing country averages (though China, Nigeria, and Sudan have no comparable education spending data).

---

[10] Sharkh and Gough (2009) expand the taxonomy further empirically and focusing solely on data for non-OECD countries in 1990 and 2000 they present a taxonomy including 'proto-welfare regimes' and informal security and insecurity regimes (and distinguish illiterate and morbidity types in the latter). Proto-welfare regimes, which are somewhat similar to potential welfare regimes, are those with highest welfare outcomes in developing countries by survival and literacy and relatively high levels of state responsibility in terms of public spending on health and education and social security revenues.

[11] Data for each country's social policies is taken from the World Bank's Country Policy and Institutional Assessment (CPIA), which is a rating of countries from 1 (worst) to 6 (best) in terms of criteria relating to policies based on a detailed research instrument of countries' policies.

In contrast, Pakistan and Sri Lanka spend a third of that, closer to 3 per cent of GDP and India, Indonesia, and Angola are in between these extremes. However, with the exception of Ghana and Vietnam, public spending on education in all the set of ten new MICs with data is substantially below even the average for developing countries in 2010–12 and public provision of health in all of these new MICs with data is drastically below the average for developing countries with the exception of Ghana, China, and Vietnam.

In terms of the World Bank's Country Policy and Institutional Assessment (CPIA) social policy regime data, Vietnam and Ghana are again at the higher end of the CPIA combined score (and China has no data for this set of variables), as too is Indonesia (though it only has one CPIA variable) and India and Sri Lanka though slightly less so. Angola and Sudan are consistently below the average for developing countries.

In terms of social outcomes, monetary and multidimensional poverty vary considerably. Monetary and multidimensional poverty remain surprisingly high in a number of the new MICs. Up to one in five Indonesians and one in three in Angola, Ghana, and Sudan live in poverty. This compares to very low poverty rates in Vietnam and Sri Lanka and very high rates in India and Nigeria and Pakistan (the latter by multidimensional poverty rather than monetary poverty which is lower). In short, there are those new MICs with lower levels of poverty (China, Pakistan by monetary poverty only, Sri Lanka, and Vietnam) and those countries with higher poverty levels (India, Pakistan by multidimensional poverty only, Nigeria) and those with moderate levels of poverty (Angola, Ghana, Indonesia, and Sudan).

If one were to seek to characterize welfare regimes, four distinct types are evident in these new MICs (see Table 3.5). Based on the data in Table 3.4 one can identify countries by lower or higher poverty levels (relative to the averages) and stronger and weaker welfare regimes (relative to the averages). In the lower poverty, stronger welfare regime category would be China and Vietnam. In the lower poverty, weaker regime would be Pakistan by monetary poverty and Sri Lanka. In contrast in the moderate or higher poverty, stronger welfare regime category would be Ghana. Most new MICs (Angola, India, Indonesia, Nigeria, and Pakistan by multidimensional poverty and Sudan) would though fall in the moderate or higher poverty and weaker welfare regime category.

In sum, in most of the group of new MICs with growth and structural change, the state has yet to expand drastically welfare security via collective public insurance in the public provision of education (which for the poor is some kind of protection possibly against future unemployment) and health (which for the poor is insurance against ill-health costs and relatedly loss of earnings) with the exception of perhaps of a small number of new MICs. Rising inequality has been driven by the increased capture of the richest, suggesting consolidation of political and economic power. At the same time social

Table 3.4 Welfare regimes: social spending, social policy, and social outcomes in selected new MICs

	Social spending as % of GDP				Social policy regime (1 = low; 6 = high)				Social outcomes	
	Public education		Public health		Social inclusion and equity	Equity of public resource use	Social protection rating	Average across social policies	Poverty headcount (% of population)	
	1995–2000	2010–12	1995–2000	2010–12	2005–12	2005–12	2005–12	2005–12	$2.50 poverty 2012	Multidimensional poverty, 2010
East Asia and the Pacific										
China	1.9	–	1.8	2.9	–	–	–	–	10.8	12.5
Indonesia	1.1	3.3	0.7	1.1	–	4.0	–	4.0	20.2	15.5
Vietnam	–	6.3	1.7	2.8	4.0	4.4	3.4	3.9	6.0	4.2
South Asia										
India	3.7	3.7	1.1	1.2	3.7	4.0	3.5	3.7	39.1	53.7
Pakistan	2.6	2.2	0.8	1.0	3.0	3.5	3.2	3.2	8.5	44.2
Sri Lanka	3.1	1.9	1.7	1.4	3.7	3.5	3.6	3.6		5.3
Sub-Saharan Africa										
Angola	2.6	3.5	2.1	2.1	2.7	2.5	2.6	2.6	31.4	–
Ghana	4.1	6.8	1.7	3.7	3.9	3.9	3.8	3.9	26.7	30.4
Nigeria	–	–	0.8	1.1	3.2	3.5	3.4	3.4	42.0	43.3
Sudan	1.0	–	0.9	1.9	2.4	2.5	2.6	2.5	33.9	–
Aggregate (mean)										
East Asia and Pacific	4.9	5.5	3.9	4.7	3.1	3.4	2.8	3.1	32.8	24.1
South Asia	3.4	3.9	2.1	2.1	3.5	3.6	3.3	3.5	27.4	37.2
Sub-Saharan Africa	3.8	4.5	2.0	3.0	3.1	3.2	2.9	3.1	55.8	60.3
All developing countries	4.2	4.7	2.8	3.5	3.3	3.4	3.1	3.3	34.8	33.5
Aggregate (median)										
East Asia and Pacific	4.7	5.0	2.7	3.2	2.9	3.4	2.6	3.0	21.8	15.6
South Asia	3.0	4.0	1.7	1.4	3.7	3.8	3.5	3.7	33.8	44.2
Sub-Saharan Africa	3.4	4.3	1.8	2.4	3.2	3.4	3.0	3.2	55.7	66.1
All developing countries	3.8	4.5	2.3	3.0	3.4	3.5	3.2	3.4	26.7	27.2

Source: Data processed from OPHI (2014) and World Bank (2015).

Table 3.5 Stylized types of welfare regimes in selected new MICs

| | | Welfare regime characteristics (based on social spending and social policy) | |
		Stronger	Weaker
Welfare regime outcomes (based on poverty headcount)	Lower	China and Vietnam	Pakistan (by $2.50 poverty) and Sri Lanka
	Moderate or higher	Ghana	Angola, India, Indonesia, Nigeria, Pakistan (by multidimensional poverty), and Sudan

Source: Author's elaboration.

spending and social policy has—in general—not been that much better than developing-country averages which in part explains the rise in post-tax Gini and also the lower than expected responsiveness of poverty to growth. Ghana and Vietnam may be exceptions to some extent and one might assume China perhaps, although it has data gaps.

In light of the noted rise in inequality in new MICs and the weaker than might be expected welfare regimes despite growth and new wealth, in section 3.4 we revisit the seminal work of Simon Kuznets on inequality and economic development in order to discuss more fully why the countries where most of the world's poor live have experienced economic development with rising inequality accompanied by weaker welfare regimes at least to date.

3.4 **Kuznets revisited**

In this section it is argued that although the Kuznets (1955, 1963) hypothesis, that during development inequality rises then falls, has been largely rejected in terms of a universal law, such an 'inverted-U' type pattern is evident in the new MICs, at least in terms of the 'upswing' of the inverted-U. Most of the set of ten new MICs, where much of global poverty is concentrated, have experienced economic growth with structural change and rising inequality.

3.4.1 KUZNETS AND THE CROSS-SECTIONAL DATA

A good point of departure is to revisit the Kuznets hypothesis via the data for all developing countries. It was thought from the mid 1950s until the 1990s, based on Simon Kuznets' famous inverted U-shaped curve that inequality rises in the early stages of development and then falls later and thus that rising inequality was inevitable for countries transitioning from agricultural/rural economies to non-agricultural/urban economies. What has happened since the Cold War? Figure 3.3 shows national inequality, 1990–5 versus 2010–12 using the post-tax

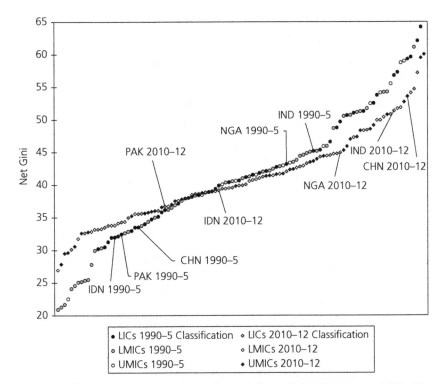

Figure 3.3 All developing countries (ascending order): net Gini, 1990–5 versus 2010–12

Source: Data processed from Solt (2014).

Gini coefficient (from Solt, 2014). The pattern is quite notable in terms of the post-tax Gini: inequality has fallen in some countries and risen in others producing a 'scissors-type' effect in the plot as more equal countries have become less equal and less equal countries have become more equal. As noted before, the post-tax Gini for all developing countries (within-country) was 40.7 in the early 1990s and fell lightly to 40.3 in the most recent time period.

Figures 3.4 to 3.6 focus on contemporary inequality in 2010–12 and show the net Gini versus other variables relevant to the Kuznets hypothesis. The dispersal of plots shows there is little in the way of any relationship in the contemporary cross-sectional data. Figure 3.4 plots the post-tax Gini versus GDP PPP per capita. This figure shows that the dispersal of the plots reveals no inverted-U curve in the cross-sectional data.[12] This is in

---

[12] Estimates in the text are 2011 PPP. Alvaredo and Gasparini (2015, p. 21) do, very cautiously, identify a U-shaped curve using 2005 PPP data but the upswing of the curve is entirely in sub-Saharan Africa and the downswing is entirely in HICs.

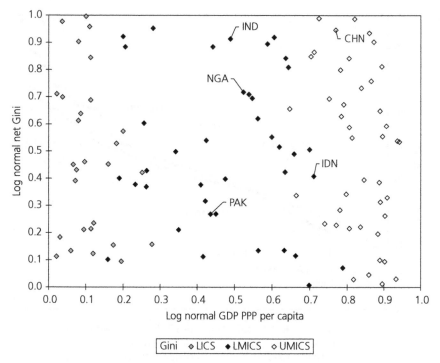

Figure 3.4 Net Gini versus GDP PPP per capita, 2010–12

Source: Data processed from Solt (2014) and World Bank (2015).

keeping with the view that there is no universal Kuznets curve, though the inverted-U curve may be found in some countries in time-series data.[13] Kuznets posited that it was the structural change of GDP and employment in particular that increased inequality. Figures 3.4 to 3.6 show the post-tax Gini versus agriculture as proportion of GDP and also versus agriculture as a proportion of employment.[14] The figures illustrate again the lack of any systematic relationship in the cross-sectional data for agriculture as a proportion of GDP or the proportion of employment in agriculture (and there is no relationship in the pre-tax Gini data either). These figures for GDP PPP per capita and agriculture as a proportion of GDP and employment are of importance as it would suggest that rising inequality in new MICs is a pattern evident in those countries rather than a general pattern across all countries.

The countries experiencing rapid growth since 1990 and where global poverty is concentrated—the set of ten new MICs—have experienced rising

[13] See discussion in Bruno et al. (1998), Deininger and Squire (1998), Fields (2001), Hellier and Lambrecht (2012), and Palma (2011).

[14] There are fewer plots for employment in agriculture (% of total employment) due to data availability in LICs.

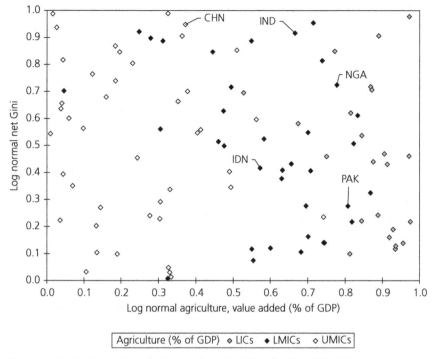

Figure 3.5 Net Gini versus agriculture, value added (% of GDP), 2010–12

Source: Data processed from Solt (2014) and World Bank (2015).

inequality from relatively low levels of inequality in the early 1990s. So, while there may be no universal law in the cross-sectional plots, the experience of post-1990 MICs has been that growth and structural change have been accompanied by rising inequality in the time-series data. This is consistent with Kanbur (2011) (see also discussion in Kanbur, 2005) in which it is noted that the Kuznets curve is not visible in cross-sectional data but is visible in some time-series data for specific countries. Indeed, as far back as the late 1990s, Deininger and Squire (1998, p. 279) noted that the failure to find the Kuznets curve overall did not mean that it does not exist for individual countries (and in their data they found that in four of forty-nine countries the Kuznets hypothesis was empirically supported).

3.4.2 THE ORIGINAL KUZNETS HYPOTHESIS REVISITED

Given the lack of visibility of a universal Kuznets curve but an unequivocal rise in inequality in the set of ten new MICs driven by the capture of the richest, it is worth revisiting exactly what Simon Kuznets argued, in his

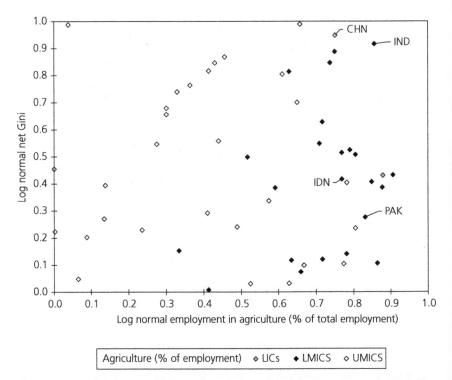

Figure 3.6 Net Gini versus employment in agriculture (% of total employment), 2010–12

Source: Data processed from Solt (2014) and World Bank (2015).

presidential address to the 1954 American Economic Association (Kuznets, 1955) and in a later article (Kuznets, 1963). Kuznets postulated that an inverted U-shape relationship existed between income and inequality: Kuznets characterized the income structure as follows: 'widening in the early phases of economic growth when transition from the pre-industrial to the industrial civilization was most rapid; becoming stabilized for a while; and then narrowing in the later phases' (1955, p. 18). This was based on what Kuznets called 'perhaps 5 per cent empirical information and 95 per cent speculation, some of it possibly tainted by wishful thinking' (p. 26).

The theoretical basis for Kuznets was a dual economy model as per the Arthur Lewis model (see discussion in Chapter 4). Indeed, Kuznets' presidential address that led to the seminal paper on the hypothesis took place the same year (1954) that Lewis published his own seminal work on the dual model. Lewis and Kuznets, however, differed somewhat on distributional questions and the inevitability of rising inequality. Kuznets (1955, p. 18) argued that inequality would increase in the earlier stages of industrialization if new industry had 'shattering effects' on long-established pre-industrial economic and social institutions as 'to destroy the positions of some of the lower groups more rapidly than opportunities elsewhere in the economy may be created for them' (p. 25) or if in the early stages the drivers of development—meaning the owners of capital—might maintain or increase their share of GNI due to the speed of wealth creation. The squeeze in the share of GNI to the poorest 40 per cent in the set of ten new MICs and the rise in share to the top decile is consistent with this, as too is the weaker change in the data on employment in agriculture. The responsiveness of poverty to growth in the set of ten new MICs would also support these assertions. Lewis (1954) in comparison made several references to distribution but did not discuss it explicitly in great depth. He did not see rising inequality as inevitable but did note the visibility of spatial inequality resonating with new MICs today or the earlier hypothesis of this book that new MICs are collections of LIC units with a set of core MIC units:

There are one or two modern towns, with the finest of architecture, water supplies and communications and the like, into which people drift from other towns and villages which might almost belong to another planet. (p. 147)

Although Lewis (1976) argued that development was in its early stages at least inegalitarian because economic development does not simultaneously start in every part of the economy, Lewis did not see a rise in inequality as inevitable. Lewis discussed inequality implicitly in terms of the traditional and modern sector and wage differentials. In considering savings too, Lewis highlighted that 'the central fact of economic development is that the distribution of incomes is altered in favour of the savings class' (p. 157). Although inequality was largely implicit in the Lewis model (in wage differentials between modern and traditional sectors) and central to the model, it was not presented as a distributional question but one of transfer between sectors, positing that 'the increase of the capitalist sector involves an increase in the inequality of incomes' (p. 159).

Distribution for Kuznets was though the unambiguous primary focus in that he argued that agricultural economies (developing countries) start as relatively equal societies (as per the set of new MICs at the end of the Cold War) and as the economy develops, the population migrates to non-agricultural sectors, where average incomes are higher, as is inequality. Thus initially, inequality worsens because of the higher proportion of national income in the industrial sector and the higher proportion of profits in national income. The early benefits of economic growth go to those with control over capital and better education (meaning the non-poor or skilled labour in today's new MICs). In time, as more of the population move out of the traditional, rural, agricultural sector to the modern, urban, industrial sector and real wages in industry begin to rise, income inequality decreases. However, one could wonder what might happen if output moves out of agriculture but labour does not to the same extent, as is the situation with today's new MICs or if there is premature deindustrialization in new MICs as per the Rodrik (2015) thesis, or at least a declining share of manufacturing in GDP or employment (see Chapter 4). This may in part be related to the fact that the Lewis model was a closed economy model in the first instance and a significant difference with today's new MICs is they are integrated into the world economy by their output and labour force into contemporary global trade and investment patterns of the international division of labour and capital. Thus the Lewis turning point and/or decline in inequality may be delayed by relocation of capital or migration of labour.

Returning to Kuznets (1955, pp. 7–8), one can note a set of assumptions that if held would lead to inequality increasing during economic development: that average income per capita is lower in rural than urban populations; that inequality is lower among the rural population (relative to the urban population); thus the increasing proportion of urban population (as is visible in the new MICs and across developing countries) increases the proportion of the less equal part of the income distribution and the relative difference in income per capita between rural and urban populations will not fall in the course of economic growth. Instead, it may be stable or indeed, increase as urban productivity per capita increases more rapidly than in productivity per capita in agriculture. Kuznets argued that if all of the above holds then inequality overall will rise. Put another way: incomes rise due to an inter-industry shift away from agriculture and this leads to a rise in the income differential between the agricultural and non-agricultural sectors. It is plausible that urbanization itself of the population may be a more important driver in new MICs than the shift in employment away from agriculture. Given that income is likely to be more equal in agriculture than in non-agriculture, the structural shift away from agriculture causes an increase in inequality. This certainly seems to be the case with the new MICs, where those countries experiencing structural change of output away from agriculture have experienced rises in inequality.

Kuznets (1955, p. 17) argued that the only way to offset the rise in inequality due to the inter-sectoral shift away from agriculture would be for a rise in the share of lower income groups within the non-agricultural sector. This, in the new MICs would likely mean those working in the urban informal service sector. Kuznets posited that in democracies once the early phases of industrialization pass, various forces combine to bolster the income share of the lower income groups within urban populations, as previously established migrants become better organized and adapt and/or grow in political strength which leads to more redistributive policies. Acemoglu and Robinson (2002) discuss the political economy of Kuznets and offer two models of late capitalism: 'autocratic disaster' with high inequality, low output; and 'East Asian miracle' of low inequality and high output. They argue these arise either

Table 3.6 Political regimes: quality of democracy and governance in selected new MICs

	Quality of Democracy (POLITY)		World Governance Indicators (average of six dimensions)	
	2000	2010	1995–2000	2005–10
East Asia and the Pacific				
China	–7.00	–7.00	–0.46	–0.54
Indonesia	6.00	8.00	–0.73	–0.55
Vietnam	–7.00	–7.00	–0.47	–0.51
South Asia				
India	9.00	9.00	–0.18	–0.22
Pakistan	–6.00	6.00	–0.82	–1.03
Sri Lanka	5.00	4.00	0.36	–0.43
Sub-Saharan Africa				
Angola	–3.00	–2.00	–1.59	–1.10
Ghana	2.00	8.00	–0.21	0.06
Nigeria	4.00	4.00	–1.07	–1.11
Sudan	–7.00	–2.00	–1.55	–1.56
Aggregates (mean)				
East Asia and Pacific	1.07	1.13	–0.48	–0.43
South Asia	0.43	5.50	–0.51	–0.66
Sub-Saharan Africa	0.62	2.62	–0.71	–0.70
All developing countries	1.24	2.78	–0.57	–0.54
Aggregates (median)				
East Asia and Pacific	3.00	4.00	–0.46	–0.47
South Asia	5.00	5.50	–0.40	–0.65
Sub-Saharan Africa	0.00	3.50	–0.68	–0.66
All developing countries	2.00	5.00	–0.54	–0.52

Sources: CSP (2015) and Kaufmann and Kraay (2015).

because inequality does not increase with development, or because political mobilization is too limited. The degree of democracy or responsiveness of governance in the set of new MICs is very mixed (see Table 3.6). Two measures to assess the relative quality of democracy and governance are respectively the POLITY quality of democracy data set and the World Bank's World Governance Indicators. The former, POLITY, is composed of elements that seek to capture the qualities of executive recruitment, the constraints on executive authority, political competition, and the institution-alized qualities of the governing authority. The data is scaled as follows: 10 is a full democracy; 6 to 9 is a democracy; 1 to 5 is an open anocracy (a regime of political instability and ineffectiveness); minus 5 to 0 is a closed anocracy; and minus 10 to minus 6 is an autocracy. In the data presented in Table 3.6 for 2010, China, and Vietnam are autocracies and Angola and Sudan are closed anocracies. The remainder are democracies of various degrees, notably Ghana, India, and Indonesia are close to full democracies. Nigeria and Pakistan are respectively a closed and an open anocracy.

The latter indicator of governance is the aggregate of six dimensions of governance: voice and accountability (perceptions of the extent to which a country's people are able to participate in selecting the government and the extent of freedom of expression and association); political stability and absence of violence; government effectiveness (perceptions of the quality of public services and civil service); regulatory quality (perceptions of whether the government is able to formulate and implement policies that promote private sector development); rule of law (perceptions of the quality of contract enforcement, the police, and the courts and likelihood of crime) and control of corruption (including petty and grand forms and capture of the state by elites and private interests). Higher values indicate better outcomes. In the more recent data all of the selected new MICs are negative bar Ghana (though India is close to zero) though they are close to the developing country averages. Angola, Nigeria, Pakistan, and Sudan have particularly negative data vis-à-vis developing country averages.

The discussion on democracy and governance points towards some of the contradictions of political change: China and Vietnam are not democracies but do have reasonable governance relative to developing country averages. At the same time countries such as India are full democracies but have weak governance vis-à-vis developing country averages. One could speculate that the expansion of social policies are increasingly visible in some new MICs today due progressive elites or elites that rely on power without democracy and thus rising living standards (China and Vietnam) or differing forms of political mobilization (India and Indonesia). One could note the expansion of health insurance and social protection in Indonesia or Vietnam for example or the rural employment guarantee programme or commitments to social security in India to name but a few examples. Thus it may be that new MICs are on the cusp of reaching a Kuznets turning point in political change. Data in World Bank (2015, pp. 12, 45) would suggest a substantial expansion of social policies at least in UMICs in the form of conditional and unconditional cash transfers, school feeding programmes, unconditional in kind transfers (e.g. food programmes), public works programmes, and school fee waivers is taking place although coverage differs substantially across types of countries by income and region.

3.4.3 THE EMPIRICAL LITERATURE RELATED TO THE KUZNETS HYPOTHESIS

How do such ideas match the wider empirical literature? In terms of the inevitability, likelihood or otherwise of rising inequality during economic growth and economic development, there has been a wide range of research pursuing such questions, the sum of which is as follows: there are too many country specifics to make a generalization. The original Kuznets hypothesis was based on urban–rural wage differentials. In a review of empirical studies on this matter, Lindert (2000) argued that historical data from the UK and US, although too incomplete to make conclusions, do not establish the support for a trend in sectoral (or occupational) wage differentials in a way to support Kuznets. Lindert posits that the fall in pay differentials in the twentieth century was driven by the expansion of trade unions, labour market regulation, and education expansion (see also Goldin and Katz, 2008) which would be consistent with a political mobilization thesis.

Turning to the literature based on developing countries, a number of empirical studies in the 1970s initially supported the Kuznets hypothesis (Ahluwalia, 1976a, 1976b; Ahluwalia et al., 1979). As Kanbur (2011) notes such papers took on significance because, although based on cross-sectional data they were interpreted as inter-temporal causal relationships. However, in the 1980s and 1990s a series of new studies led by Anand and Kanbur (1984, 1993a, 1993b) questioned or rejected the inverted-U (see also Adelman and Robinson, 1989; Ravallion, 1995) whilst others found a positive association between growth and income inequality (e.g. Barro, 2000; Galor and Zeira, 1993; Perotti, 1993). The present consensus as noted before is that the inverted-U cannot be found in cross-sectional data as illustrated above across all countries but may exist in some developing countries.[15] Indeed, Kuznets himself only found a rising trend or upswing in the data he used, not an inverted-U (his downswing of the inverted-U was based on theory and a data simulation).

In the 1990s and 2000s, the empirical literature diverged due to methodological issues. In an attempt to further explore Kuznets' thesis, some have posited that the inequality and growth relationship depends on the level of economic development or differs in democratic and non-democratic countries (see Barro, 2000; Deininger and Squire, 1998; List and Gallet, 1999; Perotti, 1996). Clearly, in the set of ten new MICs there are a range of levels of economic development and democratic/institutional configurations as noted, that make it difficult to generalize across countries such as China, Vietnam, Indonesia, and India though one commonality across many of the set of ten new MICs is an institutional history of systematic, state economic planning

---

[15] The shape of the inverted-U curve has taken various alternative shapes including an italicized-*N*, an inverted-*J* or an L-curve. In the largest review of literature on advanced countries, and with reference to wealth rather than income inequality, Roine and Waldenström (2014, pp. 38, 72) outline each but conclude on an inverse-*J* curve at least for industrialized countries:

The *N*-shape corresponds to an increase in inequality over industrialization followed by a decrease over the twentieth century and again an increase since around 1980. The *U*-shape would be a situation where inequality is high before and during the period of industrialization, then declines over the twentieth century, and increases again after around 1980. Finally the *L*-shape corresponds to the *U*-shape but without the up-turn around 1980...The proper characterization of wealth inequality over the path of development hence seems to be that, so far, it follows an inverse *J*-shape with wealth being more equally distributed today than before industrialization started.

(e.g. the REPELITA planning in Indonesia or the Planning Commission in India or state economic planning in China and Vietnam) that is counter to the post Cold War framework for a liberal market economy in the developing world as defined by the 'Washington Consensus' that was largely about rolling back the state (see Williamson, 1990 and Chapter 4).

It is worth clarifying that there are actually at least two debates that are worth separating related to Kuznets here. The first, the relationship Kuznets hypothesized from growth to inequality. The second, a trade-off that Kuznets implied on inequality to growth or reverse causation. The former has no systematic relationship in the empirical literature as noted. The latter literature has to some extent greater consensus for developing countries and suggests that high and/or rising inequality hinders future growth in developing countries at least but country or regional factors are important (see discussion of Cunha Neves and Tavares Silva, 2014). The latter is then particularly relevant to the new MICs for the future (see discussion in Chapter 5).

The relationship of growth to inequality, which was the central focus of Kuznets, however, is more complex and, in spite of numerous attempts, no systematic empirical association from growth to inequality has been reported in the empirical work (see for discussion, Adams, 2003; Deininger and Squire, 1998; Dollar and Kraay, 2002; Easterly, 1999). In fact, the dominant view is that inequality is not an outcome of growth but plays a role in determining the pattern of growth and thus poverty reduction (Bourguignon, 2003, p. 12). This does not necessarily mean that growth has no impact on distribution; rather, there are too many country specifics to make a generalization. A question follows as to what drives changes in distribution.[16]

3.4.4 DRIVERS OF DISTRIBUTIONAL CHANGE

To return to the question of the meta-welfare regimes and political change and public policy of Wood and Gough, an important question is if inequality is likely to rise with economic growth and structural change, what can public policy do to counteract this likely rise? Although Kuznets argued that the upswing of the inverted-U curve was driven by structural change, urban–rural wage differentials, he argued that the downswing was driven by political change. Kuznets (1955, p. 7) noted, two groups of forces seem to share the long-run pattern of inequality: the concentration of savings (resonating with

---

[16] Many of the discrepancies between studies could be due to methodological differences (see, for discussion, Forbes, 2000; Knowles, 2005; Lopez, 2005). Most notable are the data sets used: the original Kuznets curve was based on historical data for the first half of the nineteenth century for three developed countries (USA, UK, and Germany) and reference was made to India, Ceylon (now Sri Lanka), Prussia, and Puerto Rico. The 1970s studies were primarily based on cross-sectional, not time-series data and many of the 1990s studies were based on new, larger, 'high quality', temporal, data sets.

Lewis) and its impact on capital incomes versus political decisions and taxation.[17] The empirical literature has identified a set of factors some of which can be influenced by governments and some of which are less amenable (see review of Cevik and Correa-Caro, 2015). For example, fiscal policy can reduce income inequality (see Auten and Carroll, 1999; Benabou, 2000; Feenberg and Poterba, 1993; Muinelo-Gallo and Roca-Sagales, 2011); the liberalization of trade and investment can raise inequality (see Barro, 2000; Milanovic, 2005); and financial development can lower income inequality (see Galor and Zeira, 1993; Banerjee and Newman, 1993; Clarke et al., 2006). One way of grouping factors is as exogenous or endogenous drivers of changes in national inequality. The former relate to such factors as shifting global trade and finance patterns and technological change. The latter factors pertain to domestic policies such as national macroeconomic policies, labour market polices, wealth inequality policies and more generally fiscal policy (taxation and transfers), and government spending on public goods. Such policies can usefully be categorized by what they seek to achieve in terms of influencing distribution: first, policies to reduce disparities in disposable income such as tax and transfers; second, policies to reduce disparities in individual's endowments such as policies on wealth or education and labour market policies or policies to increase the value of assets owned by the poorest. Third, reduction of risk and resultant income losses and additional costs such as health insurance or unemployment insurance.

Dabla-Norris et al. (2015, p. 27) empirically argue that the drivers of changes in the market Gini across a data set of almost 100 countries for 1980–2012 are labour market flexibility, financial deepening, and technological progress. They argue globalization proxied as financial openness has been less significant but reinforcing and it is health outcomes that mitigate some of the rises in inequality. They further note financial openness, technological progress, and labour market easing of regulations are associated with increased capture of the richest. They find governments can reduce inequality via redistributive spending and healthier societies tend to be more equal, suggesting a role for public health spending in the welfare regime.

The sources of growth have also been thought to be important in shaping the distributional benefits of growth. The sources of growth may be divided sectorally (agriculture and non-agriculture), or by factors (labour or capital), or by drivers of growth (structural change or commodity-led). Some empirical work has argued that agricultural growth is the most important sectoral growth for poverty reduction, and increases in agriculture productivity the

---

[17] Piketty et al. (2006), however, argue with reference to France that it was the adverse war-time shocks in between World War I and World War II that decreased (wealth) inequality and the subsequent redistributive policies that prevented inequality rising afterwards. Those war-time shocks related to the destruction of infrastructure and productive capacity rather than taxation and regulation according to Piketty and Zucman (2013).

most effective for the reduction of poverty (Bourguignon and Morrisson, 1998; Gallup et al., 1999; Ravallion and Datt, 2002; Timmer, 1997; Thirtle et al., 2001). Loayza and Raddatz (2010) have empirically linked the structure of output growth in terms of the sectoral composition of growth and how that determines poverty reduction linked to skilled and unskilled labour and the capital- or labour-intensiveness of sectors. They note that the largest contributions to poverty alleviation come from the unskilled labour-intensive sectors of agriculture, construction, and manufacturing as opposed to mining, utilities, and the services sector (pp. 137, 142). Adelman (2000) earlier argued that the factor intensity of growth determines the distribution of benefits. Natural resource growth and/or capital-intensive growth are unequalizing because such factors are unequally distributed. Capital-intensive growth raises the share of income in the wealthy group because they are the capital owning class.

Changes in the level of inequality can also be driven by changes governments have little control over such as global patterns and trends in international trade, commodity prices, or international investment which may, for example, impact on the relative export prices of different commodities, and that in turn has an impact on national inequality in terms of who controls and produces different commodities domestically (e.g. some crops may be labour-intensive or grown by smallholders and other crops are capital-intensive and grown on plantations). Further, wage differentials between skilled and unskilled labour may be driven to a considerable extent by the international division of production (Indonesia has no control over minimum wages in China for example, and yet the countries compete in textile production).

There are, though, a set of drivers that government policy can—potentially—have significant control over, such as the amount and distribution geographically and socially of public spending on the provision of free or subsidized education and health (and its impact on human capital distribution), the set of social policies, including direct transfers to poorer groups in society or labour market interventions such as minimum wage setting and enforcement and trade union laws. All of which points towards the following: governments can have some influence over levels and trends in inequality even if economic growth and structural change are likely to trigger rising inequality, but this requires active policy regimes (e.g. social spending, transfers, and policies) orientated to that end and thus shaping the distribution of the benefits of growth.

Furthermore, empirical research on the drivers of changes in inequality have identified different drivers in different regions and countries, with some commonalities across regions supportive of the preceding discussion. For example, in East Asia, Sharma et al. (2011) attributes changing inequality to structural change itself; an increase in the skills premium for skilled workers due to growing demand for skilled workers; educational attainments and barriers to labour mobility. In Indonesia specifically, changes in inequality have been linked to changes in world prices of mining commodities relative to estate crops (Yusuf et al., 2013) and the sectoral contributions to growth (Suryahadi et al., 2012). Further, changes in government policies for the formal labour market including an increase in severance payments, the strengthening of labour unions, rising minimum wages, reduced demand for unskilled labour, and an increase in informality in lower wage employment which together have impacted on inequality in terms of skilled and unskilled urban and rural sectors (Yusuf et al., 2013). Large transfers, notably regressive fuel subsidies and compensation for their reduction have also played a role (Yusuf and Resosudarmo, 2008).

In South Asia, and India in particular, somewhat similar factors are drawn out by Mazundar (2012) including again the sectoral composition of growth and service-sector-led growth (which is more unequal in wages). As well as structural change in the migration of agricultural labour to the urban informal sector, the targeting of state benefits to a small formal sector, and changes in social spending and education policies that neglect primary education in favour of tertiary education have all contributed to rising inequality.

Much work has taken place on Latin America's inequality trends because of the high level of inequality and also the reported decline in inequality over the last decade in particular. For example, Cornia (2009, 2012) argues that in the 1990s rising income inequality in Latin America was a result of global factors—changes in trade, foreign direct investment and financial liberalization, and a rise in migration. In contrast, the fall in inequality in the 2000s was due to domestic policy interventions such as the equalization of the distribution of human capital, targeted social spending, and improvements in tax-to-GDP ratios. Labour markets interventions, including rising real minimum wages (after two decades of decline) and a growing number of people covered by formal contracts, as well as macroeconomic stability and stable exchange rates also contributed to the fall in national inequality.

In a different vein, Birdsall et al. (2011, p. 14) argue empirically that 'social democratic' regimes (e.g. Brazil, Chile, and Uruguay) have surprisingly been more likely to reduce inequality than 'left populist' ones (e.g. Argentina, Bolivia, Ecuador, Nicaragua, and Venezuela). However, both 'social democrat' and 'left populist' regimes were more likely to reduce inequality than non-left regimes (e.g. Colombia, Costa Rica, Mexico, and perhaps Peru). This is due not only to higher levels of social spending but to more progressive public spending and policies overall, as well as the macroeconomic framework. On the social-spending side, this includes spending on cash transfers targeted at the poor, increases in spending on health and education that reach the lower and middle quintiles, as well as expansion of basic services and education spending focused on primary and secondary schooling. This is consistent with Lustig et al. (2012) who argue that the declining inequality trend in Latin

America is due to two reasons. First, that there was a fall in the premium of skilled labour over unskilled labour, measured as returns to education and due to labour market policies and the expansion of basic education. They posit that one would expect the skill premium to rise if growth is based on open trade and open markets, but this can be counteracted by the expansion of basic education which makes low-skilled labour less abundant and shifts labour demand. Second, that there were higher and more progressive government transfers such as Oportunidades in Mexico and Bolsa Familia in Brazil.[18]

Returning to global factors, others associate changes in inequality with economic openness, and in particular the impact of that economic openness on the relative global or regional demand for skilled labour (vis-à-vis unskilled labour) as well as demographic factors, international migration, and remittances (e.g. Anderson, 2005; Chusseau and Hellier, 2012; Goldberg and Pavnick, 2007; Harrison et al., 2011).

In the case of the post-1990 MICs experiencing growth and structural change, it seems their exception to the overall rule (that inequality need not rise during growth and economic development) is of significance. Further, falls in inequality in Latin America, albeit from high levels, demonstrate that MIC governments have the capacity to address inequality and build stronger welfare regimes.

3.5 Conclusions

The chapter's thesis has been threefold: first, that poverty has not been reduced as much as one might expect, given the extent of economic growth. There has been a disappointing responsiveness of poverty to growth in new MICs. Second, that the uneven responsiveness of poverty to growth in new MICs is not because rising inequality is inevitable during economic growth in general, but that the Kuznets hypothesis that inequality rises during structural change has reappeared in the set of new MICs identified and it is in such countries where most of the world's poor live. Finally, it is

---

[18] Resonating with this, others also link the decline in inequality in Latin America to the expansion of education; minimum wage increases (given that the minimum wage sets a floor for wages and for state benefits) and more progressive government spending and transfers (see Azevedo et al., 2013; Battiston et al., 2011; Campos et al., 2012; Cruces et al., 2011; Esquivel et al., 2010; Gasparini et al., 2011; Gasparini and Cruces, 2010; Gasparini and Lustig, 2011; López-Calva and Lustig, 2010;). For example, the expansion of public transfers in Brazil and across the region is the factor most often cited as a cause of falling inequality (see Azevedo et al., 2011; Barros et al., 2010; Bérgolo et al., 2011; Lustig et al., 2012). Soares et al. (2009), find that conditional cash transfers in Brazil, Mexico, and Chile cost less than 1 per cent of GDP and have accounted for 15–21 per cent of the reduction in inequality.

posited that the relatively weak responsiveness of poverty to growth in new MICs is less due to initial levels of inequality as one might expect, but rather rising inequality during economic development which has dampened poverty reduction and skewed the benefits of growth away from the poorest.

The chapter has discussed conceptual and empirical debates on the relationship between poverty, inequality, economic growth, and economic development. The chapter has also considered the factors that might explain the relatively weak responsiveness of poverty to growth in new MICs and revisited the seminal work of Simon Kuznets. The chapter has argued that the dismissal of the Kuznets hypothesis is premature given data from the set of new MICs discussed.

In sum, although there is no universal Kuznets law that inequality will rise during economic growth and economic development, a number of large populous countries where the world's poor are concentrated have experienced rising inequality with economic growth since 1990. Factors contributing to the disappointing responsiveness of poverty to growth in the set of ten new MICs are rising inequality during structural change and also the nature of social spending and social policy or the welfare regime. All of this discussion would suggest that poverty ought to be considered within the context of the broader processes of economic development connected to the welfare regimes or types of late capitalism. In Chapter 4 we turn to theories of the causes of absolute poverty and the relationship between poverty and distribution and economic development or how the new MICs raise questions about poverty theory itself.

4 The poverty paradox

Why are some people still poor?

4.1 Introduction

The arguments presented thus far can be summarized as follows: at the end of the Cold War the world's absolute poor lived in poor countries. Today most of the world's poor live in countries that, although not rich by OECD standards, nevertheless have experienced substantial rises in GDP PPP per person. This should reorientate our attention towards asking questions about national distribution and it's relationship with absolute poverty.

The argument of this chapter is threefold: first, that existing theories of global poverty require revisiting because of the changes in global poverty outlined in Chapters 2 and 3. Orthodox theoretical explanations of poverty have tended to imply that the poor are poor because they do not have what they need to be defined as not poor, for example, the ownership of, or access to, assets or the holding of certain values over others, rather than theorizing about the structural causes of poverty at a societal level. Put another way, studying poverty has become to some considerable extent about studying the poor at an individual (or household) level but that is not the same as studying poverty and structural causes at a societal level. Second, that, given the changes in global poverty, poverty theory requires a reorientation to place more emphasis on questions of national distribution and the analysis of poverty needs to be better integrated within the study of the processes of economic growth and economic development. Indeed, a poverty paradox of late capitalism has emerged that this chapter empirically demonstrates: most developing countries have or will have in the foreseeable future the domestic resources to address absolute poverty at a national level and yet poverty is likely to persist despite those available resources. Furthermore, there is a second layer of the poverty paradox which is that even if people's consumption grows sufficiently to leave absolute poverty it could take the average poor person over one hundred years to reach a level of consumption which is likely to correspond to fully escaping poverty in the sense of being permanently secure from falling back into poverty rather than at risk of poverty during economic slowdowns or other stressors. This chapter discusses the first layer of the poverty paradox and Chapter 5 focuses on the second layer. Third, that much of global poverty could be ended via redistributive social policy potentially funded, for example, by the national public funds currently spent on regressive fossil-fuel subsidies that largely benefit elites and the upper-middle classes (as they are more likely to drive cars and use greater amounts of household electricity than lower income classes) and if redirected such subsidies would cover the cost of the poverty gap in many MICs.

The chapter is structured as follows: Section 4.2 reviews theories of poverty. It is argued that theories of poverty require a shift in their balance of attention to distributional questions and questions of the structural nature of poverty within societies. Section 4.3 presents the empirical basis for a structural theory of absolute poverty. The section argues that global poverty is 'nationalizing' and global poverty is largely and increasingly concentrated in countries that have the domestic resources to end absolute poverty. However, without redistribution, given existing levels and trends in inequality, absolute poverty in MICs may persist even with economic growth for the foreseeable future. Section 4.4 then discusses the theoretical connection of poverty, distribution, and economic development by revisiting the work of Arthur Lewis as a meta-framing. The differing forms of late capitalism in MICs are discussed. Section 4.5 concludes.

4.2 **Theories of poverty**

Existing theories of global poverty require revisiting in light of changes in global poverty previously outlined. Theories of absolute poverty have tended to overemphasize the micro-level to the detriment of the macro-level and often describe the symptoms of individual poverty rather than the underlying societal causes.

To date, poverty has been largely measured and defined in terms of deficits or a set of deficits and a poverty line set based on those, be that monetary or multidimensional poverty-related in nature. Effectively, this has often meant deficits or gaps in material opportunities or outcomes, for example, in the quantity or quality of income, nutrition, health, and education. However, none of these are underlying causes of poverty in themselves. Deficits in well-being describe the immediate consequences of poverty rather than present a theory on the causes of poverty. Hulme (2013) argues that theorizing about poverty has often been neglected in development theory under the assumption poverty automatically falls as the economy grows. One could argue that poverty has not only been neglected but when poverty is researched it is often in a vacuum, disconnected from the processes of economic development or societal distribution questions. Harriss (2007, p. 5) puts it eloquently thus:

The way in which [poverty] is conceptualised in mainstream poverty research, poverty becomes a tangible entity, or a state that is external to the people affected by it: individuals or households fall into it, or are trapped in it, or they escape from it. It is not seen as the consequence of social relations or of the categories through which people classify and act upon the social world. Notably the way in which poverty is conceptualised separates it from the social processes of the accumulation and distribution of wealth, which depoliticises it.

The assertion here is that focusing solely on conceptualizing and measuring poverty without pursing causal questions beyond the immediate consequences of poverty is neglectful. Explanations of individual deprivation ignore the study of social relations and inequalities in income, expenditure, wealth, and ultimately power and the governance structures that determine the welfare regime of country.

One should ask: Is poverty the characteristic of an individual or a society? In short, studying the 'poor' is not the same as studying poverty. This distinction is important as the difference between individual (or household) analysis and social structure is a central contention in theories of poverty. An individual might be able to get better educated and get a job and possibly move out of poverty as some theories emphasize (see discussion in Beeghley, 1988) but individuals cannot change the unemployment rate or education opportunities across a society nor the welfare regime or the growth regime (the macro-economic orientation) which are a product of, amongst other things, the forms of late capitalism pursued in a country.

Notable surveys of the causes of absolute poverty include those by Dercon and Shapiro (2007) and Ravallion (2013).[1] The latter, Ravallion (2013), provides a survey of theories of poverty and outlines two types of theories or models as follows: Model 1 is that poor people do not have the potential to be anything else due to their own 'bad' behaviour. Poverty is necessary and to be accepted (implying the welfare regime should be minimal). Ravallion contrasts this with Model 2, that poverty is due to market and governmental failures that justify anti-poverty policies (and a more significant welfare regime) which are not only consistent with economic growth but an important source of growth in themselves. In contrast, the former reference, the empirical survey of Dercon and Shapiro's (2007) is based on the longitudinal data sets from developing countries. This draws out the causes of remaining in, or escaping from, poverty which are identified as asset-based (e.g. changes in economic and social assets) but also social exclusion, discrimination, or being located in remote or otherwise disadvantaged areas. Dercon and Shapiro link descent into poverty to temporary shocks such as illness and health-related expenses; social and customary expenses (e.g. costs of marriages

---

[1] See also review of Davis and Sanchez-Martinez (2014).

and funerals); high-interest private loans; crop disease; and drought and irrigation failure. A question then follows as to how such factors are distributed across any given society.

Expanding the above surveys, one could say that theories of absolute poverty fall into three types, as follows: (i) material theories or deprivational and deficit theories; (ii) subjective, or cultural and behavioural theories; and (iii) structural and distributional or relational theories. Each theory of poverty implies a different type of state response or 'public responsibility' in terms of the social policy or the welfare regime or more generally the governance of growth, meaning the management of growth processes and distribution of opportunities from and benefits of growth and economic development. For illustration, if poverty is caused by individual failure such as laziness (as subjective, or cultural and behavioural theories suggest) then there is little role for the state in terms of an interventionist welfare regime. However, if poverty is structurally related to distribution of wealth, income, opportunities, and the nature of labour markets then there is a substantial role for a state to redistribute with an interventionist welfare regime.

The first category of theories of poverty are material theories, or deficit and deprivational theories. These are based on deprivations or deficits of something—typically productive and human assets and, relatedly, livelihood opportunities related to those assets and vulnerabilities or hazards faced or exposed to. Such theories are discussed implicitly in Ravallion (2013) and reviewed in Ruggeri et al. (2003) and Stewart et al. (2007). In such theories the poor have few private assets and/or limited entitlements or, claims on, or access to public or common assets. Thus, people are poor as they have few assets from which they can extract income and consumption. Such theories are largely individual-based—at which level these theories are logically consistent—rather than societal in unit of analysis. In some cases there may be household, village, or higher units of assessment of assets and livelihoods, but rarely societal level analysis of assets and livelihoods and their unequal distribution in the research of poverty.

A second category of theories of poverty could be labelled as subjective, or cultural and behavioural theories. These are based on deficits of culture or values and related behaviours. Such theories resonate with common labelling of the 'undeserving poor' (e.g. those of work age who are unemployed) versus the 'deserving poor' (e.g. those above retirement age or the sick or those who are unable to work) and compel the 'undeserving' poor to change behaviour to escape poverty (sometimes via controlling their access to public entitlements). This typically means deficits in work ethic, or ability to control one's fertility, or consumption choices (e.g. alcohol consumption) or parenting decisions and this is the cause of poverty. These theories are discussed in-depth and explicitly as Model I in Ravallion (2013). Such theories are often associated with the anthropologist Oscar Lewis (e.g. Lewis, 1959) and his concept of '(sub-) cultures of poverty' but have resurfaced in recent years somewhat repackaged in behavioural economics, for instance, in Banerjee and Duflo's (2012) discussion of the sub-optimal choices made by poor people due, in part, to information deficiencies, for example, on what constitutes a good diet or behavioural issues such as the present consumption bias (e.g. the trade-off of health against other needs due to insufficient resources to meet all needs). Banerjee and Duflo do argue that the behaviour of richer people is no different as does behavioural economics more generally, but that the rich have insurance and pension plans (e.g. deferred consumption) or better diets. Such behavioural issues have much more significant impacts for the poor and are to be addressed by small interventions that aim to change incentives Banerjee and Duflo argue; for example, linking entitlements to state benefits to work requirements, or attendance of clinics and school enrolment of children. In short, compelling the poor to behave differently to gain entitlement to public goods, services and transfers.[2]

Early versions of these types of cultural or behavioural theories applied to poverty argued that the poor have a deficit in their system of values which is, of course, one step beyond simply saying individuals can make bad choices whether they are poor or not. Oscar Lewis' work on Mexico argued that although poverty was imposed on families, the children of the poor were socialized into values—behaviours and attitudes—that led to an autonomous subculture that perpetuated an inability to escape poverty. In fact, Lewis (1965) presented seventy characteristics that indicated a 'culture of poverty'. These related to sense of dependency, inferiority, and marginalization. In such 'culture of poverty' theories individuals (or their close family and friends) are the cause of their poverty and to blame for their poverty due to 'bad' values such as laziness, inability to defer gratification, bad decision-making regarding fertility and consumption, 'bad' lifestyle choices, 'bad' parenting, and poor beliefs relating to the valuing of education, for example. The normative conclusion is that poverty is a result of an individual's own failings. Thus the

---

[2] Such ideas have been popularized more broadly in, for example, Thaler and Sunstein (2008) and in research in behavioural economics. This research seeks to challenge to a central tenet of mainstream economics, *homo economicus*—'the notion that each of us thinks and chooses unfailingly well' (Thaler and Sunstein, 2008, p. 6). Instead, human beings are very much influenced by their context and respond to that context or their 'choice architecture'—the organization of the context in which people make their decisions (p. 3). This then makes a case for 'libertarian paternalism', i.e. public policy to influence choices or decisions (but not by coercion) or 'nudge' people 'in a way that will make the choosers better off, as judged by themselves' (p. 5). On the one hand the challenge to orthodox economics is strong in terms of a central assumption of rational human beings. On the other hand, the paternalism inherent in this sits uneasily in a democratic system.

implied welfare regime or public responsibility to intervene is minimal (and could even be counterproductive if it encourages certain behaviours).

The two categories of poverty theory above, broadly speaking, represent orthodox theories in the sense of they represent large international organisations and their thinking on poverty to a considerable extent and/or national narratives on poverty. A heterodox or alternative group of theories in contrast forms a third category of theories of poverty and this category may be labelled as structural, distributional, or relational theories. Such theories, although well utilized in OECD countries have in general been less systematically applied at a macro or societal level to developing countries to date under the assumption that they are less of relevance if (almost) everyone is poor. In other words, if a country is poor and most of the population is poor then the distribution of wealth, income, and opportunities is irrelevant in explaining the causes of high poverty rates. Once a country is no longer unequivocally poor or has substantial domestic wealth then the assumption that such theories are irrelevant to explaining poverty requires questioning. Sen (1983) for example argues that although in terms of absolute deprivations, capabilities are likely to be set across societies, poverty relates to the society in the sense that the resources required to expand capabilities are dependent on what is available in a given society. Both entitlements and endowments are unlikely to be distributed equally in a developing country unless it is a very poor country. Thus the distribution of entitlements and endowments plays a major role in poverty in any society. Sen sums up the situation thus: 'poverty is an absolute notion in the space of capabilities but very often it will take a relative form in the space of commodities or characteristics' (Sen, 1983, p. 335).

Examples of approaches to poverty which have sought to bring in aspects of a more structuralist approach would include (but are not be limited to): the literatures on asset accumulation (e.g. Moser, 1998), multidimensional poverty (e.g. Alkire and Foster, 2011), relational aspects of wellbeing (e.g. Gough and McGregor, 2007), 'welfare regimes' (e.g. Wood and Gough, 2006), intersecting and social inequalities, the intergenerational transmission of poverty and poverty dynamics (e.g. Hulme et al., 2001). Structural, distributional, or relational theories are based on the structural position of the poor within the distribution of wealth and income and their labour-market position. The poor's hierarchical location in the social structure determines the choices people have and their consequences. The social structure continually recreates a population of poorer people because income/consumption levels at the lower end of the distribution start low and at best grow at the mean rather than at the rate of richest population. Even if the income/consumption at the bottom of society were to rise faster than at the top of society given the low starting point it would take a long time to make any large difference to the level of inequality. In terms of inequality, the stability of the social structure exists as people at each level use their resources to protect their advantage and pass that advantage on to their children in the intergenerational transmission of inequality.

Furthermore, the poor operate in informal, volatile, and insecure labour markets such as seasonal agricultural wage labour or informal urban service sectors leading to large fluctuations in income/consumption at different points in time. Access to public entitlements and public goods and assets may be haphazard and mediated via the non-poor who may have perceptions about the 'deserving' and 'undeserving' poor and/or demand informal payments to allow the poor access to their state entitlements that diminish the net value to the poor. Structurally, and resonating with Dercon and Shapiro (2007), discrimination on the grounds of social inequalities or social identity such as lower caste or gender is likely to further exacerbate the situation of the poor, not only in terms of mediating access to expanded livelihood possibilities from growth, but to claims on the state's new resources generated by growth (or claims within the household too). In short, such theories of poverty argue that poverty is caused by structural factors such as the distribution of wealth and thus income; the distribution of education and human capital and the related stratification of labour markets (the existence of lower and more highly rewarded labour markets, which may also be characterized by uncertainty, informality and differing prospects to raise incomes). Poverty is also caused by discrimination and prejudice faced by the poor as a result of perceptions of hierarchy and status which condition inequality and resource access in terms of class, gender, ethnicity, sub-national geography, and age. Such theories may extend poverty into concepts of social exclusion, which is a framing that allows for deprivations and wealth to co-exist. It also explores the processes that generate each of these, as well as the exclusion of some groups from the benefits of economic growth (see for discussion Hills and Stewart, 2005). This is in keeping too with the components outlined by Townsend (1979) as necessary for a unified theory of poverty: the analysis and distribution of resources; the patterns of production and distribution; the forms of consumption that different resources generate; the social classes that influence relationships in the system; and the over-representation of minority groups among the poor. Another example of a structural theory of poverty is illustrated by Harriss-White (2005), who argues in favour of shifting from theories based on individual deprivation to theories based on an explanation of the unequal distribution of power, wealth, and opportunity, and thus the social processes, structures, and relationships that lead to poverty and its reproduction. She argues that it is impossible to eradicate poverty as it is created by processes of accumulation and is synonymous with capitalism itself.[3]

---

[3] She identifies the following ways in which capitalism creates poverty: petty commodity production and trade; technological change and unemployment; (petty) commodification; harmful commodities and waste; pauperizing crises; climate-change-related pauperization; and the un-required and/or incapacitated and/or dependent human body under capitalism.

In sum, much theorizing on the causes of poverty has tended not to empha-size questions of national inequality, and tended not to present poverty as a structural outcome of specific patterns of growth and distribution. This is, at least in part, due to a prevailing assumption that distribution is not a relevant factor to explaining poverty if everyone is poor. If it is no longer the case in many developing countries that everyone is poor then relational theories have a new-found relevance beyond the OECD countries. In light of this in section 4.3 we explore the empirically foundation for a structural theory of absolute poverty in developing countries by assessing the extent to which global poverty is increas-ingly becoming a question of national distribution in MICs.

4.3 The empirical foundations of a structural theory of absolute poverty

What empirical foundation does a structural theory of absolute poverty have? In this section three are presented. It is argued that, first, drawing upon the work of Palma (notably, 2011) that the GNI capture of the richest in MICs will determine the level of absolute poverty. Second, that global poverty is becom-ing a question of national distribution because most of the world's poor now live in countries, although not rich countries by OECD standards, that do have the domestic resources, at least in principle, to end absolute poverty at $2.50 per day.[4] The data shows that much of global poverty could be eliminated, via redistributive social policy, funded for example, by ending regressive fossil-fuel subsidies even allowing for compensation to the poor for the loss of the subsidy to be included in the estimates. Caveats are noted, not least the volatility of global fuel prices and the political economy of redistribution (which is explored further in Chapter 5). Third, however, projections made show that without redistribution absolute poverty in MICs is likely to persist even with future growth, given current distributional patterns, for the foreseeable future. If growth is likely to be insufficient, that too implies a stronger imperative for redistributive social policy and a structural theory of absolute poverty.

4.3.1 THE PALMA PROPOSITION

First, we discuss the Palma Proposition as an empirical basis for a structural theory of absolute poverty. The Palma Proposition (see Palma, 2006, 2011, 2013, 2014a, 2014b) is of direct relevance for structural, distributional, and

---

[4] The focus here is on monetary poverty as the cost of ending such poverty is more easily estimated than multidimensional poverty and thus can be compared to alternative uses of public finance.

relational theories of poverty related to MICs. Palma (2006) identified the following distributional attributes in all societies: 'heterogeneous tails', meaning diversity in the share of GNI captured by the richest 10 per cent and poorest 40 per cent; and 'homogenous middles', meaning uniformity in the income share of deciles 5–9 of about 50 per cent. The Palma Proposition is this: changes in income inequality are exclusively due to changes in the share of the richest (top 10 per cent) and poorest (40 per cent), leaving unchanged the income share of the middle 50 per cent in between the richest and the poorest.[5] This is based, as Palma (2011, p. 102) argues, on the fact that:

It seems that a schoolteacher, a junior or mid-level civil servant, a young professional (other than economics graduates working in financial markets), a skilled worker, middle-manager or a taxi driver who owns his or her own car, all tend to earn the same income across the world—as long as their incomes are normalised by the income per capita of the respective country.

Palma notes at the top of the distribution there is a significant difference between the GNI capture of deciles 10 and 9 (meaning the richest and second-from-richest deciles, respectively) implying these are—in general—different types of people in terms of their income and consumption levels. Palma also notes some differentiation within the 'middle' between the GNI capture of the lower middle (which he defines as those who are the 20 per cent above the poor, or deciles 5 and 6, in the distribution) versus the upper middle (which is the 30 per cent of the population below the rich or deciles 7 to 9 in the distribution). This suggests a lower-middle and upper-middle group with different expenditure/income levels. Palma (2014b) himself posits that there is a 'sub-optimal equilibrium' with regard to a specific group of Latin American MICs where inequality is high but the deciles 5 to 9 still get their share, which is as follows: the situation is more stable than one would expect (even in a democracy) because the rich do well, the 'middle' have access to cheap services (for example, domestic maids) and expanding (service sector) employment, albeit poorly remunerated, helps the poorest. As a result, in Latin America, high inequality exists with low growth and low unemployment. This contrasts with, say, South Africa, where high inequality co-exists with high unemployment and accompanying social instability. Palma discusses the high inequality, low unemployment, low growth, equilibrium thus:

[5] The observation that 50 per cent of GNI is captured by the Palma 'middle' and 50 per cent of GNI is captured by the richest and poorest forms the basis of the Palma Ratio measure of income/consumption inequality. A limitation of the Palma Ratio (the GNI capture of the top decile over the poorest four deciles) is that it only considers half of the income distribution (it ignores what happens in the middle on the assumption that share is stable); for which reason it may be best considered a measure of income/consumption concentration rather than a measure of the full distribution.

It keeps the rich blissful (huge rewards with few market 'compulsions'); it allows the middle and upper middle groups to have access to a particularity large variety of cheap services; and it does at least provide high levels of employment for the bottom 40 per cent...jobs may be precarious, mostly at minimum wages...and in activities with little or no potential for long-term productivity growth, but at least they are jobs and there are plenty of them. (pp. 28–9)

One can reasonably assume that the richest 10 per cent in MICs are likely to be urban dwellers in higher positions in the state or businesses or owners of significant capital. Further, the middle 50 per cent are likely to be skilled workers and those working formally and informally around manufacturing hubs or the state sector but as lower or mid-ranking employees, not senior managers. This is why Palma also refered to the median class as an administrative class. Finally, given the labour force data for new MICs, most of the poorest 40 per cent are likely to be unskilled, agricultural smallholders and wage labourers (some with small land-holdings and some without), living at subsistence or close to subsistence. Given absolute poverty rates in many new MICs in the order of 20 to 30 per cent, a further population is likely to be in this poorest 40 per cent which is a group above absolute poverty but only just and which one might call a 'precariat' in keeping with Standing (2011) (see Chapter 5). When people cross the line out of poverty they enter into this group. This group lives a precarious life, not poor on a day-to-day basis, but not too far away from absolute poverty either, and thus insecure, or vulnerable to poverty during economic slowdowns, or other stressors and shocks. They may include urban informal sector workers, for example.

If, as the economy grows, the primary sector which includes agriculture as well as extractive industries (though the latter has few employment opportunities) and much of the poorest 40 per cent of population who are likely to be unskilled labour, grows at a slower rate than other sectors, then the result is structural change in the composition of GDP and the income share of GNI to these 40 per cent gets squeezed (judging by the new MIC data presented in Chapter 3). At the same time there is a limited amount of employment expansion in urban, high productivity manufacturing (much less than its expansion in proportion of GDP) and most employment expansion is in urban informal (under)employment, low productivity service sector employment (i.e. domestic cleaners, child carers, cooks, and so forth) triggering a stronger dynamic for urbanization. In terms of poverty—at whatever poverty line—real rural incomes for the poorest 40 per cent are likely to start at a low initial point and grow slowly in the sense that they may barely cover rises in food prices as urban growth fuels increases in food demand and agricultural labourers with little education will find it difficult to find manufacturing sector jobs via urban migration. Indeed, most new jobs will be in urban informal, low productivity employment that is likely to be barely above a subsistence urban poverty line, but probably still higher than rural subsistence in strict monetary terms. This is likely to be where the 'precariat' group are. In contrast, those in the Palma 'middle' will see their 50 per cent capture of GNI likely sustained via the maintaining of the value of real wages due to employment in manufacturing or the state as both are traditionally highly unionized groups of public sector workers and industrial workers, although actual substantive increases in real wages may be reduced gradually by increasing tax contributions. Those in the top 10 per cent are likely to see much more substantial rises in their incomes with economic growth, given the prevailing distribution of productive, financial, and human assets. Additionally, if members of this group occupy senior positions in the state, and there are the close relationships between state and business that exist in any society, they will have more access to state resources and largesse (or rent-seeking opportunities).

In sum, the impact of economic development on poverty levels at any given poverty line and assuming growth is accompanied by structural change is dependent on the outcome of competition between the richest and the poorest. In electoral systems this might entail the emergence of political parties that pull the 'middle' towards the poorest (e.g. the Workers Party and Lula in Brazil) rather than political parties that pull the 'middle' towards aligning with the richest. If the middle group are actually barely out of absolute poverty and quite vulnerable to shocks then it is plausible they may be more likely to align with the poor and exert more pressure for redistribution, or new political parties may emerge that renegotiate the social contract. If the 'middle' is more secure and thriving from employment guarantees of positions within the administration of the state, and the cheap and abundant supply of service labour from rural areas, it may be that the 'middle' is likely to politically align with the richest. That said, as incomes rise in the 'middle' and those groups start paying indirect tax, business licences, and so forth, their perception of their interest may change.

The visible way such implicit (or explicit) social contacts are evident is in the welfare regime and in social policy, most crudely via spending levels on public goods that save money for those at the lower end of the income distribution vis-à-vis the private market for health and education; and the set of policies and programmes around poverty such as cash transfer programmes and social safety nets; and overall commitments to social spending and social policy. If the 'middle' is insecure, demand for social insurance policies may expand and align the 'middle' with the poor as noted. However, if one takes a broader look at developing countries a lot of social welfare is actually provided to the upper-middle classes, especially formally employed and state-employees—they have pension plans, health insurance, unemployment benefits, and so forth. In short, welfare provisions do not necessarily follow 'demand' or greatest need. Copestake (2003) drawing on Figueroa takes three somewhat similar groups as unskilled workers (akin to the poorest four deciles), skilled workers (the Palma 'middle') and capitalists (the top decile).

He posits that unskilled workers are unable to turn their numbers into political capital due to poverty, a collective action problem and lack of cultural capital—meaning discrimination. At the same time, skilled workers would likely oppose the fiscal costs of free education, subsidized financial services, and social protection for fear of seeing their own employment opportunities weakened (a labour aristocracy argument) and have mixed feelings about subsidized financial services and social protection as the benefits are offset by their fiscal costs to them. Meanwhile, capitalists may support free education to the extent that there are skill shortages, but may oppose subsidized financial services and social protection due to any increase in self-employment, raising the costs of labour and reducing profits. The poorest 40 per cent—together with some or all of the 'middle'—may be able to negotiate a (marginally) better capture of GNI from the richest 10 per cent, though the poorests' capture of GNI is likely to diminish during growth and structural change if incomes at the top rise faster than the average and consequentially over time the richest decile take a growing share of GNI (assuming stability of the GNI share to the Palma 'middle') as has happened in the new MICs. However, if most taxpayers are in the top decile and much of the middle are vulnerable to economic slowdowns, this is likely to leave relatively little political will behind more progressive welfare regimes. That is unless there is elite buy-in to broader progress where the dominant political party has a monopoly on power and needs to justify that monopoly via rising living standards and security for most of society (e.g. China, Vietnam, and for periods of history Indonesia and other countries in which one political party dominates). One could imagine that a progressive welfare regime would redistribute—as far as is politically acceptable—relatively cheap transfers from the gains of growth to the poorest and this would lift many of the poorest and make many of the 'precariat' slightly more secure. Although global factors may, in some cases, push inequality upwards via the skilled versus unskilled labour premium, governments can and do intervene with social transfers, expansion of basic education, and rising minimum wages to attempt to address rising inequality during economic development as noted in Chapter 3.

All of this is—of course—a set of hypotheses that require further developing, refining and, as is plausible, testing at country level. There are also questions of demographics such as changes in fertility and dependency rates during development. This would have implications for inequality in the process of development (see for discussion de la Croix and Doepke, 2003; Sarkar, 2005). Further, MICs are likely to have differing technological specialization beyond the relatively crude differentiation into agriculture/subsistence versus industrial/modern. This could also have an effect. Indeed, Roine and Waldenström (2014) suggest a new Kuznets curve based on technological developments that start a shift; not the sectoral shift of agriculture to industry, but a shift from traditional industry to technologically intensive industry. The rewards accrue to a small proportion of the population who are skilled workers; that is, if a given technology makes skilled workers more productive and there is an increase in the relative demand for those workers. The supply of skilled workers then determines whether their wages rise or not, based on Tinbergen's (1974, 1975) theory that states that the returns to skills are a competition between education and technology. In contrast, Lindert and Williamson (2001) argue that it is the shift towards market orientation (domestic to export) of agriculture that causes inequality to rise.

What requires further theory building would be how the 50 per cent of GNI came to be captured in the first place by the Palma 'middle'. That would require some major research of the history of income and consumption inequality in a range of developing countries to identify commonalities. Nel (2008, pp. 24–9) proposes a historical framework based on asset concentration, the mode of incorporation into the world economy, economic modernization and governance, among other factors. While Dabla-Norris et al. (2015, p. 27) with a sample of almost 100 developing countries for the period 1985–2010 find that the following factors raise the income share of the poor: access to education, improved health outcomes, and redistributive social polices (e.g. transfers). In contrast, labour market flexibility and technological progress reduce the income share of the poor.

An implication of the above discussion and the Palma Proposition is that the capture of GNI by the richest in society will determine the GNI capture of the poorest 40 per cent and thus play a role in level of absolute poverty in MICs because for most MICs the headcount for absolute poverty at $2.50 or multidimensional poverty is below 40 per cent of the population. The correlations between $2.50 or multidimensional poverty and the top decile capture are consistent with this view in MICs overall and in LMICs and UMICs separately (with one exception of multidimensional poverty in LMICs due to some LMICs having multidimensional poverty above 40 per cent of the population) (see Table 4.1).

In sum, the level of absolute poverty is a function of the capture of the top decile—the richest—in MICs. This would imply that poverty is not only about studying the poor. The important question is does the 'middle' really hold fifty per cent of GNI with such stability across and within countries? Cobham and Sumner (2013a, 2013b) and Cobham et al., (2015) confirm Palma's thesis of the relative stability of the middle 50 per cent income or consumption share as do Alvaredo and Gasparini (2015). Cobham and Sumner (2013a, 2013b) and Cobham et al. (2015) find support for Palma's proposition across a wide range of tests and—surprisingly—across pre- and post-tax and transfer measures for a set of countries with data available to access. Table 4.2 shows that in terms of the temporal stability *within* countries, the Palma proposition holds. The relative stability of the Palma 'middle' is much lower (the coefficient of

Table 4.1 Correlation of poverty headcount and share of GNI to top decile, 2010–12

		$2.50 Poverty headcount (% population)	Multidimensional poverty headcount (% population)
LICs	Pearson Correlation	0.213	–0.126
	Sig. (2-tailed)	0.286	0.541
	N	27	26
LMICs	Pearson Correlation	0.554**	0.305
	Sig. (2-tailed)	0.001	0.101
	N	30	30
UMICs	Pearson Correlation	0.661**	0.655**
	Sig. (2-tailed)	0.007	0.002
	N	15	19
All MICs	Pearson Correlation	0.324*	0.296*
	Sig. (2-tailed)	0.030	0.039
	N	45	49

Note: ** Correlation is significant at the 0.01 level (2-tailed). * Correlation is significant at the 0.05 level (2-tailed).
Source: Author's estimates based on data from Edward and Sumner (2015), OPHI (2014) and World Bank (2015).

Table 4.2 Cross-country and temporal variance of income and consumption shares, 1990–5 and 2010–12

	Richest 10%	Middle 50%	Poorest 40%
Temporal within-country variance with equal weight to every observation			
Grand mean	0.32	0.52	0.17
Coefficient of variation	0.25	0.07	0.29
Min	17.14	30.67	5.70
Max	59.86	59.49	29.90
Temporal within-country variance with equal weight to every country			
Mean of means	0.31	0.51	0.17
Coefficient of variation	0.23	0.07	0.25
Min	20.58	36.93	7.85
Max	55.19	55.67	25.01
Cross-country variance			
Mean	0.31	0.52	0.18
Coefficient of variation	0.26	0.08	0.27
Min	17.82	30.67	6.74
Max	59.86	57.27	27.70

Note: See for discussion Cobham and Sumner (2013a, 2013b) and Cobham et al. (2015); Grand mean = the sum of all observed values divided by total number of observations; Mean of means = the mean of all countries' means (number of observations per country varies).
Source: Estimates based on World Bank (2015). Table adapted from Cobham et al. (2015).

variation) than that of the poorest 40 per cent or richest 10 per cent. In the cross-country analysis, the 'middle' capture half of GNI on average and the richest 10 per cent capture, on average, three times their population share whilst the poorest 40 per cent population capture half of their population share. The capture of the 'middle' five deciles is 0.52 across the observations. If one considers all observations, almost 90 per cent of all observations for the 'middle' are above 45.00 and below 56.00. The relative variance of the 'middle' is substantially lower than the richest decile or poorest four deciles. Over time there is even a convergence: The stability of shares has increased since the Cold War. Not only does the share of the 'middle' vary consistently less across countries than do the shares of the top 10 per cent and bottom 40 per cent; all three are more stable across countries in 2010–12 than in 1990–5 (the 'middle' has a coefficient of variation which is consistently a third of that of the top 10 per cent or the poorest four deciles). In short, the data shows that changes in inequality are a contest between the richest and poorest for capture of the half of GNI not captured by the 'middle'. This implies a nationalization of poverty in MICs.

4.3.2 THE NATIONALIZATION OF POVERTY

In providing a foundation for structural theories of absolute poverty we next consider the extent to which one can empirically contend that absolute poverty is in the process of nationalizing, meaning increasingly the prospect of eliminating absolute poverty is within domestic resource capability (rather than necessarily requiring additional external resources). We can estimate the poverty gap as a proportion of GDP. This estimation generates a theoretical cost of eliminating poverty at whatever poverty line taken (here, $2.50). However, what poverty gap might be considered to be affordable to address with domestic resources alone? What exactly constitutes domestically afford-able is open to question and of course may be said to differ from country to country. There are various reasons as to why the resources may be nationally available but not used to end poverty such as state capabilities and the political economy of redistribution preferences. The purpose here is to solely support an argument that absolute poverty is no longer explicable by the fact that countries have insufficient domestic resources to address absolute poverty.

If we consider $2.50 poverty, what do we find? First, Table 4.3 shows the $2.50 poverty gap as a proportion of GDP. Figure 4.1 shows the shift of the poverty gap curve leftwards between 1990–5 and 2010–12. Table 4.3 shows the global cost of ending $2.50 poverty has fallen from 2 per cent of world GDP in 1990 to 0.5 per cent in 2012. It is further projected to fall to just 0.1 per cent by 2030 based on moderate economic growth and the continu-ation of contemporary distribution trends.[6] In LMICs and UMICs, the current cost of ending poverty in 2012 was estimated at 1.3 per cent and 0.2 per cent of GDP, respectively across the groups with projections for 2030 of 0.1 per cent

---

[6] As noted previously, moderate economic growth is defined as the International Monetary Fund (IMF) World Economic Outlook (WEO) projection minus the historical error of IMF projections which is 1 per cent.

Table 4.3 $2.50 poverty headcount (millions) and poverty gap (% of GDP) (2011 PPP), 1990, 2012, and 2030 (projection)

	$2.50 poverty count (millions)			$2.50 poverty gap (% GDP)		
	1990	2012	2030	1990	2012	2030
Total	2,381.4	1,447.4	663.2	2.0	0.5	0.1
LICs	310.7	446.3	289.0	32.4	14.0	3.0
LMICs	1,020.3	750.7	201.4	6.8	1.3	0.1
UMICs	1,032.6	235.7	141.4	4.5	0.2	0.1

Note: Countries grouped by current classification. Total includes poverty in HICs.
Source: Data processed from Edward and Sumner (2015).

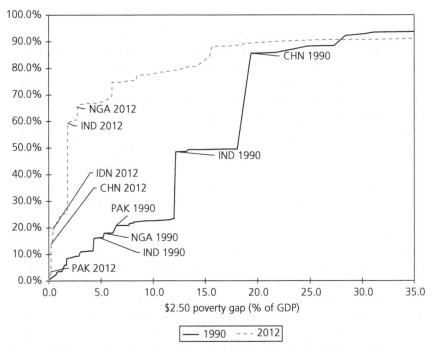

Figure 4.1 Cumulative distribution of global poverty gap at $2.50, 1990 and 2012

Source: Data processed from Edward and Sumner (2015) and World Bank (2015).

of GDP for both groupings. However, in LICs the estimate, not surprisingly, is much higher at 14.0 per cent of GDP in 2012, though falling to 3.0 per cent of GDP in 2030. What is startling in these estimates is that even another two decades more of reasonable growth in MICs would not eradicate poverty even though the total poverty gap is already a small as a proportion of GDP.

Table 4.4 shows the nationalization of global poverty by the number of countries with a total $2.50 poverty gap of less than 1 per cent, 2 per cent, and

Table 4.4 Percentage of global poverty at $2.50 in countries with a poverty gap of more than one per cent, two per cent, and three per cent of GDP, 1990 and 2012

	Countries with $2.50 poverty gap of more than 1% of GDP		Countries with $2.50 poverty gap of more than 2% of GDP		Countries with $2.50 poverty gap of more than 3% of GDP	
	1990	2012	1990	2012	1990	2012
Percentage of global poverty						
Total	96.4	78.1	91.5	40.3	89.4	33.7
LICs	13.0	30.8	13.0	30.4	13.0	30.1
LMICs	42.7	46.5	41.1	9.5	39.9	3.3
UMICs	40.7	0.8	37.2	0.3	36.5	0.3

Source: Data processed from Edward and Sumner (2015).

3 per cent of GDP, and the proportion of global poverty they represent. In 1990, almost all of global poverty (90 per cent) was in countries where the poverty gap was more than 3 per cent of national GDP. A poverty gap of greater than 3 per cent of national GDP would indicate the cost of addressing poverty is a large sum relative to domestic resources given that the substantial cash transfer programmes in Latin America are estimated to have cost about 1 per cent of GDP (see Soares et al., 2009) and military spending in developing countries averages 1.8 per cent of GDP in 2012 (World Bank, 2014). However, by 2012, only a third of global poverty was in countries with a poverty gap of more than 3 per cent of national GDP. This means that the proportion of global poverty in countries where addressing poverty is prohibitively high relative to national resources has fallen substantially.

How does this cost of ending global poverty match a proxy for available public resources that could be redistributed? We can consider national spending on regressive fossil-fuel subsidies because such subsidies are substantial in many countries and theoretically could be redirected (redirecting military expenditure would be an alternative but raises questions of national security for many countries that one could say would make the change in expenditure harder politically than for fossil-fuel subsidies). Clements et al. (2013) provide a conservative data set on fossil-fuel subsidies by their components—petroleum products (gasoline, diesel, and kerosene), electricity, natural gas, and coal—as a proportion of GDP for each country.[7] Post-tax fossil-fuel subsidies in developing countries in 2011 amounted to almost one trillion dollars in current dollars or almost two trillion in 2011 PPP dollars.[8] Estimates

[7] Alternative estimates by Coady et al. (2015, p. 19) argue the data in Clements et al. (2013) is too conservative and provide substantially higher estimates that include pricing of the externalities of fuel consumption (e.g. costs of the health impact of emissions, global warming, congestion, and so forth). They assume that the market price of energy undercharges for damages resulting from fuel consumption and that leads to a larger implied subsidy.

[8] Estimates are: $895 billion (in current dollars) and $1,865.4 billion (2011 PPP).

show that much of global poverty could be eliminated via redistributive social transfers funded at a national level by ending such regressive fossil-fuel subsidies. Such subsidies largely benefit the upper-middle classes and elite and if redirected would easily cover the cost of the poverty gap if redirected to transfer programmes in MICs.[9] Of course, removing the fuel subsidy would have some impact on the poor via, most significantly, kerosene which is used for cooking, so an allowance has to be made to compensate effectively, leaving the poorest no worse off than with the fossil-fuel subsidies. The administrative costs of new or expanded social transfer programmes would, potentially, be covered by the administrative costs formerly associated with the fuel subsidy programme. Targeting would, of course, be complex. There are further caveats too; not least that food prices may rise due to the removal of the subsidy due to transportation costs though theoretically such indirect benefits are included in the estimates via the adjustment for benefits.

Arze del Granado et al. (2012) in a sample of twenty developing-country case studies during the 2005–9 period, including several of the new MICs such as Indonesia, Sri Lanka, India, and Ghana, find that, on average, the richest 20 per cent of households gain six times more from such subsidies than the poorest 20 per cent of households. The former capture, on average, 43 per cent of the total subsidy, the latter capture just 7 per cent. It is worth reiterating that the distributional impact of the subsidies does vary by specific product. For example, gasoline is most regressive and kerosene the least. Subsidies to natural gas and electricity are highly regressive. Arze del Granado et al. (2012, pp. 2239–40) estimate the average benefits of all fossil-fuel subsidies and the welfare impact in terms of consumption quintiles. Although the poorest quintile benefits just 7 per cent from the subsidies in total, this accounts for 6 per cent of their total household budget on average. Furthermore, the poorest quintile captures 19 per cent of the kerosene (cooking fuel) subsidy, demonstrating how important compensation for the poor is, given that the kerosene subsidy accounts for 2 per cent of the poorests' household budget on average.

If we convert all subsidies into 2011 PPP dollars and allow full compensation for the poorest quintile in line with the average welfare impact in the Arze del Granado et al. (2012) study, we find that the $2.50 poverty gap is covered by the post-tax fossil-fuel subsidy in most MICs. Table 4.5 and 4.6 show the data. Six per cent of global poverty is in countries that are not covered by the fossil-fuel data set. This leaves 94 per cent of global poverty upon which an

---

[9] Indonesia in 2015 did exactly this: a long-enduring fuel subsidy that had grown to a post-tax subsidy that Clements et al. (2013) estimated at 5.4 per cent of GDP was drastically reduced and social programmes in health, education, and cash payments expanded, and commitment to infrastructure programmes made.

Table 4.5 Proportion of total global poverty at $2.50/day not covered by fossil-fuel subsidies, 2012

	% of global poverty in countries where the total fossil-fuel subsidy would not cover the $2.50 poverty gap
Total	30.7
LICs	21.8
LMICs	6.0
UMICs	2.9
Countries with insufficient data	6.0

Source: Author's estimates based on data from Clements et al. (2013), and Edward and Sumner (2015).

Table 4.6 Poverty gap at $2.50/day versus cost of fossil-fuel subsidies: selected new MICs and aggregate groups, 2012

	% of $2.50 poverty gap filled by national fossil-fuel subsidies
East Asia and the Pacific	
China	1,432.7
Indonesia	1,043.8
Vietnam	–
South Asia	
India	225.6
Pakistan	3,101.9
Sri Lanka	–
Sub-Saharan Africa	
Angola	191.8
Ghana	172.9
Nigeria	116.4
Sudan	80.5
Aggregates	
LICs	21.2
LMICs	326.0
UMICs	1,521.3
All developing countries	479.5

Note: Aggregates = proportion of total poverty gap covered by total fossil-fuel subsidy.
Source: Author's estimates based on data from Clements et al. (2013) and Edward and Sumner (2015).

assessment can be made as to whether the cost of fossil-fuel subsidies would fill the poverty gap. Two-thirds of global poverty in 2012 could be covered or virtually covered with redistribution of fossil-fuel subsidies to social transfers to the poor (with complete compensation for the poorest quintile in those countries). The remaining 30 per cent of global poverty (covered in this data) is split between two groups of countries: a set of LICs that could not cover the poverty gap with fossil-fuel subsidies and 9 per cent of global poverty which is in twenty-two other MICs who could not cover the entire poverty gap but a proportion of it (and 2 of that 9 per cent of global poverty could mostly be covered as the cover is over three-quarters of the gap).[10] Of course if one lowered the poverty line to $2 and/or used a less conservative set of subsidy estimates then much more of global poverty would be covered.

The calculations here are intended as indicative. The estimates are an example of substantial domestic resources now available to some countries and not necessarily as advocating for the removal all fossil-fuel subsidies. The example is intended to be illustrative of the domestic resources at the disposal of many MICs. Redistributing the fossil-fuel subsidy spending might, in practice, not be easy for the following reasons: compensation may need expanding beyond the poorest quintile; as noted, the removal of the subsidies may raise transportation costs and thus prices of other goods; and— importantly—fuel prices are subject to global price fluctuations.[11] In short, the purpose of this exercise is solely to show there are now sufficient public resources at a national level—in principle—to end much of global poverty at $2.50. This is a relatively new phenomenon—that most countries may have the public resources to cover the poverty gap—even if their reallocation is not necessarily easy.[12]

[10] The MICs not able to cover the $2.50 poverty gap with fossil-fuel subsidies and of some significance to global poverty are: Brazil (fossil-fuel subsidy cover of poverty gap = 44.4% of poverty gap), the Philippines (cover = 60.1%), Sudan (cover = 80.5% of poverty gap), Cameroon (78.8% cover of poverty gap), and Zambia (cover = 43.4%), Senegal (26.7% cover), Cote D'Ivoire (48.8% cover). The following countries and islands of insignificance to global poverty could not cover the $2.50 poverty gap with fossil-fuel subsidies: Albania, Djibouti, Guatemala, Honduras, São Tomé and Príncipe, Timor-Leste, Lesotho, and Nicaragua.

[11] For example, World Bank (2015, p. 4) notes the substantial fall in energy prices. In years of higher energy prices relative to 2011 the estimates in this book will underestimate the poverty gap covered and vice versa. Although it would seem very unlikely that energy prices will remain permanently low, fluctuations in energy prices mean that the estimates here should, as noted, be viewed as indicative of domestic resources available to developing countries. There are further methodological issues on the quantification of subsidies (for discussion on measuring fossil-fuel subsidies see in particular, Kojima and Koplow, 2015). The data used here is based on the 'price-gap approach'.

[12] As recently as the early to mid 2000s, estimates of redistributive capacity, suggested that redistribution would not cover the poverty gap unless the marginal tax rates (MTRs) were exorbitant for most developing countries. Ravallion (2009) taking survey data for the early to mid 2000s, produced estimates for the $1.25 and $2 poverty gap (2005 PPP) and the necessary taxation to cover it. Ravallion estimated the MTRs for the 'rich' (which he defined as those earning more than $13 per day or living above the US poverty line) required in order to end poverty in each country. He argued that MTRs over 60 per cent would be prohibitive. While the MTRs needed to end poverty are less than 10 per cent in many of the 'old' MICs or UMICs, in many new MICs or LMICs they would have to be much higher (see for estimates, Ravallion, 2009, pp. 30–2).

In the absence of redistribution of domestic resources such as those from fossil-fuel subsidies, will economic growth alone end poverty in MICs? If economic growth is insufficient to address poverty in the foreseeable future the imperative for redistributive transfers would be stronger.

One can make projections of poverty into the future to get some sense of how easily poverty might or might not be addressed by growth alone and thus assess the case for redistributive policies. Table 4.3 presents projections for poverty in 2030 based on almost twenty years more reasonable growth (IMF projections minus 1 per cent which is the historical error of IMF growth projections—see Aldenhoff, 2007 and discussion of Edward and Sumner, 2013a, 2014; Karver et al., 2012). One finds that poverty could remain in the region of 600–700 million people worldwide, of which more than half would live in countries currently classified as MICs and the remainder would live in LICs (and there would be a small amount in HICs). In sum, even two decades more economic growth would not end absolute poverty alone. The projections are based on two assumptions: the first is that annual growth on a country-by-country basis is, as noted, equivalent to the IMF growth projections in WEO minus the historical error of such growth projections. In short, average incomes will rise at the average annual growth rate of the GDP PPP per capita data in the IMF's WEO growth projections (extended to 2030) minus 1 per cent. The second assumption is that, country-by-country, historic inequality trends since the Cold War will continue (which are extrapolated from the distribution trends of the last two decades). An essential caveat must be noted: such projections are *an inherently imprecise exercise* that merely illustrates a possible future based on the assumptions used—reasonable economic growth and contemporary distribution trends continuing will not eradicate MIC poverty in themselves.

In summary, the empirical basis of a structural theory of absolute poverty has three empirical foundations. First, drawing on the Palma Proposition outlined, the capture of GNI by the richest plays a role in poverty levels in MICs. Second, that the cost of ending poverty in many MICs already represents a small proportion of GDP and sufficient public resources are available in many MICs in the form of regressive fossil-fuel subsidies. Finally, despite those resources, absolute poverty could persist even if economic growth is reasonable due to current distribution trends. Having explored the empirical rationale or foundation for a structural theory of absolute poverty and in light of the potential affordability of ending absolute poverty on the one hand versus the continuation of poverty if simply left to growth alone, section 4.4 develops a theoretical basis and outline of a structural theory of absolute poverty by revisiting the work of Arthur Lewis as a meta-framing for late economic development and discusses the differing forms of late capitalism and their poverty and distributional-related outcomes in MICs.

4.4 The theoretical basis of a structural theory of absolute poverty

4.4.1 SOME STYLIZED FACTS

In setting the context for a structural theory of global poverty, a useful starting place is to restate some stylized facts by recapping the discussions of this book so far. Then drawing upon the meta-framing of the Arthur Lewis dual model one can theorize the broad processes of economic development in new MICs and develop a set of modes of late capitalism in terms of their welfare, growth, and political regimes.

First, to recap, a structural theory of absolute poverty could be predicated on the following: (i) as a result of a set of populous countries becoming better off and graduating to middle-income status, most of the world's poor, about a billion people, now live in MICs. However, as is argued below despite higher average income and although GDP in agriculture has fallen to lower levels, surprising proportions of the labour force remain in agriculture and fuel still contributes substantially to merchandise exports in many new MICs; (ii) although there are a billion poor people, the cost of ending $2.50 poverty amounts currently to just 1.8 per cent and 0.3 per cent of GDP in LMICs and UMICs, respectively. Even if economic growth is reasonable, current distribution levels and trends would mean $2.50 poverty would still remain even with another two decades of reasonable economic growth; (iii) in light of the above, a contemporary theory of global poverty that is structural would necessarily seek to connect poverty, distribution, economic growth, and economic development. In the following discussion the seminal works of Arthur Lewis are revisited in order to provide a meta-theoretical framing for economic development before considering the different modes of late capitalism in the new MICs.

4.4.2 REVISITING THE LEWIS MODEL

4.4.2.1 The Context for Lewis

Arthur Lewis provided one of the best-known theoretical framings for the processes of economic development (see, for discussion, Gollin, 2014). How relevant is this theory to contemporary economic development in new MICs? Although Lewis was writing up to sixty years ago (see in particular, Lewis, 1954, 1969, 1972, 1976) it is clear that a number of issues of economic development, that are pertinent in the new MICs, were clear to Lewis. For example, the question of the benefits of growth and changes in distribution during growth.[13] A useful point of departure, as with the discussion of Kuznets in Chapter 3, is to consider what Lewis actually said. At the outset it is also worth acknowledging the empirical support for the Lewis model presented in Bourguignon and Morrisson (1998) who find economic dualism to be an important explanatory factor in cross-country differences in inequality.[14] This connection of dualism and distribution was developed by Lewis in the context of post World War II which was a period dominated by meta-theories of economic development and 'catch-up' for developing countries such as the 'Big Push' or 'Critical Minimum Effort' (Rosenstein-Rodan, 1943; Leibenstein, 1957), 'Balanced versus Unbalanced Growth' (Hirschman, 1958, 1963; Streeten, 1959) and the 'Stages of Economic Growth' (Rostow, 1960). These theories explored questions about the linkages and integration of the national economy with the global economy, and the relationship between sectors (agriculture, industry, and services) (see Tribe et al., 2010 for further discussion). Some of these had much to say on the issues that interested Lewis. For example, Rosenstein-Rodan (1943, p. 202) was concerned with agrarian 'excess population' or 'disguised unemployment' in agriculture and the transfer of this low- or zero-productivity population to the industrial sector some twenty years prior to Lewis's own writing.

4.4.2.2 The Two-sector Model

The Lewis (1954) model of economic development is one of two sectors: the 'capitalist' or 'modern' sector which expands on the basis of a cheap supply of labour from the 'subsistence' or 'traditional' sector. Lewis did not intend the term 'capitalist' or 'modern sector' to be taken to mean the urban or industrial sector. Nor, conversely was the subsistence or traditional sector synonymous with the rural or agriculture sector.[15] Lewis argued that the capitalist sector may be privately or publically owned and includes manufacturing, plantations, and mines, for example, and 'is that part of the economy which uses reproducible capital, and pays capitalists for the use thereof' (Lewis, 1954, p. 146). In contrast, the 'subsistence' sector is 'all that part of the economy which is not

---

[13] See also, written at the same time, Kaldor's (1955–6, p. 83) review of different theoretical attempts, to understand the 'laws' of distribution.

[14] They find that country differences in inequality can be explained by the relative labour productivity in non-agriculture sectors versus agriculture sectors, and these factors are more robust than variables such as GDP per capita or average levels of schooling. They also find that integration of countries into the world economy and the basis upon which this takes places can be significant to economic development.

[15] Indeed, Lewis (1979) later on had to reiterate that the two sectors he outlined were modern or capitalist and traditional or subsistence—not industrial and agricultural, nor urban and rural—because many had taken 'capitalist' to mean strictly industrial and urban and 'subsistence' to mean strictly rural and agricultural. He also switched to 'abundance' of unskilled labour rather than 'surplus labour' (noting that the latter seemed to cause 'emotional distress' to some).

using reproducible capital. Output per head is lower in this sector than in the capitalist sector, because it is not fructified by capital' (p. 146). Lewis posited that the capitalist sector could apply to capitalist agriculture, mining, or plantations as well as to industry. Further, the capitalist sector is not necessarily the private sector, and can equally apply to state capitalists who as Lewis put it, could accumulate capital faster than private capitalists because they can 'force or tax' the subsistence sector in addition to having profits to reinvest (p. 159). This is of significance to at least two new MICs, China and Vietnam, though a number of new MICs might potentially fall under this state capitalist label, notably, Indonesia (given state-directed economic development in the 1980s and 1990s), as well as both Angola and Pakistan which both had a level of government consumption expenditure as a proportion of GDP above the average for developing countries over the 1990–2012 period.

Lewis next sought to characterize his two sectors as follows: the capitalist or modern sector Lewis argued is characterized by higher wages and higher marginal productivity of labour compared to the subsistence sector. It has capital-intensive production and a demand for labour. The subsistence or traditional sector, in contrast, is characterized by low wages, low productivity, and an over-supply of labour and labour-intensive production relative to the modern sector. Thus labour moves from the traditional sector to the modern sector which absorbs the labour and promotes and sustains industrialization by increasing output per worker. Lewis put it as follows:

The key to the process is the use which is made of the capitalist surplus. In so far as this is reinvested in creating new capital, the capitalist sector expands, taking more people into capitalist employment out of the subsistence sector. The surplus is then larger still, capital formation is still greater and so the process continues until the labour surplus disappears. (1954, pp. 147, 151)

Attempting to consider this empirically in the new MICs is not easy. Although, as noted, traditional and agriculture categories are not synonymous, there has been some shift from agriculture to non-agriculture in the new MICs. There is also a significant proportion of people in new MICs working in the informal, low-capital, low-productivity urban service sector (ILO, 2015). This means that abandoning subsistence does not necessarily imply moving into productive, capital-intensive sectors and thus poses a challenge to Lewis' dualistic model that has been discussed by scholars.

In almost all of the set of ten new MICs growth has been accompanied by structural change away from agriculture if one compares agriculture as a proportion of GDP for 1990–5 and 2010–12. That said, the role of manufacture exports in export-led growth has been mixed and many of the set of new MICs fuel exports have played a significant role in export-led growth. Further, transformation in terms of employment in agriculture as a proportion of total employment is much less evident than agriculture value added as a proportion of GDP. There is in fact a mismatch evident between GDP in agriculture and labour force in agriculture. This means that structural transformation is evident in terms of output but much less so in terms of employment. One could assume that much, though not all, of the traditional sector is likely to be agriculture-based and characterized by low productivity, and it may seem surprising that substantial proportions of the labour force remain in this sector despite structural change in output and large rises in GDP PPP per capita. However, one should not assume that in new MICs the shift away from agriculture in output and employment is entirely to modern, high productivity manufacturing. In some cases that shift has been to services and those services are likely to be low-productivity urban services. Table 4.7 considers structural change in the new MICs in terms of the expansion of GDP in manufacturing and services as agriculture declines as a share of GDP. If one considers manufacturing value-added as a proportion of GDP in the set of ten new MICs experiencing economic growth and structural change, one finds substantial contributions from manufacturing in China and Indonesia over 1990–2012, and moderate contributions in India, Pakistan, Sri Lanka, and Vietnam. One finds employment in the broader category of industry (which is largely manufacturing as non-manufacturing industry tends to be capital-intensive) to be typically close to one in five of all jobs, though in Ghana employment in industry has tended to be closer to one in ten jobs over the period. Of course, none of the above covers specifically the concepts Lewis was referring to in more than a general sense. Table 4.7 shows a declining share of agriculture in employment in all new MICs though there are a number of data gaps. The extent of the shift away from employment in agriculture to other sectors has been uneven since the Cold War. China, India, Indonesia, and Ghana have recorded notable falls in employment in agriculture. However, Pakistan and Sri Lanka have experienced little change. What is surprising is that all of the new MICs with data retain a third to a half of their labour force in agriculture despite substantial economic growth and structural change. The changes in employment in industry have not been that substantial since the early 1990s. The rising share of employment in the service sector is clearly evident in some of the new MICs, such as China, Ghana, Indonesia, and Sri Lanka but much less so in India and Pakistan.

In sum, the data, though patchy, shows that most new MICs retain large though declining proportions of their labour force in agriculture and industry in general has expanded not much more than a fifth of employment. The service sector is where employment has expanded more so for countries as agriculture has declined. In short, the overall shift since the early 1990s in the structure of employment is—in general—one from agriculture to services and rather less so of agriculture to industry and manufacturing.

This transition of employment between sectors was pivotal to Lewis in the model as were wages and 'surplus labour':

Table 4.7 Selected new MICs: shares of GDP and employment by sector, 1990–5 versus 2010–12

	Structure of GDP (% of total by sector)								Structure of employment (% of total by sector)					
	Agriculture		Industry (including manufacturing)		Manufacturing		Services		Agriculture		Industry (including manufacturing)		Services	
	1990–5	2010–12	1990–5	2010–12	1990–5	2010–12	1990–5	2010–12	1990–5	2010–12	1990–5	2010–12	1990–5	2010–12
East Asia and the Pacific														
China	21.8	9.6	44.0	45.8	33.0	31.3	34.2	44.7	56.9	35.8	22.1	29.1	21.0	35.1
Indonesia	18.1	13.9	40.2	44.4	22.3	22.3	41.7	41.6	50.9	37.5	15.9	20.4	33.1	42.1
Vietnam	32.9	19.5	26.7	38.3	14.3	17.8	40.3	42.2	–	47.9	–	21.2	–	30.9
South Asia														
India	28.4	18.2	26.2	30.7	15.9	16.9	45.4	51.1	60.5	49.1	15.7	23.6	23.7	27.4
Pakistan	25.8	25.0	24.7	21.3	16.9	14.1	49.5	53.8	48.5	45.1	19.0	20.7	32.4	32.1
Sri Lanka	25.1	12.0	25.9	30.3	15.2	18.0	49.0	57.7	41.9	37.4	21.5	19.6	33.1	40.6
Sub-Saharan Africa														
Angola	15.9	8.8	51.5	61.3	5.1	6.3	33.2	30.0	5.1	–	20.6	–	66.6	–
Ghana	43.6	26.8	22.2	25.0	9.9	6.7	34.1	48.2	62.0	41.5	10.1	15.4	27.9	43.1
Nigeria	32.5	22.7	44.3	23.5	5.8	7.2	23.3	53.7	–	–	–	–	–	–
Sudan	39.7	26.3	12.3	26.1	6.1	6.7	48.0	47.7	–	–	–	–	–	–
Aggregates (mean)														
East Asia and Pacific	28.9	18.7	23.9	26.1	13.7	12.8	47.2	55.2	48.2	38.0	19.6	19.8	30.7	42.1
South Asia	28.3	19.6	23.1	26.1	12.5	12.5	48.6	54.4	53.7	48.1	15.8	18.0	28.2	32.8
Sub-Saharan Africa	31.3	24.9	25.7	26.9	11.4	9.9	43.8	48.2	57.5	30.9	11.2	17.4	28.8	50.2
All developing countries	25.8	17.4	27.6	28.0	14.7	12.0	46.9	54.6	38.2	27.1	19.7	21.0	39.6	51.2
Aggregates (median)														
East Asia and Pacific	24.7	18.6	15.7	20.8	10.9	8.0	44.0	56.0	50.9	37.5	16.7	20.4	33.1	40.4
South Asia	28.4	17.9	24.7	24.4	14.2	13.7	48.6	53.0	54.5	47.1	17.4	20.2	28.0	31.6
Sub-Saharan Africa	33.2	24.0	22.6	23.3	9.7	7.7	45.0	48.4	62.0	35.0	10.1	15.3	27.8	49.5
All developing countries	22.1	14.1	28.4	26.6	14.0	12.3	47.0	53.9	35.5	26.8	20.6	20.4	39.2	52.1

Note: Data for employment in manufacturing is not available in World Bank (2015).
Source: Data processed from World Bank (2015).

From the point of view of the effect of economic development on wages, the supply of labour is practically unlimited ... the wage which the expanding capitalist sector has to pay is determined by what people can earn outside that sector ... in economies where the majority of people are peasant farmers, working their own land, we have a more objective index, for a minimum at which labour can be had is now set by the average product of the farmer. (1954, pp. 145, 148)

Therefore, in the Lewis model, capitalist owners reinvest profits and this increases the size of capital stock in the modern sector increasing labour demand and expanding output, further increasing profits and thus reinvestment and generating future demand for labour. A set of factors sustain growth and structural change: the surplus labour supply contains wage growth; the marginal cost of labour is constant; the average wage is equal to the marginal wage rate; and total agricultural output remains the same but industrial production rises as labour moves. These sustain growth and structural change either up until the surplus rural labour is exhausted, or when capital accumulation is faster than population growth (thus there is a decline in rural labour surplus), or when changes in the terms of trade between the two sectors lead to higher urban wages, or when new technology in the subsistence sector raises production and wages. When the supply of labour is exhausted—the Lewis 'turning point'—the increasing demand for labour leads to higher wage levels and this adversely impacts on the profit level and the rate of reinvestment and capital stock.

Once again, these questions are not easy to explore empirically in the set of new MICs. It is likely to be true that the supply of labour at least to a point has been 'unlimited' but education levels may determine the use of that labour. Certainly in the late 1980s, many of the new MICs had, and still do have, substantial proportions of population still working in agriculture despite rapid urbanization. Which might imply the turning point has yet to be reached or that prevailing levels of education are a bottleneck to faster growth. All the new MICs in the early 1990s had reasonable levels of literacy suggesting that a more skilled labour force would not be a bottleneck. Only in Pakistan was the literacy rate below 50 per cent in the early 1990s. Even in Ghana, Nigeria, and Sudan, literacy rates were in the order of 50–60 per cent. Lewis argued that a scarcity of skilled labour could be a bottleneck on expansion but only temporarily until education could be expanded, which for the new MICs has happened in terms of primary school net enrolments but issues around the quality of primary education and the expansion of secondary and tertiary education remain.

Looking ahead, Lewis (1954, p. 172) argued that the process must stop, however, when capital accumulation has caught up with population, so that there is no longer surplus labour. This can happen as noted, if capital accumulation is proceeding faster than population growth; if the terms of trade turn against the capitalist sector; if the subsistence sector becomes more productive in the technical sense; and if the workers in the capitalist sector need more to live on by imitating the 'capitalist way of life', as Lewis put it. Of relevance to the turning point and set of new MICs is that Lewis (1954) has a short section on an open economy where he outlines the role of immigration and capital export which could postpone the turning point at which rising wages undermine capitalist surplus and end the period of rapid accumulation. In this open economy model, productivity changes accrue to the importing or advanced country, leading to immiserizing growth in the less advanced countries. In short, the turning point could be avoided by immigration or exporting capital to countries with abundant labour at a subsistence wage.[16] Given that in many sectors, such as textiles, the East Asian new MICs have developed substantial capacity, but become less cost competitive in recent years, this would lend support to this thesis. Indeed, the orthodox 'middle-income trap' is related to this point (see Chapter 5).

In terms of openness and contemporary economic development in Rodrik (2015) outlines a hypothesis of premature deindustrialization of developing countries in so far as there is a declining share of manufacturing in GDP or employment. Rodrik posits that the inverse U-shaped curve in manufacturing in which the downturn of the curve—deindustrialization as he defines it and the expansion of the service sector—to date has solely been associated with advanced economies. However, he argues deindustrialization is now visible in developing countries and that the inverse-U shape has shifted downwards because late industrializers are running out of industrial opportunities sooner, at lower levels of output than early industrializers. In short, developing countries are turning into service economies without full industrialization first, with a small number of exceptions. He notes the well-known importance of manufacturing in terms of its potency for economic growth, productivity, labour absorption, and trade. The causes of the shifting curve, he hypothesizes, relate to trade liberalization of manufacturing which has opened up manufacturing sectors without a strong comparative advantage and, further, the fall in the relative price of manufactures in advanced countries may have pushed down prices in developing countries manufacturing too as developing countries liberalize their economies. Rodrik posits this will have far-reaching consequences on political change in developing countries if a large working class fails to materialize and make political demands. If instead urban production is largely informalized, then non-elite political organization and common interests are much harder to generate. In short, it could be that in new MICs the transition to

---

[16] Lewis posited that capital export would be the easiest route due to trade unions' likely opposition to immigration. Lewis also noted the deterioration in the terms of trade for primary products based on the surplus supply of labour. He argued that the terms of trade between rich and poor countries would be determined entirely by relative labour productivity in food. For example, if there is low labour productivity in coffee production in a poor country the terms of trade will be unfavourable to those producers of coffee.

industrial and manufacturing output, employment, and exports has peaked much sooner than expected and in a number of new MICs it is the service sector that is increasingly providing employment expansion whilst manufacturing output may be stagnant or even contracting. Such a process is visible in Indonesia. The proportion of GDP in manufacturing steadily rose from 20.7 at the end of the Cold War to a peak of 29.1 per cent in 2001 then gradually fell back to 21.9 per cent in 2012, a level close to Indonesia in 1990. Such a pattern is also evident in some of the other new MICs. China's proportion of GDP in manufacturing has been flat at about 30 per cent for the entire period. In contrast, India, Pakistan, and Sri Lanka have fluctuated around 15–20 per cent of GDP throughout the period, whilst Angola, Ghana, Sudan, and Nigeria have similarly fluctuated around 5–10 per cent of GDP. Given the lack of major manufacturing expansion at least in shares of GDP or employment in any of the new MICs it is not surprising that employment growth has been in the service sector which of course has distributional consequences. One should though look beyond the share of manufacturing in GDP or employment and towards shares of external trade (see below discussion and Singh, 1977).

4.4.2.3 The Lewis Model and Distributional Questions

Although elsewhere, Lewis (1954, p. 9) went as far as to say in his theory of economic growth, 'it should be noted our subject matter is growth, and not distribution', implicitly Lewis dealt with a range of distribution questions in espousing the dual model. Take for example, the assertion that capitalists have a 'direct interest in holding down the productivity of the subsistence workers' (1954, p. 150). In terms of inequality, and rural–urban inequality in particular, in contrast to Kuznets, Lewis argued that inequality is higher in overpopulated, under-developed countries than in advanced industrial countries because agricultural rents are so high in the former (p. 159). As noted in Chapter 3, Kuznets took countries in earlier stages of development to be more equal. And it is the inter-sector relationship that is a central question for Lewis. Not considered was the possibility of urbanization without a related or accompanying structural change away from agriculture, be that output or employment. As discussed in Chapter 1, in many developing countries, urbanization has occurred with only limited structural economic transformation in output away from agriculture since 1990. Even in the new MICs with structural economic transformation in output as noted, structural change in employment has lagged behind whilst at the same time rapid urbanization has been experienced in many (though not all) new MICs. However, there is no evidence in the cross-sectional data of a new Kuznets curve based on urbanization of the population. Figure 4.2 presents the net Gini versus urbanization (proportion of population) and demonstrates there is no relationship across the cross-sectional data between urbanization and a new Kuznets curve

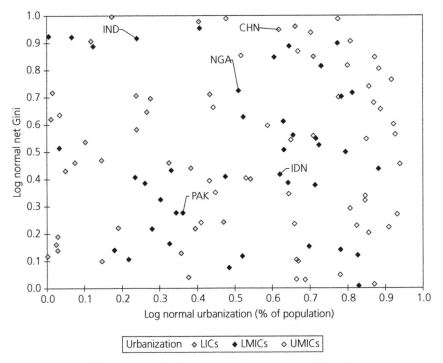

Figure 4.2 Net Gini versus urbanization rate (% of population), 2010–12

Source: Data processed from Solt (2014) and World Bank (2014).

based on urbanization as migration rather than a shift away from agriculture of output and/or employment.

However, one theory posited for urbanization without structural change of output and employment away from agriculture is that in many countries economic growth has been driven by natural resource exports and thus commodity prices and this has driven a different kind of urbanization and change to that envisaged by Lewis and of relevance to the new MICs. Table 4.8 shows that although agriculture, ores, and metals have become a smaller proportion of merchandise exports, such exports are still significant to Indonesia and Ghana to some extent. Further, many of the set of ten new MICs have a substantial proportion of merchandise exports in fuels. Vietnam and India, even at the lower end of the range, have about a tenth to a fifth of merchandise export in fuels. Ghana and Indonesia both have more a third of merchandise export in fuels and Nigeria and Sudan are almost entirely dependent on fuels for merchandise exports. Many of the new MICs with data do, though, have a substantial proportion of exports in manufacturing: China has over 90 per cent; Vietnam, India, Sri Lanka, and Pakistan have approximately two-thirds or more other exports in manufactures; and

Table 4.8 Selected new MICs: structure of exports, 1990–5 versus 2010–12 (or nearest available years)

	Agricultural raw material exports, ores and metals (% of merchandise exports)		Fuel exports (% merchandise exports)		Manufactures exports (% of merchandise exports)	
	1990–5	2010–12	1990–5	2010–12	1990–5	2010–12
East Asia and the Pacific						
China	4.2	1.9	5.3	1.6	78.8	93.6
Indonesia	9.5	14.7	32.7	32.5	46.6	35.9
Vietnam	0.0	4.1	–	10.8	–	66.3
South Asia						
India	6.2	6.7	2.3	18.0	73.3	63.6
Pakistan	7.6	3.9	1.2	4.1	80.8	73.8
Sri Lanka	5.3	4.5	0.3	0.3	65.9	68.2
Sub-Saharan Africa						
Angola	–	–	94.2	–	–	–
Ghana	31.9	10.2	9.4	36.0	–	–
Nigeria	0.6	5.6	96.6	86.8	7.7	14.2
Sudan	36.8	1.5	0.1	92.6	0.7	4.0
Aggregates (mean)						
East Asia and Pacific	10.0	12.1	7.0	6.9	32.4	42.4
South Asia	4.5	6.8	5.1	5.1	64.6	56.0
Sub-Saharan Africa	23.6	25.5	16.1	13.4	15.9	24.0
All developing countries	13.4	15.1	13.5	17.6	30.6	35.1
Aggregates (median)						
East Asia and Pacific	4.8	5.4	2.1	0.6	24.1	33.0
South Asia	4.7	5.6	1.1	1.5	73.3	65.9
Sub-Saharan Africa	11.5	14.2	1.2	1.1	7.2	14.2
All developing countries	5.3	8.3	1.6	4.6	24.3	26.6

Source: Data processed from World Bank (2015).

Indonesia has about a third of exports in manufactures. In short, although some of the new MICs are manufacturing exporters others have more mixed exports and some are dependent on fuel exports.

Gollin et al. (2015) have argued that if natural resource exports such as agriculture raw materials, ores, metals, or fuels are significant then urbanization without substantial structural change is likely. They explain this as follows: given price differences between international prices and local production costs, natural resource exports generate a considerable surplus. If this surplus is spent mainly on urban goods and services, the growth drives urbanization, and if manufactured goods are imported, then urban employment tends to be in non-tradable services. Gollin et al. argue that if countries specialize in the export of urban-produced manufacturing goods and tradable services, structural transformation occurs. Further, they argue that the main driver of intra-country migration is the urban–rural wage gap and this is a product of rural push factors via rising food production that releases labour or rural poverty that then pushes rural migrants to cities and/or urban pull factors such as increases in urban wages that attract rural migrants, or pro-urban government policies that raise urban wages, resonating with Lewis and those writing since on the Lewis model.[17]

There are other criticisms of the Lewis model in terms of the validity of the central assumptions, such as an abundance of labour in the subsistence sector. Neither Lewis nor Kuznets accounted for the possibility that the employment effects of low wages could increase the wage bill and create a functional distribution of income-favouring labour (Ranis, 2004, p. 5). In terms of urban–rural migration, in reality, intra-country migration is often circular (back and forth and seasonal) rather than permanent, and substantial remittances (relative to the rural economy's size) are likely to flow back to rural areas in rapidly urbanizing countries. Further, there is a contradiction noted by Kirkpatrick and Barrientos (2004): the Lewis closed economy model implies the need to expand the capitalist/industry sector, while the Lewis open economy model implies the need to raise productivity in the subsistence/agriculture sector. Rising urban unemployment also raised question marks for the Lewis model (Harris and Todaro, 1970).

Rising urban wages were the real puzzle for Lewis. He argued that unions and large-scale employers exploited economies of scale and could enforce restrictions on recruitment leading to rising wages. In many developing countries, and notably in new MICs, rather than unlimited labour in the agriculture sector migrating to a modern setting, migration has been to low productivity, underemployment or urban informal, self-employment. This means that higher average incomes in non-agricultural sectors vis-à-vis the higher cost of urban living may not hold if migration is circular and remittances largely flow from urban to rural, and much urban employment or underemployment is in the informal sector. That said, several new MICs (e.g. Indonesia, China, and Vietnam) have deliberately sought to foster rural manufacturing.

In sum, although with limits, the Lewis model of economic development does provide a theoretical meta-framing for considering distribution and structural change during economic development in the new MICs. However, there are

---

[17] Since Lewis wrote, the literature has sought to identify such labour push factors (e.g. rises in agricultural productivity that allow agricultural labour to move to the modern sector by reducing the 'food problem'—see Schultz, 1953 and also Gollin et al., 2004) and labour pull factors (e.g. rises in non-agricultural productivity or an 'industrial revolution' attracts underemployed labour from the traditional to the modern sector) as the drivers of structural change. There have also subsequently been various extensions of the Lewis model. For example, in terms of the inter-sectoral terms of trade (Fei and Ranis, 1964); that inter-sectoral labour allocation is affected not only by the inter-sectoral wage gap but the probability of finding a formal sector job (Harris and Todaro, 1970); the two urban informal sectors, one of which is dynamic and tied by subcontract to the urban formal sector and the other of which is an informal 'sponge' sub-sector (Ranis and Stewart, 1999); cross-country labour movements and remittances (e.g. Kindleberger, 1967); and the role of self-reinforcing social and economic exclusion (Copestake, 2003).

different modes of economic development accross the new MICs which we turn to next. We discuss a taxonomy of MICs and in doing so differentiate between the forms of economic development or types of late capitalism since the Cold War and their characteristics and their outcomes in terms of poverty and distribution.

4.4.3 TYPES OF LATE ECONOMIC DEVELOPMENT: CATCH-UP CAPITALISM SINCE THE COLD WAR

What types of late economic development or 'catch up' capitalism are associated with more or less equitable socio-economic outcomes? Whilst Arthur Lewis can provide the theoretical meta-framing for economic development, comparative capitalism studies in both the varieties of capitalism literature and the welfare regimes literature previously noted have argued that there is a diversity of forms to contemporary capitalism (e.g. Amable, 2003; Esping-Andersen, 1999; Hall and Soskice, 2001; North, 1990; Wood and Gough, 2006). The varieties-of-capitalism approach is a reaction to the latter (social policy or welfare regimes) literature shifting the focus from states and labour to firms and how institutions shape their behaviour. Across both literatures, attempts to theorize have for the most part been largely conceptual and OECD- or advanced-nation-based (e.g. Esping-Andersen, 1999; Hall and Soskice, 2001; Schroder, 2013; Weimar and Pape, 1999).

The varieties-of-capitalism literature (e.g. Hall and Soskice, 2001; Yamamura and Streeck, 2003; Streeck and Yamamura, 2005), including that literature labelled as 'national business systems' (notably, Whitley, 1991, 1999), focuses on firms as central actors or the engines of growth in capitalist economies and emphasizes the multiplicity of institutions that influence firms' behaviour in any given society. The literature distinguishes between models of capitalism: liberal market capitalism (e.g. USA) and coordinated market capitalism (e.g. Germany and Japan). The first is characterized by competitive markets and formal contracting. The latter is characterized by institutional mechanisms of coordination that determine firm behaviour. Different regulatory regimes exist in different countries that coordinate labour and corporate governance and these, in turn via firms, determine national economic performance as do other supply-side factors such as financial systems.[18]

---

[18] One recent empirical example of models of late capitalism is that of Judge et al. (2014) who utilize Whitley's (1991, 1999) framework to assess how different models of capitalism are associated with more or less equitable wealth creation which they define as GDP per capita and the inverted Gini coefficient. The Whitley (1991, 1999) 'national business systems' framework has been empirically validated by various scholars (e.g. Bowen and De Clercq, 2008; Dobbin and Boychuk, 1999; Ioannou and Serafeim, 2012; Redding, 2005; Witt and Redding, 2013). Whitley identified four institutional dimensions which collectively interact and coalesce on the form of the model of capitalism or 'national business system'. First, the role of the state: the state has a major influence on the economy via state expenditures and state regulatory quality. Second, the financial system and equity market financial

Furthermore, to the two forms of capitalism another has been added, state-led market capitalism (e.g. in the new MICs, China or Vietnam).

One can posit that in order to understand the socio-economic characteristics and outcomes of different forms of contemporary or late economic development inherent in the new MICs, one ought to conceptualize new MICs as interwoven 'growth regimes' and 'welfare regimes' within the broad process of economic development outlined in the Lewis model. The first, 'growth regimes', are how the macro-economy is orientated (as per the comparative capitalism literature above). The second, 'welfare regimes', relate to how welfare is provided in terms of public responsibility (or otherwise) for collective well-being security (as per the welfare regimes literature). In the era since the Cold War both growth and welfare regimes have come to be dominated by the 'liberal market economy' model inherent in the comparative capitalism literature above. In the developing world since the Cold War this has come to be defined by the 'Washington Consensus' as per Williamson (1990). Williamson's (1990) original 'Washington Consensus' was a set of ten policy recommendations as follows: fiscal discipline (avoidance of large fiscal deficits); public expenditure priorities (the reallocation of public spending from subsidies towards growth-supporting investments such as primary education and health care and infrastructure); tax reform (a broader tax base and reduce marginal tax rates); financial liberalization and market-determined interest rates; unified and competitive exchange rates; trade liberalization of imports; liberalization of foreign direct investment regime (barriers to entry); privatization of state-owned enterprises; elimination of market-impeding regulations and legal protection of property rights. The Washington Consensus, as promoted and practiced by the international financial institutions became a wholesale attempt to dismantle the developmental state as well as promoting global integration (Kanbur, 1999; Rodrik, 2002; Stiglitz, 2005). Much discussion has centred on the concept of a post or augmented Washington Consensus (see Rodrik, 2002; Stiglitz, 1998a, 1998b). Perraton (2005), though, suggests the difference was 'rather less than the rhetoric suggests' and

---

systems (large and liquid equity markets distribute capital) versus credit market based financial system (banks and the state allocate capital via an administrative process). Third, human capital in terms of skill development and 'control system': the former is the education and training system and the latter in the strength of organized labour and trade unions in terms of collective bargaining. Finally, national cultural norms in trust relations (e.g. perceptions of corruption levels as inverse trust) and authority relations (drawing from cultural psychology, power distance cultural norms can assess how in 'low power distance' societies authority figures can be challenged whilst in high power distance authority figures are less likely to be questioned—see Triandis, 2001). Judge et al. (2014) then using fuzzy set analysis empirically identify six models of capitalism: three associated with more equitable and three less equitable forms or 'configurations' of capitalism (the former are more typical in OECD, the latter are more typical in developing countries). They find that more equitable capitalism is associated with lower power distance and better training systems, and higher state expenditures.

noted the post-Washington Consensus only repudiates fiscal discipline, and liberalization of the capital account and tight monetary policy. Elsewhere there is only caution or sequencing rather than opposition to trade and foreign investment regime liberalization and privatization of state-owned enterprises.

If one seeks to build an empirical analysis to differentiate types of late capitalism in MICs by their growth regime and welfare regimes one needs variables to capture aspects of these regimes. Inevitably such an exercise is crude as it is based on available proxies and data sets. If one reviews all the variables used in this book to discuss MICs one can take a set of proxies to analyse the different types of MICs (see Table 4.9). For example, the growth regime can be characterized by the extent of the role of the state in economic activity, and growth policies such those related to the extent of global integration and protection afforded to national businesses (e.g. industrial policies such as tariffs), and structural change in the form of the structure of exports given that growth since 1990 has been export-orientated under globalization and the two sources of export-led growth have been fuel exports and manufacturing exports. Additionally, one can add the institutional aspects of the growth regime as per the comparative literature above: specifically, the quality of democracy (the POLITY data discussed in Chapter 3), and the extent of

Table 4.9 Stylized growth and welfare regimes: types, characteristics, outcomes, and proxies

	Growth regime	Welfare regime
Regime type	Extent to which regime is consistent with the liberal market economy of the Washington Consensus and the strength of institutional development or not	Extent to which the regime reflects a minimalist or maximalist acceptance of public responsibility for collective wellbeing security
Regime characteristics and outcomes	General government final consumption expenditure (% of GDP) Tariff rate, applied, weighted mean, manufactured products (%) Manufactures exports (% of merchandise exports) Fuel exports (% of merchandise exports) Quality of democracy (POLITY) (quality of executive recruitment, the constraints on executive authority, political competition, and institutionalized qualities of governing authority). Voice and accountability (WGI) (the extent to which a country's people are able to participate in selecting the government and extent of freedom of expression and association)	Tax revenue (% of GDP) Health expenditure, public (% of GDP) Share of GNI to richest decile Share of GNI to 'middle' (deciles 5–9) Proportion of population living on less than $2.50 per day (population in absolute poverty) Extent of political stability and absence of violence (WGI)

Note: Data from Edward and Sumner (2015) and World Bank (2015).
Source: Author's elaboration.

voice and accountability (from the World Governance Indicators—WGI— and also discussed in Chapter 3). In contrast, the welfare regime can be characterized by the overall extent of tax collection to fund public services, and by spending on key public goods, notably public spending on health as well as the welfare regime outcomes in terms of inequality via the share of GNI to the richest and the 'middle' (decile 5 to decile 9) and poverty levels at $2.50 per day and the extent of political stability and the absence of violence.

To reiterate, the exercise is crude and the choice of variables is to a considerable extent driven by data availability for a large number of MICs. Within the overall approach taken here to characterize late capitalism a growth regime is assessed by the extent to which it is consistent with the liberal market economy of the Washington Consensus (minimal state and minimal interference in markets) and institutional characteristics such as democracy and voice and accountability. The welfare regime is assessed by the extent to which the regime reflects a minimalist or maximalist acceptance of public responsibility for addressing collective well-being security.

Taking this set of twelve variables, if one performs a cluster analysis, one finds four clusters or forms of late capitalism in contemporary MICs (see Table 4.10). There is sufficient data coverage to cluster seventy of the 105 MICs and of the set of ten new MICs all but Angola have sufficient data to be included. The most important or discriminating variables are the structure of exports (and if exports are dominated by fuels or manufactures), followed by the distribution variables, notably the poverty headcount, and the share of GNI captured by the richest decile of population. That means that these are the variables that are driving the clustering. Thus whilst it may seem surprising to see how certain countries are clustered together in the analysis, the clustering of countries itself is more dependent on these variables as they have the strongest discriminatory power in the data set. This clustering ought to be seen as one largely driven by export structure and distributional variables. Of course if one changes the variables the clustering may change to.

Interestingly, growth regimes' variables in terms of the Washington Consensus orientation (proxied in this analysis by state involvement in the economy and by tariffs) differ surprisingly little across the clusters, demonstrating the pervasive nature of liberal market economics since the Cold War with only limited differentiation in terms of cluster averages. For example, government spending and tariffs do not differ enormously between or within groups. Welfare regimes, on the other hand, do differ considerably across and even with groups. Some countries do spend substantially more on public health for example (which here is taken as a proxy for wider public goods spending). Welfare regime outcomes do differ considerably too in terms of differing poverty levels in different types of MICs.

Overall the four clusters or types of MICs can be outlined as follows: there are two groups of mixed-export MICs, one group of manufactures-exporting

Table 4.10 Characteristics of clusters of middle-income countries

Types of MICs		Growth regime						Welfare regime					
		Gov't exp.	Tariffs	Manuf. exports	Fuel exports	Demo-cracy	Voice and acc.	Tax revenue	Health exp.	Share of richest	Share of 'middle'	Poverty	Political stability
Mixed exporters I (with high inequality and high poverty rates)	Mean	17.3	9.9	37.8	10.7	4.2	−0.4	23.6	3.8	41.5	47.0	47.7	−0.2
	N	10	10	10	10	10	10	10	10	10	10	10	10
	Std. dev.	8.5	4.2	22.8	12.5	6.0	0.6	14.9	2.3	8.0	5.0	17.6	0.7
Mixed exporters II (with moderate inequality and moderate poverty rates)	Mean	15.1	6.9	29.5	12.0	5.6	−0.2	18.3	3.3	31.3	51.9	13.5	−0.3
	N	20	20	20	20	20	20	20	20	20	20	20	20
	Std. dev.	4.4	4.2	17.6	11.4	5.2	0.6	5.1	1.2	5.9	2.3	7.1	0.5
Manufactures exporters	Mean	14.8	7.4	71.8	6.1	4.9	−0.2	16.5	3.4	31.2	51.8	12.0	−0.3
	N	24	24	24	24	24	24	24	24	24	24	24	24
	Std. dev.	4.9	5.3	9.0	5.7	5.4	0.7	5.2	1.6	5.9	2.9	11.9	0.9
Fuel exporters	Mean	12.6	11.3	9.3	71.0	0.4	−0.9	14.0	2.5	31.7	52.1	16.9	−1.0
	N	16	16	16	16	16	16	16	16	16	16	16	16
	Std. dev.	2.8	4.7	7.9	21.2	5.8	0.6	8.7	1.2	5.1	2.3	12.1	0.9

Note: Indicators are listed in Table 4.9.

Source: Author's estimates based on data from Edward and Sumner (2015) and World Bank (2015).

MICs, and one group of fuel-exporting MICs. The characteristics of the four clusters of MICs are discussed in turn: first, there is a group of MICs which are mixed exporters with very high poverty levels and a high inequality (the GNI share of the rich). These are largely the pseudo new MICs noted in Chapter 1 and many are from sub-Saharan Africa. Second, there is a group of MICs which are mixed exporters with moderate poverty levels and less unequal than the group above. This group is largely former planned or socialist economies as also noted in Chapter 1 but also includes the new MIC, Indonesia. Indonesia is, though, somewhat of an outlier as it has fuel as a proportion of exports significantly higher than the group average and its welfare regime indicators are also weaker than group averages (notably in public health expenditures). The welfare regime is—in general—weaker in the first group of mixed export MICs and stronger in the second group of former planned economy MICs. This is largely due to the fact that the poverty rate is much higher in the former group (though there is a much larger standard deviation than the latter group). Public spending on health is about the same. Third, there is a group of manufactures-exporting MICs. These MICs have moderate poverty levels. This group had stronger welfare regimes in general in terms of moderate poverty levels (relative to other clusters), and moderate tax revenue and health expenditure. This group includes China, India, Pakistan, Sri Lanka, and Vietnam. India is potentially an outlier in some of the characteristics of this cluster as it has substantially higher fuel exports than the group mean and much higher poverty levels than the group mean. India and Pakistan also have weaker welfare regimes. Finally, there is a group of fuel exporting MICs. These MICs have moderate poverty levels but generally weaker democracies and higher levels of political instability. This includes Nigeria and Sudan and also Ghana. This group has weaker welfare regimes in general in terms of lower levels of tax collection and health spending as well as moderate poverty levels noted. Ghana is possibly an outlier in this group as it has much lower fuel export dependency than the group mean. It also has a stronger welfare regime than group averages. In contrast, the welfare regimes of Nigeria and Sudan are very weak.

What should one conclude from this taxonomy of MICs? First, that the structure of exports is by far the most important variable in differentiating MICs, followed by distributional and poverty variables. Second, that, by the indicators here at least, growth regimes do not differ that much across or within groups in terms of the extent of the pervasive Washington Consensus orientation. Third, that better welfare regimes in general are to be found in the manufactures-exporting MICs but even so outliers persist in this group and the other groups demonstrating heterogeneity.

All of these types of late capitalism do share common characteristics—one not yet discussed in depth is that substantial proportions of the population remain either in absolute poverty or in insecurity not far above the absolute poverty line. That is to say most of the population lives below the $10 per day indicative security-from-poverty line. In Chapter 5 we broaden the discussion of this book beyond the absolute poor to include the burgeoning insecure or 'precariat' who are just above the poverty line because this insecure group forms the basis of a second layer to the poverty paradox which can constrain countries' future growth, poverty reduction, and political change. The chapter discusses how, as countries progress from low to middle income, if high or rising inequality is not mediated by governments a new kind of middle-income poverty trap may emerge based on the burgeoning precariat group. The precariat is what some of the absolute poor will become as growth continues. As the absolute poor move into this insecure group poverty is potentially perpetuated in a way which is likely to lead to slower growth and slower political change in a self-reinforcing mechanism in new MICs.

4.5 Conclusions

The previous chapters have discussed the changes in the developing world, the resultant shifts in global poverty since the end of the Cold War and sought to provide an explanation of the uneven responsiveness of poverty to growth in new MICs. In short, there has been substantial economic growth, and the world's poor now live in countries that are better off than the poorest countries but do not yet have the structural characteristics of developed countries. Such patterns also mean that global poverty is in the process of nationalizing, meaning that redistributive social policy is affordable for many of the countries where the world's poor are concentrated. Furthermore, if global poverty is increasingly a question of spatial and social inequalities, and distributional patterns of economic growth and economic development, then poverty ought to be framed and approached as a distribution question. This too would imply greater focus on redistributive social policy rather than relying largely on economic growth to address poverty.

This chapter has presented three arguments. First, orthodox theories of global poverty are dominated by explanations of poverty that suggest that the poor are poor because they lack what they need to be defined as not poor such as assets or values. Put another way, orthodox theories of poverty simply describe poverty rather than explain it, and focus on the poor themselves rather than the societal causes of poverty, which above a certain level of development are distributional in nature. Second, that the changes in global poverty discussed imply that theories of the causes of poverty should give greater emphasis to questions of national distribution and the pattern of economic development. Finally, that much of global poverty could now or in the foreseeable future be eliminated with redistributive social policy.

The chapter reviewed theories of global poverty and compared three types of theory as follows: (i) material theories, or deficit and deprivational theories, (ii) subjective, or cultural and behavioural theories, and (iii) structural, distributional or relational theories. The first group of theories are based on material deprivations or deficits of something, for example, insufficient assets to generate incomes from. The second group are based on deficits in values and, relatedly, behaviours, for example, insufficient control over one's fertility or insufficient valuing of educational attainment. The third group of theories are based on the structural position of the poor, for example, the distribution of wealth and income and access to, and rewards from, labour markets.

The discussion then considered the empirical and theoretical foundation for a structural theory of poverty. This would be that global poverty is nationalizing, and much of global poverty is now or will soon be concentrated in countries that have the domestic resources to end poverty. Without redistribution, absolute poverty in MICs may persist even with economic growth. The chapter discussed the theoretical foundation of the Arthur Lewis dual model in terms of economic development in new MICs and develop a taxonomy of late capitalism in terms of growth and welfare regimes which found that the structure of exports and distribution variables differentiate MICs.

One aspect that MICs share, not yet fully discussed, is that a substantial proportion of the population live in either absolute poverty or in insecurity above the poverty line, meaning most of the population lives below a $10-per-day security-from-poverty line. In Chapter 5 we broaden the discussion of this book beyond the absolute poor to include the burgeoning insecure or 'precariat' who are just above the poverty line because this is a second layer to the poverty paradox of late capitalism and has implications for future economic development in MICs.

5 Slowdown capitalism

Is there a new middle-income poverty trap?

5.1 Introduction

In Chapter 4 the basis for a structural theory of absolute poverty was made. That basis is a two-layered poverty paradox which is as follows: the first layer is defined as the paradox that absolute poverty persists despite the national resources being already or soon in existence to end absolute poverty and, further, that such poverty may persist for the foreseeable future even with reasonable growth due to prevailing patterns and trends in inequality. The poverty paradox is common across the new MICs but the extent of poverty and thus the intensity of the paradox differs according to the mode of late capitalism pursued. The different forms of late capitalism outlined also share a common characteristic that forms a second layer of the poverty paradox or in some sense may even contribute to an explanation of the poverty paradox itself and that is the subject of this chapter. This is that the poverty paradox extends further than the absolute poor. The second layer of the poverty paradox can be defined as follows: some people may pass the line and move out of absolute poverty but the risk of falling back into poverty can extend much further and reaching a level of consumption corresponding to a full escape from the risk of falling back into poverty could take over a hundred years given current patterns of and trends in inequality. In short, escaping absolute poverty is not the same as permanently escaping poverty because the risk of poverty extends to far higher consumption levels than a few dollars a day. This chapter outlines a thesis of an alternative middle-income trap on this basis that may hinder future growth and governance prospects and thus the chapter seeks to reconnect further poverty and the processes of economic development. In outlining a middle-income poverty trap this chapter widens the lens to include both absolute poverty and this burgeoning group of people in new MICs who are barely above the poverty line and indeed are poor by OECD country standards. The chapter discusses how rising inequality across the new MICs is slowing down the journey from poverty to secure lives. Not only is the burgeoning precariat group already substantial in size in MICs this group is what some of the current absolute poor will join when they cross the absolute poverty line. In short, even when absolute poverty falls, it is simply replaced by a new type of poverty in the form of highly insecure lives. Poverty is perpetuated in a different way because those who are no longer in absolute poverty are vulnerable to stressors and shocks such as ill-health or growth slowdowns pushing them back into absolute poverty. The failure of growth to lift sufficient people into a more secure group quicker is due to rising inequality dampening consumption growth at the lower end of the distribution and this is the cause of the trap. The trap is likely to lead to weak and slow future growth due to slower growing domestic demand and limited governance reform due to a weak and slowly expanding tax base, both of which in themselves form a self-reinforcing mechanism.

This trap provides the foundations for a new kind of development cooperation between OECD countries and countries at middle-income levels. Counter to the interpretation that the dwindling numbers of LICs and the nationalization of global poverty mean foreign aid and development cooperation more broadly are no longer required in all but the very poorest countries, the poverty paradox and middle-income poverty trap suggest development cooperation could remain important for many years to come. It is argued that as global poverty nationalizes development cooperation needs to adapt to the contemporary problems faced by MICs which are not related to insufficient resources but to the issues faced at middle-income level which are quite different to those experienced at low-income level.

The MIC trap outlined in this chapter is different to the orthodox middle-income trap. It is a theorem about the challenges of transitioning from middle-income towards the levels of development of more advanced nations. It is presented in this chapter not as a final theory but as a hypothesis to be further discussed, refined, and tested to assess what utility it has, what determines if countries enter such as trap, and what might determine how countries circumnavigate or avoid such a trap.

The arguments of this chapter can be summed up as follows: first, if inequality is not mediated during economic growth and structural change, MICs may, in the future, face a new kind of middle-income poverty trap. Second, that this middle-income trap is neither inevitable nor unavoidable. It can be characterized as follows: rising inequality constrains the growth of a secure middle-income group and instead creates a new 'precariat' group living precarious lives, just above absolute poverty but not by a large margin, and not in a sufficiently secure position to drive economic growth and pay significant taxes and thus drive political change and expand significantly welfare regimes. In short, there is an opportunity cost of rising inequality during economic development and that cost is to forgo the elimination of absolute poverty and the emergence of a secure, consuming class in the foreseeable future. Third, it is this trap that provides a basis for continuing development cooperation with MICs but of a different kind to 'traditional' aid.

The chapter is structured as follows: section 5.2 presents the alternative middle-income trap. Section 5.3 considers how the trap manifests in the emergence, not of a traditional secure middle class but a precarious, near poor group or 'precariat'. Section 5.4 then discusses how the middle-income trap provides a basis for a new kind of development cooperation between OECD countries and countries at the middle-income level. The trap outlined and the burgeoning 'precariat' group could form the basis of a new approach to development cooperation: It is argued that 'traditional' aid—year-to-year supplementary resources—is less relevant over time as MICs grow. Instead, policy coherence from OECD countries to sustain growth and expand tax revenues for the state—meaning development policies such as trade policy, or regulating tax havens and illicit financial flows, and so forth—may be more in demand from MICs and appropriate for MICs. Long-run concessional lending may remain cheaper than commercial lending and thus useful for addressing via co-financing, more inclusive growth spatially via infrastructure investments designed to better link sub-national geographies and social groups to the MIC growth hubs. Donors could also consider co-financing with MICs global and regional public goods where there are high up-front costs but long-term benefits which are likely to be across regions or beyond. Finally, section 5.5 concludes.

5.2 The middle-income trap

5.2.1 THE ORTHODOX MIDDLE-INCOME TRAP

The upswing, at least, of the Kuznets inverted-U hypothesis is evident in the set of new MICs where growth has been accompanied by structural change of output. As Palma (2011) observed the downswing of the inverted-U though has 'evaporated' or at least it is not evident yet in the data. The unequal distribution of the benefits of growth sub-nationally and the only partial transformation of labour force structure (relative to GDP transformation) may generate a situation whereby rapid growth and structural transformation are accompanied by rising inequality. This may inhibit future economic growth, governance, and poverty reduction due to the emergence of a precarious group of people or 'precariat' with insufficient purchasing power to drive growth and pay significant taxes and thus influence the responsiveness of governance.

This precarious group, is what today's poor will become if poverty falls. Some have prematurely and erroneously labelled this group as a new 'middle class' in the developing world. The group is more appropriately labelled a new 'precariat' group drawing on Standing (2011). This is not to deny that such a group is better off than the absolute poor and is likely not to live in absolute poverty on a day-to-day basis. At the same time this precariat may not live too far from the absolute poverty line either. The group is likely to be vulnerable to poverty itself from shocks or stressors. For example, the precariat is vulnerable to slow downs in economic growth pushing them back into poverty and/or the factors that Dercon and Shapiro's (2007) empirical review of longitudinal data sets identified as possible causes of falling back into poverty (see discussion in Chapter 2). Growing numbers of people in this precarious group and their insecurity are the underlying cause of the new middle-income trap.

'Traps' at both low- and middle-income levels of development have been a substantial focus in the economic literature. There is a well-known low-income poverty trap which is related to the inability of a country to rise above a certain level of income per capita. There is also a well-known 'middle-income trap' which is related to loss of competitiveness at the middle-income level. Both are situations whereby countries may get 'stuck' at certain levels of development typically defined as an economic growth slowdown though this could be extended to a slowing pace of poverty reduction or governance reform or the pace of structural change.

In its original iteration, Nelson (1956) argued that the country-level low-income poverty trap exists at low levels of per capita income, whereby countries are too poor to save and invest and this results in low growth rates. Once a country passes a threshold and a rising proportion of income is saved and invested, more rapid economic growth will ensue. In short, some countries are stuck at a stable equilibrium level of low-per-capita income close to subsistence as population growth counteracts any gains in income growth.

More recently, Sachs (2005) and Collier (2007) offered a set of LIC poverty traps to explain why countries are poor, somewhat building on Nelson (1956).[1] Sachs (2005, pp. 54–61) presents a range of traps: an individual-level poverty trap (the poor are too poor to save for the future and accumulate capital); a physical geography trap (of isolated poor countries similar to Collier (2007) as discussed next); a fiscal trap (limited government resources); a governance trap/failure; cultural barriers (notably on rights, and gender inequality); a geopolitics trap (as a result of trade barriers); a constraining of innovation trap (due to small markets and weak incentives); and a demographic trap (as a result of high fertility). In short, poverty is a result of a lack of savings, the absence of trade opportunities (due to geography), technological reversal, natural resource decline, adverse productivity shocks, and population growth. The solution proposed by Sachs and others is a large

---

[1] See also Azariadis and Stachurski (2005) for a review of the literature on poverty traps. See Ghatak (2015) for a discussion of individual-level poverty traps. Ghatak argues there is a distinction between those traps which are 'friction driven' and those traps which are 'scarcity driven'. The former are market failures. The latter relate to behaviour under extreme scarcity. The former imply addressing market failures. The latter imply redistributive transfers.

increase in foreign aid to be spent on agriculture inputs, investments in basic health, investments in education, power, transport and communication services, safe water, and sanitation (Sachs, 2005, pp. 233–4).

In contrast, Collier (2007) argued that the poorest countries are afflicted by one or more of four interlocking poverty traps related to conflict, fragility, and governance: a conflict trap (especially civil war); a natural resource trap—abundance of which makes 'democracy malfunction' (p. 42); a landlocked-with-bad-neighbours trap—in the sense of poor markets—'If you are coastal, you serve the world; if you are landlocked, you serve your neighbours' (p. 57); and a 'bad governance in a small country' trap. Collier noted that the traps could be broken out of by some countries. Collier argued that globalization is not going to solve these problems left to itself—the poorest countries need to diversify into manufacturing trade. Temporary protection from successful exporters in Asia in certain sectors such as textiles is required. International laws and charters which shape behaviour and support 'heroes' are important in areas of managing natural resource revenues, democracy, public budget transparency, and investment.

Such discussions of LIC poverty traps have limited meaning for countries with much higher-per-capita income that *have* already grown beyond low-income levels and attained middle-income status. Such countries can face instead what has been called a 'middle-income trap' (see for discussion Aiyar et al., 2013; Eichengreen et al., 2011; Gill and Kharas, 2007; Ohno, 2009). The orthodox middle-income trap is a slowdown of economic growth thought to be triggered by an inability to compete internationally either in low-wage manufacturing markets due to rising wages, or in high-value-added markets due to limited skill and innovation investments. One proposed remedy is to stimulate domestic demand. This is to be accompanied by large investments in education and infrastructure. Another remedy is the identification of new international markets in higher value-added goods. Eichengreen et al. (2013) find that growth slowdowns are less likely if countries have higher levels of secondary and tertiary education and a higher proportion of hi-tech products in their exports. However, many of the options countries face are constrained by the need to out-compete China or other parts of East and South East Asia in higher-valued-added sectors or in low-wage manufacturing.

Alternatively, Alonso et al. (2014) list a set of traps or 'bottlenecks' specific to MICs, notably, difficulties sustaining a process of technical and productive change (see also Agenor and Canuto, 2012) as well as environmental and energy challenges; additionally, achieving macroeconomic stability and integration into international financial markets while at the same time maintaining enough space for counter-cyclical macroeconomic policies (see also Ocampo, 2003; Ocampo and Griffith-Jones, 2007); and adjusting economic and social changes with the required path of institutional change (see Alonso and Garcimartin, 2013). Alonso et al. define 'traps' thus:

Those constraints to progress that result from a set of mutually reinforcing blocking factors... As countries rise up the income ladder they tend to be affected less by absolute shortages and more by asymmetries and bottlenecks in the development process... These bottlenecks have a similar effect to the well-known "poverty traps", insofar as they drive countries to fall into a low-level equilibrium that ends up blocking or delaying growth. (2014, pp. 4–5)

A general comment on both the low-income and middle-income traps posited to date is that they have sometimes been viewed as universal and unavoidable. However, economic growth since the Cold War would suggest that some countries at least have avoided or escaped the low-income trap altogether, and some existing MICs have sustained growth. This would mean that under certain conditions or with specific policies such traps are avoidable.

5.2.2 AN ALTERNATIVE MIDDLE-INCOME TRAP

An alternative framing to that of the orthodox middle-income trap outlined above would be to build on the discussion of this book so far. One question is whether the trap for new MICs is a poverty trap or an inequality trap. Bourguignon et al. (2007, p. 243) differentiate an inequality trap from a poverty trap. They argue that in a poverty trap the incomes of the poor do not grow beyond some threshold—they are forever poor. In contrast, an inequality trap allows for the incomes of the poor to grow over time as long as patterns of unequal relative advantage persist in the long run. Mansuri and Rao (2011, pp. 33–4) building on Rao (2006) put it as follows:

A poverty trap is a situation in which mechanisms such as credit market imperfections, corruption, dysfunctional institutions, or increasing returns to investments in health, education, or physical capital, cause a group of people and their descendants to remain in a perpetual state of poverty. In an inequality trap, by contrast, the entire distribution is stable, because... the various dimensions of inequality (wealth, power, social status) interact to protect the rich from downward mobility and prevent the poor from being upwardly mobile.

What new MICs face could be characterized as both a poverty and an inequality trap give the trap is driven by rising inequality during structural change delaying the expansion of a consuming class. However, henceforth the discussion refers to the trap as a middle-income poverty trap because it implies a large population in or near poverty for a considerable time to come despite the growth and resources middle-income status implies. A way of framing this new middle-income trap is as follows: rising inequality during economic development slows down an already long journey from absolute poverty (at for example, less than $2.50) to secure lives (at over $10 as indicative) and thus constrains the growth of the group of population living secure lives. Figure 5.1 shows various trajectories and the time in years they

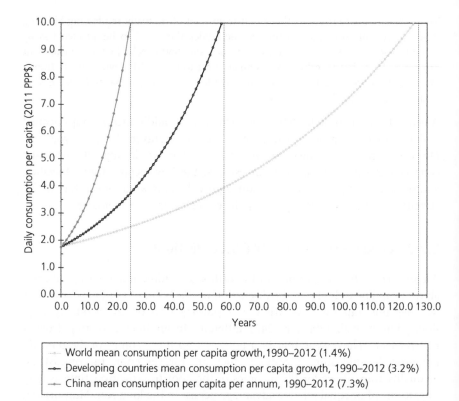

Figure 5.1 Years taken for median consumption of the $2.50 poor to reach security from poverty at $10 per day at various average annual consumption growth rates

Note: Median of $2.50 poor = $1.75.

Source: Data processed from World Bank (2015).

would take from a starting point set at the median consumption of the poor at under the $2.50 poverty line (which is $1.75 in 2012 or year zero on the figure). If consumption of that person grows at the average annual consumption per capita growth for all developing countries since the Cold War, it would take almost sixty years for the average poor person in 2012 to reach $10 per day consumption. That is likely to be longer than the average life expectancy for the $2.50 poor. Worse, if one took a slower rate such as the world average annual consumption rate annual growth, 1990–2012, it would take almost 130 years for the average poor person now to reach security from poverty. If inequality rises during economic development this length of time is likely to be extended further if consumption growth at the lower end of the distribution falls below the average for the whole country. On the other hand, if public policies were put in place to address rising inequality and inequality falls and the consumption growth rate at the lower end of the distribution increases relative to the average then the length of time to go from $2.50 to $10 could be reduced. If one took lower poverty lines such as the $2 poverty line the journey would take even longer as it lowers the starting point in year zero (the median of the $2 poor is $1.50 in 2012). Alternatively one could aim for much higher growth rates so the consumption of the poor in all countries in the developing world would need to grow at China's 1990–2012 average consumption per capita under which the journey would still take a generation.

The impact of a prolonged journey from poverty to security is the very slow expansion of a secure, consuming group in middle-income countries. This is likely to hinder future economic growth due to constraining domestic demand and also hinder tax collection and an accompanying governance transition as the state remains reliant on a narrow tax base to fund its functions.

Without a substantial secure, consuming group, growth and development are likely to remain vulnerable to external global markets and the precarious group are likely to be vulnerable to falling back into poverty during economic slowdowns or other serious external shocks. This alternative middle-income problem may be particularly framed by spatial and social inequalities hindering poverty reduction noted in Chapter 2 because of the relative disconnect of sub-national geographies and social groups. These spatial and social inequalities too may hinder future growth and structural change.

A relevant body of studies considers the instrumental reasons for why high or rising inequality matters to future rates of growth and poverty reduction, as well as good governance, and so forth. Many have argued that high or rising inequality not only reduces economic growth and also slows down poverty reduction not only through lower growth but also via the distribution of the growth increment. Nissanke and Thorbecke (2006, p. 1343) sum up the debate: high and rising inequality, (as the set of new MICs now find themselves with), can lead to rent-seeking, social tensions, political instability, a poor median voter, and imperfect capital markets. In turn, these can lead to less secure property rights, increased uncertainty, greater demands for redistribution, a reduction in investment opportunities which in turn lead to lower investment, higher taxation, and lower economic growth.

Cunha Neves and Tavares Silva (2014) review the empirical research on the relationship of inequality-to-growth and the potential transmission channels of: imperfect credit markets; fiscal policy; socio-political instability and savings.[2] They conclude that the empirical literature is inconclusive overall because of differences in data quality and coverage, estimation methods, and the choice of inequality indicator and that different channels have differing impacts across

---

[2] Rehme (2001) posited that unequal societies create redistributive pressures leading to distortionary fiscal policy that reduces future growth. Kaldor (1955–6) argued that the rich have a higher propensity to save.

countries and that country and regional specifics are important. Despite the lack of an overall conclusion in the empirical literature, Cunha Neves and Tavares Silva (2014) do note that—in general—the cross-sectional data has tended to find that income inequality has a negative impact on growth (e.g. Alesina and Rodrik, 1994; Berg and Ostry, 2011; Birdsall and Londono, 1997; Castello and Domenech, 2002; Clark, 1995; Deininger and Squire, 1998; Knowles, 2005; Ostry et al., 2014; Perotti, 1996; Persson and Tabellini, 1994). However, when panel data are utilized income inequality has a positive impact on growth across the sample, though underlying this may be negative impact in LICs and MICs (see Barro, 2000; Castello, 2000; Deininger and Olinto, 2000; Forbes, 2000; Halter et al., 2014; Li and Zou, 1998). The extent of openness to trade and investment could be of importance (Agénor, 2002; Barro, 2000; Milanovic, 2005). In particular, research suggests that the socio-political instability channel is important (see Alesina and Perotti, 1996; Keefer and Knack, 2002; Perotti, 1996; Svensson, 1998) but the other channels have contradictory evidence. Further, one might add a set of studies that have found that redistribution can be good for growth or at least have a neutral impact on growth (Easterly and Rebelo, 1993; Ostry et al., 2014; Perotti, 1996).

That there is either a negative impact of inequality on growth overall or in developing countries specifically suggests a threshold effect. Cornia et al. (2004) find a distinct non-linear relationship between income inequality and economic growth. They argue that low levels of inequality are bad for growth, but also that high levels of inequality can have serious negative consequences. Cornia et al. (2004), who use a data set of seventy-three countries to identify critical threshold levels of inequality, conclude that rising inequality can assist growth, but only up to a Gini value of 0.30; a Gini value above 0.45 impedes economic growth. Most of the set of ten new MICs are already close to or above this level in both their pre- and/or post-tax Gini.

Dabla-Norris et al. (2015, pp. 6–7) concur empirically, based on 159-country data set that a higher net Gini is associated with lower output growth in the medium term and find an inverse relationship between the national income share of the rich and economic growth. They find as the income share of the richest quintile increases, GDP slows in the following five years. Conversely, an increase share of national income to the poorest quintile increases future growth. The positive association between disposable income share and higher growth holds for the quintile above the poorest quintile: in short the poorest 40 per cent or the Palma 'poor'. In a similar vein, Brueckner and Lederman (2015) find that on average if the Gini rises by 1 percentage point, GDP per capita is reduced by 1.1 per cent over five years. However, that in LICs increases in inequality raise GDP per capita and in MICs and HICs increases in inequality reduce GDP per capita.

Birdsall (2007) argues further that income inequality in developing countries matters for at least three reasons: i) where markets are underdeveloped, inequality inhibits growth through economic mechanisms; ii) where institutions of government are weak, inequality exacerbates the problem of creating and maintaining accountable government, increasing the probability of economic and social policies that inhibit growth and poverty reduction; and iii) where social institutions are fragile, inequality further discourages the civic and social life that underpins effective collective decision-making that is necessary to the functioning of healthy societies. In the same vein, there are further political arguments, noted not only by Birdsall but others too (e.g. Beitz, 2001; Wade, 2005), that high or rising inequality distorts the processes of decision-making and that inequality may also be a threat to democratic participation. Nel (2006, 2008), for example, discusses in depth, theoretically and empirically, the socio-political consequences of inequality. He empirically links higher levels of inequality to weaker democratic participation, corruption, and civil conflict. Growing inequality can lead to political instability because elites co-opt the political system and public investment is lowered (see Karayalcin and McCollister, 2005; Knack and Keefer, 1995). In a similar vein, Acemoglu and Robinson (2012) argue that the main reason nations fail is that their political institutions become focused on elites and institutions become extractive.

In sum, rising inequality is likely to hamper future development. In section 5.3 we consider the manifestation of the new 'middle-income trap' more specifically. That is, that rising inequality produces a burgeoning 'precariat' or vulnerable group that is unable to drive future growth and political change.

5.3 The burgeoning precarious group in new MICs

5.3.1 THE LIMITATIONS OF ALL POVERTY LINES

As noted in Chapter 2, poverty measurement, and the specification of poverty lines, has become a dominant part of much research on poverty since poverty-related research emerged in the 1960s and 1970s. Indeed, a substantial scholarly effort has focused on measuring poverty in ever more precise ways (or at least using measurement perceived to be ever more precise). This is useful but as noted previously the pursuit of an ever-increasing desire for precision may be a distraction from greater discussion on the causes of global poverty. To reiterate, Harriss (2007), for one, has argued that it is the excessive fetishization of poverty measurement that has distracted from understanding and addressing the causes of poverty which are not immediately measurable or quantifiable (at least not to anywhere near the same extent).

As a point of departure it is worth noting that poverty is not a 'condition'; rather poverty for many of those likely to be counted as poor is an experience, and often a transitory experience depending on exactly where the poverty line is drawn and when data are collected. In other words, the volatility of income/ expenditure evident in longitudinal studies (as discussed in Dercon and Shapiro, 2007) would suggest that perfect monetary poverty lines are impossible to set because whether a person is counted as poor may be due in a large part to when the data are collected. Relatedly, the impossibility of precise poverty line setting is yet further demonstrated by the typically observed clustering of a sizeable proportion of the population not too far above the poverty line. Unless the poverty line is set at a much higher level than absolute poverty, the sensitivity of poverty estimates relate to where any poverty line is set, as noted in Chapter 2. This is also true with regard to non-monetary poverty measurement to some extent. The situation is compounded by the fact that there may be nothing necessarily different between individuals above and below a given poverty line. National poverty lines are theoretically better, given their basis on a minimum nutritional intake of, typically, 2,100 calories, and their inclusion of some non-food necessities. However, even national poverty lines have limited meaning as different people require different calorific intake, and the minimum calories can be met at much lower cost through poor quality diets. Furthermore, large proportions of the population may be measured as non-poor but still living in poverty from time to time or may be at risk of poverty from growth slowdowns or other stressors and shocks such as illness. This illustrates the underlying issue that people do not escape poverty in one big jump into a middle-class lifestyle, but in a series of steps. Pritchett (2006) makes a convincing case for a spectrum of poverty lines, with poverty persisting to much higher levels of per capita expenditure. This is based on an idea that people do not move out of poverty, but move out of poverty of different levels of severity.

Research on poverty dynamics and vulnerability to poverty has become increasingly prominent since the 1990s (see Chambers, 1989; Dercon, 2006; Moser, 1998; Sen, 1981, 1999). Such literature on longitudinal poverty analysis in developing countries has expanded (see, for example, Addison et al., 2009; Baulch, 2011). Studies imply that policy interventions should distinguish between the chronic poor (meaning here the longevity of poverty episode) and the transient poor (see Baulch and McCulloch, 1998; Hulme et al., 2001): It has been argued that poverty policy needs to include measures to reduce risks and fluctuations, for example, by introducing safety nets and insurance schemes. In sum, while it is useful to estimate absolute poverty and trends in absolute poverty, one needs to not forget there is usually a large group of people who sit just above but precariously close to the absolute poverty line. It is this group we turn to next.

5.3.2 INDICATIVE ESTIMATES OF THE PRECARIOUS GROUP

The thesis of this section is that economic growth with rising inequality in the set of new MICs has led to a situation whereby a new burgeoning group has emerged. This group is not a secure middle class but a precarious group and thus can do relatively little to power domestic demand. Further, their position only slightly above poverty constrains the expansion of tax revenue and thus improvements in the responsiveness of governance (see also discussion in Sumner, 2012d). Kuznets (1955, p. 22) foresaw to some extent this pattern and referred to this group as the 'intermediate income classes'. Regarding under-developed countries, he argued that they have no middle classes: 'there is a sharp contrast between the preponderant proportion of the population whose average income is well below the generally low countrywide average, and a small top group with a very large relative income excess'.

This book so far has focused on absolute global poverty defined as both a $2.50-per-day threshold and in terms of multidimensional poverty. However, poverty could be said to extend further when one considers security from poverty and the implied life expectancy of various consumption levels. To illustrate the possible size of this new precarious group we can make estimates for $2.50–$10 per day expenditures.[3] The basis of these cut-offs is somewhat arbitrary but grounded at the lower end, on the poverty line used earlier in this book and at the higher end on a $10 poverty line which as also noted previously is a threshold which has been associated with greater security from poverty.[4] Furthermore, ten dollars is associated with a life expectancy of about 65 years (see Figure 5.2). Although $10 per day may sound extravagant when compared to an absolute poverty line of $1 or $2 a day it represents a consumption level of the poorest in the OECD countries as it is the upper limit of the poorest decile in OECD countries in 2012.

The data show (see Table 5.1) that the group in between $2.50 and $10 has doubled in size from 1.6 billion people in 1990 to 3.2 billion people in 2012 or from a third of the world's population to almost half of the world's population. Even when China is excluded the numbers in this precarious group were almost 2.5 billion in 2012 or 44 per cent of the world's population.

If growth is reasonable (taking the IMF growth projection minus historical IMF error on its own projections as before) and distribution trends continue, this group could grow to almost 4 billion people in 2030. This group is worthy

---

[3] Alternatively one could focus on insecure employment and take ILO (2015) estimates.
[4] To recap, the line is based on the 10 per cent probability of falling back below the national poverty lines in Mexico, Brazil, and Chile (López-Calva and Ortiz-Juarez, 2014) and additionally Indonesia (Sumner et al., 2014).

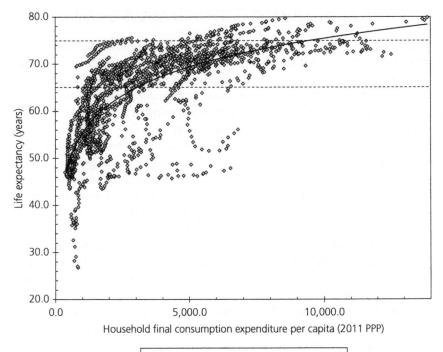

Figure 5.2 Life expectancy (years) versus household final consumption expenditure per capita in developing countries, 1990–2012

Source: Data processed from World Bank (2015).

Table 5.1 Indicative estimates of the precarious group ($2.50–$10.00 per capita), 1990, 2010, and 2030 (projection)

	Millions of people			% of population		
	1990	2012	2030	1990	2012	2030
Total	1,611.1	3,247.4	3,920.0	31.5	47.0	47.2
Total excluding China	1,340.0	2,453.3	3,470.0	33.7	44.1	50.6
LICs	76.2	279.8	706.0	19.4	37.7	61.0
LMICs	646.2	1,535.0	2,175.0	37.5	61.1	69.3
UMICs	672.1	1,287.8	915.5	35.7	54.1	34.4

Note: Countries grouped by current classification. Total includes HICs.

Source: Data from Edward and Sumner (2015).

of greater attention in research and public policy because their expansion may potentially have wider societal implications.

Of the three billion people currently in this precariat group, almost half live in China and India and 40 per cent are living in other MICs. Not surprisingly, less than 10 per cent live in LICs. The precariat group will, though, decline in current UMICs in numbers by 2030 as people in China move above $10 per day (given the high rate of consumption per capita growth), but this precarious group will remain an issue for LMICs and other UMICs even in 2030. Such a precarious group is clearly visible in the set of new MICs: in India and China in 2012 the precarious group (the $2.50–$10 group) was over half of the total population, which was also the case for Angola, Ghana, Nigeria, and Sudan. While in the new MICs with lower absolute poverty such as Indonesia, Pakistan, Sri Lanka, and Vietnam the precariat represented approximately two-thirds or more of the population. This emerging precarious group is too poor to be a traditional middle class judging by the consumption levels but has been labelled as such by some erroneously.

5.3.3 THE PRECARIOUS GROUP VERSUS THE MIDDLE CLASS

There is a long and rich history of class analysis in sociology and classical political economy, dating back to Aristotle, Mill, Ricardo, Smith, Marx, Weber, and others. For Aristotle and Marx, the middle class were property owners. In contrast, for John Stuart Mill, the middle classes were defined by level of income rather than source of income. Weber (1922) viewed stratification in terms of class, status, and power. Class is discussed in contemporary sociology in terms of types of assets and productive processes, labour markets, and occupational resources (see review in Torche and López-Calva, 2012). The middle classes are those who do not own the means of production, but control skills and knowledge or authority as a source of power. In short, the type as well as the amount of assets matters, as does some sense of security.

Contemporary sociological analysis of class places a particular emphasis on economic security (see, for discussion, Erikson and Goldthorpe, 1992; Goldthorpe and McKnight, 2006). For example, Standing (2011, pp. 7–8) from whom the concept and term 'precariat' is taken, drawing upon Weber (1922), sums up contemporary sociological thinking on class as a combination of the social relations of production and position in the labour process (meaning status). Standing (2011) notes that, in contemporary labour markets, key distinctions are made between employers, employees, and the self-employed; but also between wage-workers (paid by piece-rate or time-rate) and salaried employees. He summarizes, with an implicit emphasis on industrialized countries, thus:

At the top is an 'elite'... Below the elite comes the 'salariat' [with] stable, full-time employment... concentrated in large corporations, government agencies and public administration... Alongside the salariat... is a (so far) smaller group of 'proficians' [referring to] the traditional ideas of 'professional' and 'technician' [or] those with bundles of skills that they can market earning high incomes on contract, as consultants or independent own-account workers... Below the proficians, in terms of income, is a shrinking 'core' of manual employees, the essence of the old 'working class'... Underneath these four groups, there is a growing 'precariat' [meaning those in insecure employment], flanked by an army of unemployed and a detached group of socially ill misfits living off the dregs of society.

Recently a body of empirical studies related to developing countries has emerged in response to the growing data broadly speaking based on the precarious group discussed. This literature has referred to 'new middle classes'; more often than not defined by daily expenditure per capita. For example, Cárdenas et al. (2011, p. 17) in their study of Latin America's 'global middle class' sums up the literature on this group thus:

The middle class has been calling the attention of researchers because of its role in explaining comparative development. A variety of channels have been explored, including those linking the middle class to long run economic growth, democratic attitudes, and entrepreneurship.

As is immediately evident, one could ask whether we should assess the 'middle class'—a social identity—in terms of daily expenditures, or by some other component of the expenditure distribution. Like the preceding discussion, many of the recent studies are based on absolute definitions of expenditure per capita per day (all of these studies use 2005 PPP), including a range from $2 per day to $13 per day (Ravallion, 2010a); or stipulating two ends of the middle class, such as $2–$4 per day and $6–$10 per day (Banerjee and Duflo, 2008), or $2–$10 per day and $10–$20 per day (ADB, 2010; AfDB, 2011); or defining a 'global middle class' as the group living on between $10 and $100 per day (Kharas, 2010). Others have taken the literal middle of the income/expenditure distribution in terms of the middle three expenditure quintiles (Easterly, 2001).

Of course the definition taken determines the size of this group. Taking the $2.50 poverty line at the lower end and a $10 line at the top end (both in 2011 PPP), there is certainly a burgeoning group of people, most of whom live in MICs. However, whether this group has a cohesive identity as a social class is an open question given that their main shared characteristic is likely to be insecurity of varying degrees.

If the precarious group in new MICs—regardless of if it is a coherent class—were more secure it might have potential to have a transformatory impact on governance. As incomes increase, people's perceptions may shift from a preoccupation with freedom from hunger and poverty towards a desire for civil and political rights and freedoms or holding governments to account. Further, as countries become richer in per-capita income, government revenue as a proportion of GDP rises as does individual income tax and tax on goods and services (as empirically discussed in IMF, 2011, pp. 53–4 and see Table 5.2). As people's expenditures rise above poverty levels their consumption patterns

Table 5.2 Taxation indicators in selected new MICs, 2011

	Tax revenue and social contributions (as % of GDP)	Tax capacity (maximum possible tax revenue as % of GDP)	Tax effort (ratio of actual revenue to tax capacity)
East Asia and the Pacific			
China	18.9	39.1	0.48
Indonesia	11.9	28.0	0.42
Vietnam	24.1	36.8	0.65
South Asia			
India	33.7	29.6	0.53
Pakistan	9.9	22.3	0.44
Sri Lanka	12.5	21.9	0.57
Sub-Saharan Africa			
Angola	12.7	17.9	0.60
Ghana	16.9	32.7	0.52
Nigeria	11.0	21.3	0.39
Sudan	–	–	–
Aggregates (mean)			
LICs	17.0	26.0	0.65
MICs	24.1	37.3	0.64
HICs	34.2	45.1	0.76

Note: Nigeria data is for 2012.
Source: Data processed from Fenochietto and Pessino (2013, pp. 16, 25–6).

shift, resulting in an increasing exposure to indirect and sales taxes, and perhaps formal (and informal) payments for state services for example, for small business licenses though probably not income taxes (given the levels of income implied as less than $10 consumption would mean an income not much higher if savings are minimal as most of income is consumed and employment is likely to be in the informal sector). As average income rises, total tax revenue as a proportion of GDP rises; as does revenue from individual income tax, corporate tax, and taxes on goods and services (see data in IMF, 2011). At the same time as average income rises, aid is becoming less and less significant in new MICs. There is thus a shift from external funding in the form of aid towards non-aid and domestic sources such as taxation. Hypothetically, this implies a shift in accountability from state-to-donors to state-to-domestic taxpayers and/or domestic capital or natural resource related-capital interests (see Brautigam et al., 2008; Moore, 2007). In short, a politically engaged and taxpaying population may be more likely to exact demands on government. Empirical evidence for this is provided by Devarajan et al. (2011, p. 15), suggesting that there is a positive relationship between the level of tax revenue and the extent of voice and accountability in a country (using the World Governance Indicators for voice and accountability); but that there is a threshold at 49 per cent of GDP after which, with excessively high levels of taxation, the relationship is inverted. However, as the authors note (p. 15):

Since the tax-to-GDP ratio in most developing countries is below this level, one can assume that most [developing countries] are situated on the rising part of the relationship where increases in the level of taxation are associated with more accountability.

Interestingly, Devarajan et al. (2011, p. 13) also note that governance and secondary education have a strong association even after controlling for various variables.

Taxation data for the new MICs would suggest that although tax revenue has risen slightly, as a proportion of GDP, across all developing countries since the 1990s, tax revenue is below the Devarajan et al. threshold in the set of the new MICs (see Table 5.2) meaning that additional tax revenue would improve governance responsiveness in general. Tax revenue is in fact weak in the set of new MICs. Only in India and Vietnam is the tax revenue estimate at or above the MIC average. All other countries in the set of new MICs are closer to the LIC average or even substantially below. Estimates for Angola, Indonesia, Pakistan, Nigeria, and Sri Lanka are as low as 10–13 per cent. Two other measures are 'tax capacity' and 'tax effort' which Fenochietto and Pessino (2013) develop for 113 developing countries. They define tax capacity as the maximum level of tax revenue a country could achieve. Tax effort is then the ratio of actual revenue to tax capacity. They note that most European countries with high levels of development have tax effort of close to 90 per cent of capacity. This means that there are relatively low levels of tax evasion in European countries compared to developing countries, the latter of which only collect two-third of the tax revenue that could be achieved. Only Angola and Vietnam are close to this average for developing countries in the set of new MICs with the other new MICs collecting around half of the tax revenue that could be collected. Indonesia, Nigeria, and Pakistan's estimates were as low as 39 to 44 per cent.

The ability to collect taxes and the preferences of the non-poor for redistributive policies, may become increasingly important for poverty reduction in MICs. However, if a large part of the 'middle' are still vulnerable to poverty, there will be limitations to expanding the tax base for some time to come. If there is little support among the more secure upper-middle classes for paying more taxes, such policies will also be constrained by domestic political economy factors. For example, Cárdenas et al. (2011, p. 19) are sceptical of tax rises for the upper-middle classes based on the attitudes expressed in the World Values Survey in Latin America:

The status quo . . . is a very low level of income taxation for the middle classes. Given their attitudes and political say, it is very unlikely that the expansion of the middle class will result in greater levels of personal income taxation. This is the main difference in tax structures compared to the developed world.

OECD (2011) discusses in some considerable detail preferences for the amount of income redistribution via fiscal policy, notably what households gain and the quality of public services. It also discusses what role what it labels the 'middle sector' plays in Latin America in shaping fiscal policy and redistribution, and the impact of fiscal policies on the middle 'sector'. It notes (pp. 23, 147) that:

The net effect of fiscal policy for middle-sector families, while marginally positive, is not large, and they benefit most from in-kind services such as education and health care...[However], if these services are of low quality, the middle sector [meaning the middle group] is more likely to consider itself a loser in the fiscal bargain and less willing to contribute to financing of the public sector.

In short, if some of the population opt for private education and health, as is evident in many MICs given the size of private provision, this could undermine the social contract for the provision of public goods that the poor benefit from.

Other factors that determine preferences for redistribution in the literature, are thought to be: personal experiences of social mobility (Piketty, 1995), national and regional cultural and social values (Alesina and Giuliano, 2009), the extent of impacts of (higher) taxation on leisure consumption (Meltzer and Richards, 1981), levels of university education (Daude and Melguizo, 2010; Torgler, 2005), and attitudes to prevailing levels of meritocracy (Alesina and Angeletos, 2005). Support for redistribution is undermined by low institutional capacity in tax administration, the quality of state services, and pessimistic views of social mobility (Gaviria, 2007; Torgler, 2005).

In sum, a new middle-income trap that hinders both future growth and political change has been hypothesized based on rising inequality in the new MICs during economic development. The creation of a burgeoning group of people who are not absolute poor but not far above absolute poverty and poor by OECD standards is of significance. Due to rising inequality during economic development, the journey from absolute poverty towards secure lifestyles is slower than it need be. Not only does rising inequality constrain absolute poverty reduction, rising inequality constrains future growth in the sense of weak domestic demand (as peoples' incomes are insufficient to drive demand significantly) but also may constrain future improvements in governance responsiveness as few people have sufficient incomes for the state to tax. It is this new middle-income trap that provides a rationale for a different kind of development cooperation with countries at middle-income level.

5.4 The middle-income trap and the future of development cooperation

How does the middle-income trap outlined form the basis for a new kind of development cooperation? One conclusion that might be drawn from the dwindling numbers of LICs and the nationalization of global poverty in the foreseeable future is that development cooperation—foreign aid—is no longer necessary for all but a small number of the poorest countries, whether they are defined as LICs, LDCs, or FCASs. Given the economic size of the poorest countries the amount of official development assistance (ODA) they can effectively absorb is questionable (see discussion in Glennie and Sumner, 2014). Thus, ending aid to MICs might imply a much smaller annual global ODA budget, or greater use of ODA budgets for global and regional public goods (see discussion in Sumner and Mallet, 2012).

One can certainly argue that 'traditional' aid—meaning resource transfer—is likely to become increasingly irrelevant for most MICs as domestic resources grow further. However, new forms of development cooperation based on addressing the middle-income poverty trap would improve incomes of those living in absolute poverty and the precariat groups and by an emphasis on infrastructure and thus spatial inequality seek to ensure rising inequality does not hinder future growth and governance reform. For example, policy coherence from richer countries on matters such as trade policy or tax havens and illicit financial flows may be of importance in sustaining growth and collecting tax revenues for social policy in MICs and MICs may still be interested in long-run concessionary lending, given prevailing interest rates on ten-year treasury bonds in many new MICs. One could thus imagine an evolved form of development cooperation based on long-run concessionary lending, possibly with a component of co-financing by MICs themselves for long-run infrastructure and better linking of sub-national geographies and social groups to the growth process. Further, co-financing between donors and MICs could extend across borders to global and regional public goods where the up-front costs are expensive and the benefits to growth and poverty reduction are long term and across regions.

Overall, aid levels are already low in MICs relative to LICs, LDCs, and FCASs in terms of aid dependency (see Figure 5.3). In fact even in the poorest countries aid has been declining over the last decade though it remains much higher than in MICs.

In terms of the wider set of new MICs, it is clear that, as Figure 5.4 shows, those new MICs with drastically rising GDP PPP per capita and structural change already have very low ODA/GNI ratios (e.g. Angola, China, India, Indonesia, Nigeria, Pakistan, and Sri Lanka). However, many of the pseudo MICs highlighted in Chapter 1, where GDP PPP per capita has not risen drastically retain ODA/GNI ratios in the order of 5–10 per cent of GNI suggesting that for the pseudo MICs at least, moderate ODA may be important for some time (e.g. Senegal and Zambia). That said, even these 'poor MICs' have experienced drastic drops in aid dependency since the early 1990s.

Development cooperation to MICs or countries with substantial domestic resources (however defined) may evolve considerably because ODA or

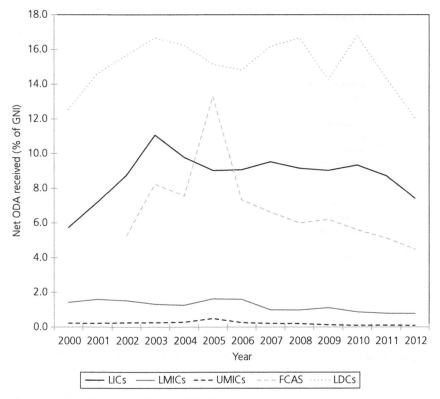

Figure 5.3 Net ODA received/GNI, 2000–12

Source: Data processed from World Bank (2015).

resource transfer will be in demand less as domestic resources expand, if not now then over the next decade if economic growth continues. However, concessional loans will still be useful even if grants are not deemed appropriate in light of expanding domestic resources. Although most MICs do have credit ratings and thus access to capital markets in principle, their ratings are often the lowest non-speculative grade investment and thus their borrowing costs are higher than one might expect. Interest rates on ten-year bonds for the eurozone, despite the events of recent years were very low (see Table 5.3). In contrast, interest rates on ten-year government bonds stood close to, or over 10 per cent even in some of the fastest growing, large MICs such as India, Nigeria, and Indonesia. Further, some new MICs have yet to even issue bonds with ten-year maturities. Concessional, long-term lending could thus remain important as a cheaper source of finance.

Drawing upon discussions in Kanbur and Sumner (2012), it is possible to argue that one could construct an approach to development cooperation with MICs. The rationale for this is to sustain MICs' economic growth to date, to

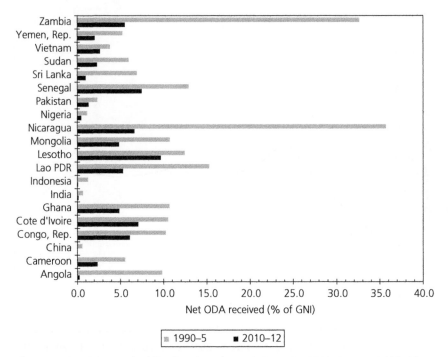

Figure 5.4 Net ODA received/GNI in selected post-1990 MICs, 1990–5 versus 2010–12

Source: Data processed from World Bank (2015).

Table 5.3 Selected new MICs, credit ratings (foreign currency), and rates of interest on ten-year government bonds, August 2015

	Foreign currency ratings (Standard & Poor's)	Rate of interest on ten-year government bonds (EU = 0.03%)
East Asia and the Pacific		
China	AA–	3.4
Indonesia	BB+	8.8
Vietnam	BB–	7.0
South Asia		
India	BBB–	7.8
Pakistan	B–	9.2
Sri Lanka	B+	–
Sub-Saharan Africa		
Angola	BB–	–
Ghana	B	–
Nigeria	BB-	16.0
Sudan	–	–

Note: If no rate of interest then government has not issued ten-year bonds.

Source: Data processed from World Bank (2015), and Standard & Poor's (2015) and trading economics (derived from monetary authorities of each country).

reduce poverty, and to improve the security of the precarious near poor, and the circumnavigation of the middle-income trap outlined, with a focus on public infrastructure and thus address issues of spatial inequality. Three components of development cooperation between OECD countries and MICs would be policy coherence; infrastructure and inclusive growth; and global and regional public goods.

Taking policy coherence first: a useful starting point would be OECD aid donors' negotiation of formal agreements on policy coherence with MICs (and MICs' own policy coherence with LICs) to sustain growth and circumnavigate slowdowns during which the precarious group might slip back into poverty. The continuing dominant position of OECD countries in global trade and investment (although this is changing) and unfavourable development policies suggests that traditional donors' most important engagement with MICs or countries with substantial domestic resources lies in policy coherence such as trade policy, tax haven policies, migration, remittances, and so forth. Such policies are likely to be important for the precarious near poor who may be more likely to be involved in the tradable sector rather than the non-tradable and/or subsistence sector where much of the absolute poor reside.

The concept of 'policy coherence' in the development-related policies of traditional donors is of course not new (see, for example, Forster and Stokke 1999). Policy coherence is typically defined as developed or industrialized countries making their own national policies more consistent with their stated objectives to promote growth and reduce poverty around the world (OECD, 2005, p. 120).[5] Often the financial benefits are highly significant. According to Picciotto (2005, p. 314), examples of potential policy incoherence, whereby developing countries are negatively affected by the policies of rich countries, include: farming subsidies and the Common Agricultural Policy (CAP); tariffs on industrial goods, such as steel and textiles, imposed by OECD countries; and patents and the protection of intellectual property rights.

A tension is that MICs themselves may not practice such policy coherence with poorer countries such as LICs, so policy coherence from OECD countries would be negotiable on MIC policy coherence with LICs. Though desirable, these could in practice imply unpopular conditionalities (imagine MICs liberalizing immigration policies towards LICs for example). On the other hand, this might potentially open the door to OECD donors and new donors from emerging MICs, working collaboratively on development cooperation with LICs. Such ways of engaging would all entail much more systematic working

---

[5] Since 2003 the Center for Global Development in Washington has published the Commitment to Development Index which has quantified policy coherence. The index scores the performance of developed countries in seven key areas—aid, trade, investment, migration, environment, security, and technology—awarding points for policies and actions which support poor countries' developmental efforts, broadly defined.

of OECD donors beyond aid ministries and perhaps even the reorganization of aid ministries into cross-governmental bodies in OECD countries. These changes might be more likely in countries with small aid ministries or units rather than donors with large, established aid ministries.

A second component of development cooperation with MICs could be OECD countries' support for inclusive growth—meaning spatially and socially inclusive—by working in low-income provinces within MICs and infrastructure development for example. This would better connect sub-national geographies and social groups to growth in order to reduce poverty but also seek to expand the numbers of the 'secure middle' population. OECD donors could work with various national and local governments and civil society organisations on inclusive policy processes such as the allocation of public expenditure and its sectoral and sub-national allocation, and spatial patterns of economic growth (regional development policy) to improve prospects for more inclusive development. How MIC central governments might perceive this is open to question—it could be seen as overly interventionist in domestic politics.[6] There is an economic rationale for donors to work on inclusive growth in MICs with a focus on low-income provinces, and around structural change, which entails connection of those areas to the broader growth processes in that country, and a sub-national focus on the poorer provinces. As highlighted, there could also be a focus on aspects of public spending that are more long-term capital investments (e.g. sea or airports) because MIC governments may face constraints due to large up-front costs or the political economy constraints of public spending in certain regions.

Finally, a third component of development cooperation with MICs and related to the concessional long-run finance discussion above is the co-financing of global and regional public goods. Such goods include national, regional, and global economic infrastructure such as regional networks of seaports and airports and so forth, where there are high up-front costs, but long-term developmental benefits to multiple countries or across regions. This focus on public goods could be extended to research on poverty and economic development and the transfer/sharing of research between MICs and LICs (and potentially vice versa) or technical assistance as a global or regional public good too (e.g. technical assistance to build well-functioning domestic tax systems).

In sum, these three areas—policy coherence; infrastructure and inclusive growth; and global and regional public goods—may form the basis for a new

---

[6] Working with advocacy groups and civil society actors to influence policy public spending priorities and regional planning and regional resource allocation, is one avenue through which external development actors could pursue broader aims. For some MICs, such policies could be seen as unwelcome interference in domestic distribution questions. Alternatively, donors working in sub-national low-income regions within MICs or with low-income groups might be (more) welcome if it was accompanied by policy coherence commitments from OECD donors.

kind of development cooperation, potentially loan-based, though at concessional rates. Such measures would go some way towards helping MICs avoid the new middle-income trap by sustaining growth as well as addressing rising inequality and speeding up the expansion of a secure population.

5.5 **Conclusion**

In previous chapters this book discussed the changes in the developing world and global poverty since the end of the Cold War and sought to account for these changes by discussing the uneven responsiveness of poverty to growth in new MICs and theories of the causes of absolute poverty. Further, the case has been presented that global poverty is in the process of nationalization, leading to the growing significance of redistributive social policy and more inclusive growth, spatially and socially.

The impact of a declining number of LICs and the nationalization of global poverty might be interpreted in such a way that foreign aid and development cooperation should be scaled back to just the poorest countries and, given the expansion of domestic resources, have no place in MICs. In this chapter such a view has been challenged and a new basis for development cooperation—largely concessional loan-based—outlined in relation to avoiding a new middle-income trap. This trap requires circumnavigating to ensure a secure population emerges that would improve growth prospects and be more likely to bring political change.

The chapter's argument has been threefold: first, that if rising inequality is not addressed with stronger social policy or welfare regimes or growth that is inclusive spatially and socially during economic development, new MICs can face an alternative trap to the orthodox middle-income trap. This trap is based on a second layer or explanatory aspect of the poverty paradox outlined in Chapter 4. That second layer of the paradox is that although people may move out of day-to-day poverty they will likely take a long time to reach secure lives and the risk of falling back into poverty could persist for over a hundred years given current patterns and trends in inequality. Second, that the alternative middle-income trap is not inevitable and may be described as follows: rising inequality during growth leads to a burgeoning group of people who are not secure or a traditional middle class, but a precarious group living not far above the poverty line. This group lacks the kind of purchasing power necessary to drive future growth and is also difficult to tax and thus expand the state's tax base. This in turn means that improvements in governance which are linked to mass taxation (rather than natural-resource-funded or an elite-funded state) may be delayed. There is then an opportunity cost to rising inequality during economic development. That cost is to forgo the elimination of absolute poverty and the emergence of a consuming class in the foreseeable future. It is this middle-income trap that could provide a logic for continuing development cooperation, but of a different kind to 'traditional' aid.

The chapter has considered existing theories of low and middle-income traps, and described the new precarious group and why it is likely to constrain future growth and improvements in governance. The implications for development cooperation of the 'middle-income trap' have also been discussed in the sense that 'traditional' aid will be of less relevance as domestic resources expand and policy coherence may be more in demand from MICs. Long-run concessional lending may be useful to address inclusive growth and infrastructure could be used to better link sub-national geographies and social groups to the growth process.

All of this may well imply some significant restructuring in the domestic reorganization of aid ministries in OECD countries. The kind of administrative unit fit for pursuing engagement with MICs is unlikely to be a large aid ministry with an existing portfolio of projects, programmes, and spending. Rather, one might imagine smaller, cross-governmental administrative units with unequivocal mandates across all departments of government in a given country, and a high level of technical capacity. Such units may well be more fit-for-purpose to facilitate the shift from spending money on projects and sectors in MICs to cultivating quite new collaborative relationships that require careful negotiation of objectives, co-financing arrangements, policy coherence agreements between parties, and working sub-nationally in MICs. Thus, in addition to technical skills, 'soft skills', and a premium on political sensitivity and negotiation would be the core skills rather than 'old school' project and programme planning and management, which will likely only matter in an ever-decreasing number of aid-dependent countries in the decades ahead.

If their objectives are global poverty reduction, OECD donors will need to stay engaged with MICs as a significant amount of global absolute poverty could easily remain in these countries, let alone numbers of the insecure or vulnerable-to-poverty population. All of the above may push donors towards helping construct, via co-financing with MICs, global and regional public goods such as infrastructure in order to reconnect sub-national geographies and social groups in MICs to the growth and economic development process and circumnavigate the new middle-income trap.

Conclusions

The discussions of this book can be summarized as follows: in 1990, approximately 90 per cent of the world's poor people lived in low-income countries (LICs), where the average income was barely above any reasonable global poverty line. Addressing global poverty was framed largely around international redistribution via aid. Now, most of the world's poor people live in middle-income countries (MICs). Even new MICs have far higher average standards of living than LICs, and are typically far less aid-dependent. However, absolute poverty in MICs amounts to a billion poor people whether defined by monetary or multidimensional poverty. And, despite notable economic development in the structure of GDP away from agriculture, a surprising amount of the labour force in new MICs remains in agriculture, and a substantial proportion of exports comes from the primary sectors such as fuel exports.

A number of countries have transitioned to MIC status and it is this shift, particularly of a few populous countries, that is key to the majority of the world's poor now residing in new MICs. While currently, average income in many MICs is still way below that of the advanced countries, over time, the cost of ending poverty is falling as a proportion of national GDP to levels where domestic resources are, in principle, available to deal with absolute poverty. This raises the question of whether global poverty requires reframing as a national distribution question in a world of fewer and fewer aid-dependent countries, either now, or at some point in the near future.

Although crossing a line in per capita income does not mean a sudden change within a country, substantially higher levels of average per capita income imply substantially more domestic resources available for poverty reduction and the value of regressive fossil-fuel subsidies corroborates this. Most importantly for aid donors the aid system, does treat countries differently if they are middle-income (or at least considers middle-income country classification to be a reason to reduce or end aid flows).

One interpretation of the shift in the geography of global poverty towards MICs is that at a certain level of average per capita income (be it of the low-income to middle-income thresholds or other thresholds), absolute poverty increasingly becomes a domestic political issue. However, even if ending poverty is within domestic financial capacity, constraints may remain. There are significant questions around economic growth patterns, and differing state and sub-national state capacities. Further, the constraints of domestic political economy may mean that support for redistributive policies is difficult to mobilize and/or maintain, particularly among the burgeoning but precarious group who are barely out of absolute poverty themselves.

In conclusion, this book has presented five central arguments which can be summarized as follows: first, that relatively few developing countries have achieved economic growth *with* structural change since the end of the Cold War. Second, that global poverty is concentrated in those countries and in a relatively small set of those new MICs who have but patterns of MIC poverty suggest that spatial and social inequality are important issues. Third, that this substantial economic growth has not reduced poverty as much as one might expect across the new MICs. Indeed, it is argued that a structural theory of poverty that takes account of distribution and economic development has increased relevance in MICs. Fourth, that there is a poverty paradox that is that addressing absolute poverty is affordable for many MICs but given inequality levels and trends, growth is unlikely to eliminate poverty in new MICs. Thus, there is an imperative for redistributive social policy and growth which is more spatially and socially inclusive. Fifth, that all of the above does not mean that development cooperation with MICs should simply be terminated due to the rise of domestic resources because MICs may face a new kind of middle-income trap related to a further layer of the poverty paradox: high or rising inequality will constrain future economic growth and poverty reduction because of the slow expansion of a secure, consuming class. At the very least there is an opportunity cost of rising inequality during economic development and that cost is to forgo the elimination of absolute poverty and the emergence of a consuming class in the foreseeable future. In light of this, foreign aid—development cooperation of the traditional sort—may not be relevant to most MICs. Instead, policy coherence and concessional lending and co-financing of long-run infrastructure, better connecting sub-national poorer regions and social groups to the economic growth poles and regional and global public goods, may present a new future for development assistance based on the new geography of global poverty.

▓ REFERENCES

Acemoglu, D. and J. Robinson (2002). 'The Political Economy of the Kuznet Curve', *Review of Development Economics*, 6(2): 183–203.

Acemoglu, D. and J. A. Robinson (2012). *Why Nations Fail: The Origins of Power, Prosperity, and Poverty*, New York: Crown.

Adams, R. (2003). 'Economic Growth, Inequality and Poverty: Findings from a New Data Set'. World Bank Working Paper 2972. Washington DC: World Bank.

Adelman, I. (2000). 'Fallacies in Development Theory and their Implications for Policy', in G. M. Meier and J. E. Stiglitz (eds), *Frontiers of Development Economics: The Future in Perspective*. Washington DC: World Bank/Oxford University Press, 103–34.

Adelman, I. and C. Morris (1973). *Economic Growth and Social Equity in Developing Countries*, Stanford CA: Stanford University Press.

Adelman, I. and S. Robinson (1989). 'Income Distribution and Development', in H. Chenery and T. N. Srinivasan (eds) *Handbook of Development Economics*, ii. Amsterdam: Elsevier Science Publishers, 951–1003.

Addison, T., D. Hulme, and R. Kanbur (2009). *Poverty Dynamics: Interdisciplinary Perspectives*, Oxford: Oxford University Press.

African Development Bank (AfDB) (2011). *The Middle of the Pyramid: Dynamics of the Middle Class in Africa*, Tunis-Belvedère: AfDB.

Agénor, P. (2002). 'Does Globalisation Hurt the Poor?' Mimeo. Washington DC: World Bank.

Agénor, P. and C. Otaviano (2012). 'Middle-income Growth Traps', World Bank Policy Research Working Paper 6210. Washington DC: World Bank.

Ahluwalia, M. (1976a). 'Inequality, Poverty and Development', *Journal of Development Economics* 3: 307–42.

Ahluwalia, Montek S. (1976b). 'Income Distribution and Development: Some Stylized Facts', *American Economic Review, Papers and Proceedings* 66(2): 128–35.

Ahluwalia, Montek S., N. G. Carter, and H. B. Chenery (1979). 'Growth and Poverty in Developing Countries', *Journal of Development Economics* 6: 299–341.

Aiyar, S., Romain Duval, Damien Puy, Yiqun Wu, and Longmei Zhang (2013). 'Growth Slowdowns and the Middle-Income Trap'. IMF Working paper. Washington DC: IMF.

Aldenhoff, F. O. (2007). 'Are Economic Forecasts of the International Monetary Fund Politically Biased? A Public Choice Analysis', *Review of International Organization* 2(3): 239–60.

Alesina, A. and G. M. Angeletos (2005). 'Fairness and Redistribution', *American Economic Review* 95(4): 960–80.

Alesina, A. and P. Giuliano (2009). 'Preferences for Redistribution'. National Bureau of Economic Research (NBER) Working Paper 14825. New York: NBER.

Alesina, A. and R. Perotti (1996). 'Income Distribution, Political Instability and Investment', *European Economic Review* 40: 1203–28.

Alesina, A. and D. Rodrik (1994). 'Distributive Policies and Economic Growth', *Quarterly Journal of Economics* 109: 465–90.

Ali, I. and J. Zhang (2007). 'Inclusive Growth toward a Prosperous Asia: Policy Implications'. Asian Development Bank (ADB) Economics and Research Department Working Paper. Manila: ADB.

Alkire, S. (2005). *Valuing Freedoms: Sen's Capability Approach and Poverty Reduction*, Oxford: Oxford University Press.

Alkire, S. (2011). 'Multidimensional Poverty and its Discontents'. Oxford Poverty and Human Development Initiative (OPHI) Working Paper. Oxford: OPHI.

Alkire, S. and G. Aguilar (2015). *High Visibility: How Disaggregated Metrics Help to Reduce Multidimensional Poverty*, Oxford: Oxford Poverty and Human Development Initiative (OPHI).

Alkire, S. and J. E. Foster (2011). 'Counting and Multidimensional Poverty Measurement', *Journal of Public Economics* 95(7): 476–87.

Alkire, S., J. M. Roche, and S. Seth (2011). 'Sub-National Disparities and Inter-Temporal Evolution of Multidimensional Poverty across Developing Countries'. Oxford Poverty and Human Development Initiative (OPHI) Research in Progress 32a. Oxford: OPHI.

Alkire, S. and M. E. Santos (2010). 'Acute Multidimensional Poverty: A New Index for Developing Countries'. Oxford Poverty and Human Development Initiative (OPHI) Working Paper 38. Oxford: OPHI.

Alkire, S. and M. E. Santos (2014). 'Measuring Acute Poverty in the Developing World: Robustness and Scope of the Multidimensional Poverty Index', *World Development* 59: 251–74.

Alkire, S., J. Foster, S. Seth, M. Santos, J. Roche, and P. Ballon (2014). 'Multidimensional Poverty Measurement and Analysis: Chapter 1—Introduction, with James Foster, Suman Seth, Maria Emma Santos, Jose Manuel Roche, and Paola Ballon'. Oxford Poverty and Human Development Initiative (OPHI) Working Paper. Oxford: OPHI.

Alkire, S., J. Roche, E. Santos, and S. Seth (2011). *Multidimensional Poverty 2011*, Oxford: Oxford Poverty and Human Development Initiative (OPHI).

Alkire, S., J. Roche, S. Seth, and A. Sumner (2015). 'Identifying the Poorest People and Groups: Strategies Using the Global Multidimensional Poverty Index', *Journal of International Development* 27(3): 362–87.

Alkire, S., J. M. Roche, and A. Sumner (2013). 'Where Do the World's Multidimensionally Poor People Live?' Oxford Poverty and Human Development Initiative (OPHI) Working Paper 61. Oxford: OPHI.

Alonso, J. (2007). *Cooperation with Middle-Income Countries*, Madrid: Instituto Complutense de Estudios Internacionales.

Alonso, J. and C. Garcimartín (2013). 'The Determinants of Institutional Quality: More on the Debate', *Journal of International Development* 25: 206–26.

Alonso, J., J. Glennie, and A. Sumner (2014). 'Recipients and Contributors: Middle Income Countries and the Future of Development Cooperation', UNDESA Working Paper. New York: UNDESA.

Alvaredo, F. and L. Gasparini (2015). 'Recent Trends in Inequality and Poverty in Developing Countries', in A. Atkinson and F. Bourguignon (eds) *The Handbook of Income Distribution*, ii, Amsterdam: North-Holland Publishing, 697–805.

Amable, B. (2003). The Diversity of Modern Capitalism. New York: Oxford University Press.

Anand, S. and R. Kanbur (1984). 'Inequality and Development: A Reconsideration', in H.-P. Nissen (ed.) *Towards Income Distribution Policies*, EADI Book Series 3, Tilburg, Netherlands: University of Paderborn, 131–67.

Anand, S. and R. Kanbur (1993a). 'The Kuznets Process and the Inequality- Development Relationship', *Journal of Development Economics* 40: 25–52.

Anand, S. and R. Kanbur (1993b). 'Inequality and Development: A Critique', *Journal of Development Economics* 41: 19–43.

Anand, S. and P. Segal (2008). 'What Do We Know about Global Income Inequality?' *Journal of Economic Literature* 46(1): 57–94.

Anand S., P. Segal, and J. Stiglitz (2010). *Debates on the Measurement of Global Poverty*, Oxford: Oxford University Press.

Anderson, E. (2005). 'Openness and Inequality in Developing Countries: A Review of Theory and Recent Evidence', *World Development* 33(7): 1045–63.

Arze del Granado, F. J., D. Coady, and R. Gillingham (2012). 'The Unequal Benefits of Fuel Subsidies: A Review of Evidence for Developing Countries', *World Development* 40: 2234–48.

Asian Development Bank (ADB) (2010). *The Rise of Asia's Middle Class*, Manila: ADB.

Auten, G. and R. Carroll (1999). 'The Effects of Income Taxes on Household Income', *Review of Economics and Statistics* 81: 681–93.

Azariadis, C. and J. Stachurski (2005). 'Poverty Traps', in P. Aghion and S. Durlauf (eds) *Handbook of Economic Growth*, Amsterdam: North-Holland, Elsevier, 295–384.

Azevedo, J., María Eugenia Dávalos, Carolina Diaz-Bonilla Bernardo Atuesta, and Raul Andres Castañeda (2013). 'Fifteen Years of Inequality in Latin America: How Have Labor Markets Helped?' World Bank Policy Research Working Paper. Washington DC: World Bank.

Azevedo, J., G. Inchauste, and V. Sanfelice (2011). 'Decomposing the Decline in Income Inequality in Latin America', mimeo, Washington DC: World Bank.

Banerjee, A. and E. Duflo (2008). *What Is Middle Class about the Middle Classes around the World?* Boston: MIT.

Banerjee, A. and E. Duflo (2012). *Poor Economics: Barefoot Hedge-Fund Managers, DIY Doctors and the Surprising Truth about Life on less than $1 a Day*, London: Penguin.

Banerjee, A.V. and A. Newman (1993). 'Occupational Choice and the Process of Development', *Journal of Political Economy* 101(2): 274–98.

Barrientos, A. (2009). 'Labour Markets and the (Hyphenated) Welfare Regime in Latin America', *Economy and Society*, February, 38(1): 87–108.

Barro, R. (2000). 'Inequality and Growth in a Panel of Countries', *Journal of Economic Growth* 5: 5–32.

Barros, R., M. De Carvalho, S. Franco, and R. Mendonça (2010). 'Markets, the State and the Dynamics of Inequality in Brazil', in L. F. Lopez-Calva and N. Lustig (eds) *Declining Inequality in Latin America: A Decade of Progress?* Washington DC: Brookings Institution and UNDP, 134–74.

Baster, N. (1979). 'Models and Indicators', in S. Cole and H. Lucas (eds) *Models, Planning, and Basic Needs*, Oxford: Pergamon, 99–103.

Battiston, D., C. Garcia-Domenech, and L. Gasparini (2011). 'Could an Increase in Education Raise Income Inequality? Evidence for Latin America'. Centro de Estudios Distributivos, Laborales y Sociales (CEDLAS) Working Paper. Argentina: Universidad Nacional de La Plata.

Baulch, B. (ed.) (2011). *Why Poverty Persists: Poverty Dynamics in Asia and Africa*, Gloucester: Edward Elgar.

Baulch, B. and N. McCulloch (1998). 'Being Poor and Becoming Poor: Poverty Status and Poverty Transitions in Rural Pakistan'. Institute of Development Studies (IDS) Working Paper 79. Brighton: IDS.

Beausang, F. (2012). *Globalization and the BRICs*, Basingstoke: Palgrave Macmillan.

Beeghley, L. (1988). 'Individual and Structural Explanations of Poverty', *Population Research and Policy Review* 7(3): 201–22.

Beitz, C. R. (2001). 'Does Global Inequality Matter?' *Metaphilosophy* 32: 95–112.

Benabou, R. (2000). 'Unequal Societies: Income Distribution and the Social Contract', *American Economic Review* 90(1): 96–129.

Berg, A. and J. Ostry (2011). 'Inequality and Unsustainable Growth: Two Sides of the Same Coin?' International Monetary Fund (IMF) Staff Discussion Note. Washington DC: IMF.

Bergolo, M., F. Carbajal, G. Cruces, and N. Lustig (2011). 'Impacto de las Transferencias Públicas en la Década de 2000: la Experiencia de los Países del Cono Sur'. Mimeo. Centro de Estudios Distributivos, Laborales y Sociales (CEDLAS). Argentina: Universidad Nacional de La Plata.

Bird, K. (2007). 'The Intergenerational Transmission of Poverty: An Overview'. Chronic Poverty Research Centre (CPRC) Background Paper. London and Manchester: CPRC.

Birdsall, N. (2007). 'Income Distribution: Effects on Growth and Development'. Center for Global Development (CGD) Working Paper 188. Washington DC: CGD.

Birdsall, N. and J. Londono, (1997). 'Asset Inequality Does Matter: Lessons from Latin America'. OCE Working Paper 1. Washington DC: Inter American Development Bank.

Birdsall, N., N. Lustig, and D. McLeod (2011). 'Declining Inequality in Latin America: Some Economics, Some Politics'. Center for Global Development (CGD) Working Paper. Washington DC: CGD.

Bowen, H. P. and D. De Clercq (2008). 'Institutional Context and the Allocation of Entrepreneurial Effort', *Journal of International Business Studies*, 39(4): 747–67.

Bourguignon, F. (2003). 'The Growth Elasticity of Poverty Reduction: Explaining Heterogeneity across Countries and Time Periods', in T. Eicher and S. Turnovsky (eds) *Inequality and Growth: Theory and Policy Implications*, Cambridge MA: Massachusetts Institute of Technology (MIT) Press, 3–26.

Bourguignon, F., F. Ferreira, and M. Wolton (2007). 'Equity, Efficiency and Inequality Traps: A Research Agenda', *The Journal of Economic Inequality* 5(2): 235–56.

Bourguignon, F. and C. Morrisson (1998). 'Inequality and Development: The Role of Dualism', *Journal of Development Economics* 57: 233–57.

Brautigam, D., O.-H. Fjeldstad, and M. Moore (2008). *Taxation and State Building in Developing Countries*, Cambridge: Cambridge University Press.

Brueckner, M. and D. Lederman (2015). 'Effects of Income Inequality on Aggregate Output'. World Bank Policy Discussion Paper 7317. Washington DC: World Bank.

Bruno, M., M. Ravallion, and L. Squire (1998). 'Equity and Growth in Developing Countries: Old and New Perspectives on Policy Issues', in V. Tani and K.-Y. Chu (eds) *Income Distribution and High Growth*, Cambridge MA: Massachusetts Institute of Technology (MIT) Press, 117–46.

Campos, R., G. Esquivel, and N. Lustig (2012). 'The Rise and Fall of Income Inequality in Mexico, 1989–2010'. World Institute of Development Economics Research (UNU-WIDER) Working Paper 2012/10. Helsinki: UNU-WIDER.

Cárdenas, M., H. Kharas, and C. Heneo (2011). 'Latin America's Global Middle Class'. Brookings Institution Paper. Washington DC: Brookings Institution.

Carr-Hill, R. (2013). 'Missing Millions and Measuring Development Progress', *World Development* 46: 30–44.

Castello, A. and R. Domenech (2000). 'Human Capital Inequality and Economic Growth: Some New Evidence', *Economic Journal* 112(478): 187–200.

Cevik, S. and C. Correa-Caro (2015). 'Growing (Un)equal: Fiscal Policy and Income Inequality in China and BRIC+'. IMF Working Paper. Washington DC: IMF.

Chambers, R. (1989). 'Editorial Introduction: Vulnerability, Coping and Policy', *IDS Bulletin* 20(2): 1–7.

Chandy, L. and H. Kharas (2014). 'What Do New Price Data Mean for the Goal of Ending Extreme Poverty?' *Brookings Institution Blog*, 5 May. http://www.brookings.edu/blogs/up-front/posts/2014/05/05-data-extreme-poverty-chandy-kharas (accessed 3 March 2015).

Chen, S. and M. Ravallion (2010). 'The Developing World Is Poorer than We Thought, but No Less Successful in the Fight against Poverty', *The Quarterly Journal of Economics* 125(4): 1577–625.

Chen, S. and M. Ravallion (2012). *An Update to the World Bank's Estimates of Consumption Poverty in the Developing World*, Washington DC: World Bank.

Chenery, H., M. Ahluwalia, C. Bell, J. Duloy, and R. Jolly (1974). *Redistribution with Growth*, Oxford: Oxford University Press for the World Bank.

Chusseau, N. and J. Hellier (2012). 'Globalization and Inequality: Where Do We Stand?' Society for the Study of Economic Inequality (ECINEQ) Working Paper 279. Verona, Italy: ECINEQ.

Clarke, G. R. G. (1995). 'More Evidence on Income Distribution and Growth', *Journal of Development Economics* 47(2), 403–27.

Clarke, G., L. C. Xu, and H. Zou (2006). 'Finance and Income Inequality: What Do the Data Tell Us?' *Southern Economic Journal* 72, 578–96.

Clements, B., et al. (2013). *Energy Subsidy Reform: Lessons and Implications*, Washington DC: IMF.

Coady, D., Ian Parry, Louis Sears, and Baoping Shang (2015). 'How Large Are Global Energy Subsidies?' IMF Working paper. Washington DC: IMF.

Cobham, A. and A. Sumner (2013a). 'Is It all about the Tails? The Palma Measure of Income Inequality'. Center for Global Development (CGD) Working Paper. Washington, DC: CGD.

Cobham, A. and A. Sumner (2013b). *Putting the Gini Back in the Bottle? 'The Palma' as a Policy-Relevant Measure of Inequality*, London: Kings College London.

Cobham, A., L. Schlogl, and A. Sumner (2015). 'Inequality and the Tails: The Palma Proposition and Ratio Revisited'. UNDESA Working Paper. New York: UNDESA.

Cobham, A., L. Schlogl, and A. Sumner (2016). Inequality and the tails: The Palma Proposition and Ratio. Global Policy 7(1): 25–36.

Collier, P. (2007). *Bottom Billion*, Oxford: Oxford University Press.

Collier, P. (2009). *War, Guns and Votes: Democracy in Dangerous Places*, London: Vintage.

Copestake, J. (2003). 'The Links between Social and Economic Development: The Sigma Economy of Adolfo Figueroa'. Wellbeing in Developing Countries (WeD) Working Paper 3. Bath: University of Bath.

Corak, M. (2006). 'Do Poor Children Become Poor Adults? Lessons from a Cross Country Comparison of Generational Earnings Mobility'. IZA Discussion Papers 1993. Bonn: Institute for the Study of Labor.

Cornia, G. A. (2009). *What Explains the Recent Decline of Income Inequality in Latin America?* ECINEQ Working Paper. Verona: ECINEQ.

Cornia, G. A. (2012). 'Inequality Trends and their Determinants'. UNU-WIDER Working Paper 2012/09. Helsinki: UNU-WIDER.

Cornia, Giovanni Andrea, Tony Addison, and Sampsa Kiiski (2004). 'Income Distribution Changes and their Impact in the Post-Second World War Period', in Giovanni Andrea Cornia (ed.) *Inequality, Growth, and Poverty in an Era of Liberalization and Globalization*, Oxford: Oxford University Press, 26–56.

Cruces, G., C. Garcia-Domenech, and L. Gasparini (2011). 'Inequality in Education: Evidence for Latin America'. UNU-WIDER Working Paper 2011/93. Helsinki: UNU-WIDER.

CSP (Centre for Systemic Peace) (2015). 'Polity IV Annual Time-Series, 1800–2014', http://www.systemicpeace.org/inscrdata.html (accessed 1 August 2015).

Cunha Neves P. and S. Tavares Silva (2014). 'Inequality and Growth: Uncovering the Main Conclusions from the Empirics', *The Journal of Development Studies*, 50(1): 1–12.

Dabla-Norris, E., K. Kochhar, N. Suphaphiphat, F. Ricka, and E. Tsounta (2015). 'Causes and Consequences of Income Inequality: A Global Perspective'. IMF Discussion Note. Washington DC: IMF.

Dadush, U. and W. Shaw (2011). *Juggernaut: How Emerging Markets Are Reshaping Globalization*, Washington DC: Carnegie Endowment for World Peace.

Datt, G. and M. Ravallion (1992). 'Growth and Redistribution Components of Changes in Poverty Measures: A Decomposition with Applications to Brazil and India in the 1980s', *Journal of Development Economics* 38: 275–95.

Daude, C. and A. Melguizo (2010). 'Taxation and More Representation? On Fiscal Policy, Social Mobility and Democracy in Latin America'. OECD Working Paper 294. Paris: OECD Development Center.

Davis, E. and M. Sanchez-Martinez (2014). 'A Review of the Economic Theories of Poverty'. NIESR Discussion Paper. NIESR: London.

de la Croix, D. and M. Doepke (2003). 'Inequality and Growth: Why Differential Fertility Matters'. UCLA Economics Working Papers, No. 803. Los Angeles CA: UCLA Department of Economics.

de Mello, L. (ed.) (2010). *Growth and Sustainability in Brazil, China, India, Indonesia and South Africa*, Paris: OECD.

Deaton, A. (2005). 'Measuring Poverty in a Growing World (or Measuring Growth in a Poor World)', *Review of Economics and Statistics* 87(1): 1–19.

Deaton, A. (2010a). 'Measuring Development: Different Data, Different Conclusions'. Paper presented at the 8th AFD-EUDN Conference, Paris, 1 December.

Deaton, A. (2010b). 'Price Indexes, Inequality, and the Measurement of World Poverty', *American Economic Review* (1): 5–34.

Deaton, A. and B. Aten (2014). 'Trying To Understand the PPPs in ICP 2011: Why Are the Results so Different?' National Bureau of Economic Research (NBER) Working Paper. Cambridge MA: NBER.

Deaton, A. and O. Dupriez (2011). 'Purchasing Power Parity Exchange Rates for the Global Poor', *American Economic Journal: Applied Economics* 3(2): 137–66.

Deaton, A. and A. Heston (2010). 'Understanding PPPs and PPP-based National Accounts', *American Economic Journal* 2(4): 1–35.

Deininger, K. and P. Olinto (2000). 'Asset Distribution, Inequality, and Growth'. The World Bank Development Research Group Working Paper No. 2375. Washington DC: World Bank.

Deininger, K. and L. Squire (1998). 'New Ways of Looking at Old Issues: Inequality and Growth', *Journal of Development Economics* 57(2): 259–87.

Demographic and Health Surveys (DHS)/ICF International (2011). *Demographic and Health Surveys Methodology: Questionnaires: Household, Woman's, and Man's,* Calverton MD: ICF International.

Demographic and Health Surveys (DHS)/ICF International (2012a). *Demographic and Health Surveys Standard Recode Manual,* Calverton MD: ICF International.

Demographic and Health Surveys (DHS)/ICF International (2012b). *Survey Organization Manual,* Calverton MD: ICF International.

Dercon, S. (2006). 'Vulnerability: A Micro Perspective'. Queen Elizabeth House (QEH) Working Paper. Oxford: QEH.

Dercon, S. and J. Shapiro (2007). 'Moving On, Staying Behind, Getting lost: Lessons on Poverty Mobility from Longitudinal Data'. Global Poverty Research Group (GPRG) Working Paper. Manchester/Oxford: GPRG.

Devarajan, S., H. Ehrhart, Tuan Minh Le, and G. Raballand (2011). 'Direct Redistribution, Taxation, and Accountability in Oil-Rich Economies: A Proposal'. Center for Global Development (CGD) Working Paper. Washington DC: CGD.

Dobbin, F. and T. Boychuk (1999). 'National Employment Systems and Job Autonomy: Why Job Autonomy Is High in Nordic Countries and Low in the United States, Canada, and Australia', *Organization Studies,* 20(2): 257–91.

Dollar, David, Tatjana Kleineberg, and Aart Kraay (2013). 'Growth still Is Good for the Poor'. World Bank Policy Research Working Paper. Washington DC: World Bank.

Dollar, David and Aart Kraay (2002). 'Growth Is Good for the Poor', *Journal of Economic Growth* 7: 195–225.

Easterly, W. (1999). 'Life During Growth'. Mimeo. Washington DC: World Bank.

Easterly, W. (2001). 'The Middle Class Consensus and Economic Development', *Journal of Economic Growth* 6: 317–55.

Easterly, W. and S. Rebelo (1993). 'Fiscal Policy and Economic Growth: An Empirical Investigation', *Journal of Monetary Economics* 32(3): 417–58.

Eastwood, R. and M. Lipton (2001). 'Pro-Poor Growth and Pro-Poor Growth Poverty Reduction'. Paper presented at the Asia and Pacific Forum on Poverty: Reforming Policies and Institutions for Poverty Reduction, Manila, Asian Development Bank, 5–9 Feb.

Edward, P. (2006). 'The Ethical Poverty Line: A Moral Quantification of Absolute Poverty', *Third World Quarterly* 27(2): 377–93.

Edward, P. and A. Sumner (2013a). 'The Future of Global Poverty in a Multi-Speed World: New Estimates of Scale and Location, 2010–2030'. Centre for Global Development (CGD) Working Paper. Washington DC: CGD.

Edward, P. and A. Sumner (2013b). 'The Geography of Inequality'. Centre for Global Development (CGD) Working Paper. Washington DC: CGD.

Edward, P. and A. Sumner (2014). 'Estimating the Scale and Geography of Global Poverty Now and in the Future: How Much Difference Do Method and Assumptions Make?' *World Development* 58: 67–82.

Edward, P. and A. Sumner (2015). 'New Estimates of Global Poverty and Inequality: How much Difference Do Price Data really Make?' Centre for Global Development (CGD) Working Paper (and Data Set). Washington DC: CGD.

Eichengreen, B., D. Park, and K. Shin (2011). 'When Fast Growing Economies Slow Down: International Evidence and Implications for China'. National Bureau of Economic Research (NBER) Working Paper. Cambridge MA: NBER.

Eichengreen, B., D. Park, and K. Shin (2013). 'Growth Slowdowns Redux: New Evidence on the Middle-Income Trap'. National Bureau of Economic Research (NBER) Working Paper. Cambridge MA: NBER.

Epaulard, A. (2003). 'Macroeconomic Performance and Poverty Reduction'. International Monetary Fund (IMF) Working Paper 72. Washington DC: IMF.

Erikson, R. and J. H. Goldthorpe (1992). *The Constant Flux: A Study of Class Mobility in Industrial Societies*, Oxford: Clarendon Press.

Esping-Andersen, G. (1990). *The Three Worlds of Welfare Capitalism*, Princeton NJ: Princeton University Press.

Esping-Andersen, G. (1999). *Social Foundations of Postindustrial Economies*. New York: Oxford University Press.

Esquivel, G., N. Lustig, and J. Scott (2010). 'A Decade of Falling Inequality in Mexico: Market Forces or State Action?' in L. F. Lopez-Calva and N. Lustig (eds) *Declining Inequality in Latin America: A Decade of Progress?* Washington DC: Brookings Institution and UNDP, 175–217.

Feenberg, D. and J. Poterba (1993). 'Income Inequality and the Incomes of Very High Income Taxpayers', *Tax Policy and the Economy* 7: 145–77.

Fei, John C. H. and Gustav Ranis (1964). *Development of the Labor Surplus Economy: Theory and Policy*, Homewood IL: Richard A. Irwin.

Fenochietto R. and Carola Pessino (2013). 'Understanding Countries' Tax Effort'. IMF Working Paper. Washington DC: IMF.

Ferreira, F., S. Chen, A. L. Dabalen et al. (2015). 'A Global Count of the Extreme Poor in 2012: Data Issues, Methodology, and Initial Results'. World Bank Working Paper. Washington DC: World Bank.

Ferrera M. (1996). 'The "Southern Model" of Welfare in Social Europe', *Journal of European Social Policy* 6(1): 17–37.

Fields, G. (2001). *Distribution and Development: A New Look at the Developing World*, Cambridge, MA: MIT Press.

Forbes, K. (2000). 'A Reassessment of the Relationship between Inequality and Growth', *American Economic Review* 40(4): 869–87.

Forster, J. and O. Stokke (1999). 'Coherence of Policies towards Developing Countries: Approaching the Problematique', in J. Forster and O. Stokke (eds) *Policy Coherence in Development Co-operation*, London: Frank Cass, 16–57.

Fosu, A. (2011). 'Growth, Inequality, and Poverty Reduction in Developing Countries: Recent Global Evidence'. World Institute for Development Economics Research (WIDER) Working Paper 2011/01. Helsinki: WIDER.

Gallup, J., S. Radelet, and A. Warner (1999). 'Economic Growth and the Income of the Poor'. Consulting Assistance on Economic Reform II, Discussion Paper 36. Cambridge MA: Harvard Institute of International Development.

Galor, O. and J. Zeira (1993). 'Income Distribution and Macroeconomics', *Review of Economic Studies* 60, 35–52.

Gasparini, L. and G. Cruces (2010). 'A Distribution in Motion: The Case of Argentina', in L. F. Lopez-Calva and N. Lustig (eds) *Declining Inequality in Latin America: A Decade of Progress?* Washington DC: Brookings Institution and UNDP, 100–33.

Gasparini, L., S. Galiani, G. Cruces, and P. Acosta (2011). 'Educational Upgrading and Returns to Skills in Latin America: Evidence from a Supply-Demand Framework, 1990–2010'. World Bank Policy Research Working Paper 5921. Washington DC: World Bank.

Gasparini, L. and N. Lustig (2011). 'The Rise and Fall of Income Inequality in Latin America'. Tulane Economics Working Paper Series. New Orleans LA: Tulane University.

Gaviria, A. (2007). 'Social Mobility and Preferences for Redistribution in Latin America', *Economia* 8(1): 55–88.

Gentilini, U. (2013). 'Banking on Food: The State of Food Banks in High-income Countries'. IDS Working Paper. Sussex: IDS.

Ghatak, M. (forthcoming). 'Theories of Poverty Traps and Anti-Poverty Policies', *World Bank Economic Review*.

Gill, I. and H. Kharas (2007). *An East Asian Renaissance*, Washington DC: World Bank.

Glassman, A., D. Duran, and A. Sumner (2013). 'Global Health and the New Bottom Billion: What Do Shifts in Global Poverty and Disease Burden Mean for Donor Agencies?' *Global Policy* 4(1): 1–14.

Glennie, J. (2011). *The Role of Aid to Middle-Income Countries: A Contribution to Evolving EU Development Policy*, London: Overseas Development Institute.

Glennie, J. and A. Sumner (2014). 'The $138.5 Billion Question: When Does Aid Work?' Center for Global Development (CGD) Policy Paper. Washington DC: CGD.

Goldberg, P. and N. Pavnick (2007). 'Distributional Effects of Globalization in Developing Countries', *Journal of Economic Literature* 45(1): 39–82.

Goldin, C. and Lawrence F. Katz (2008). 'The Race between Education and Technology'. Cambridge MA: Harvard University Press.

Goldthorpe, J. H. and A. McKnight (2006). 'The Economic Basis of Social Class', in S. L. Morgan, D. B. Grusky, and G. S. Fields (eds) *Mobility and Inequality: Frontiers of Research from Sociology and Economics*, Stanford CA: Stanford University Press, 109–36.

Gollin, D. (2014). 'The Lewis Model: A 60-year Retrospective', *Journal of Economic Perspectives*, 28(3): 71–88.

Gollin, D., R. Jedwab, and D. Vollrath (forthcoming). 'Urbanization With and Without Structural Transformation', *Journal of Economic Growth*.

Gough, I. (2000). 'Welfare Regimes in East Asia and Europe: Comparisons and Lessons'. Mimeo. Department of Social and Policy Sciences, University of Bath.

Gough, I. and McGregor, J. A. (eds.) (2007). Wellbeing in Developing Countries, Cambridge: Cambridge University Press.

Gough, I. and G. Wood with A. Barrientos, P. Bevan, P. Davis, and G. Room (2004). Insecurity and Welfare Regimes in Asia, Africa and Latin America: Social Policy in Development Contexts. Cambridge: Cambridge University Press.

Guillaumont, P. (2009). *Caught in a Trap, Identifying the Least Developed Countries*, Paris: FERDI.

Haggard, S. and R. Kaufman (2008). *Development, Democracy, and Welfare States*. Princeton, NJ: Princeton University Press.

Hall, P. A. and D. W. Soskice (2001). *Varieties of Capitalism: The Institutional Foundations of Comparative Advantage*. Oxford: Oxford University Press.

Halter, D., M. Oechslin, and J. Zweimuller (2014). 'Inequality and Growth: The Neglected Time Dimension', *Journal of Economic Growth* 19: 81–104.

Hanmer, L. and F. Naschold (2001). 'Attaining the International Development Targets: Will Growth Be Enough?' *Development Policy Review* 18: 11–36.

Harris, J. R. and M. P. Todaro (1970). 'Migration, Unemployment and Development: A Two-Sector Analysis', *American Economic Review* 60: 126–42.

Harrison, A., J. McLaren, and M. McMillan (2011). 'Recent Perspectives on Trade and Inequality', *Annual Review of Economics* 3(1): 261–89.

Harriss, J. (2007). 'Bringing Politics back into Poverty Analysis: Why Understanding Social Relations Matters More for Policy on Chronic Poverty than Measurement'. Chronic Poverty Research Centre (CPRC) Working Paper. Manchester: CPRC.

Harriss-White, B. (2005). 'Poverty and Capitalism'. Queen Elizabeth House (QEH) Working Paper 13. Oxford: QEH.

Harttgen, K. and S. Klasen (2010). 'Fragility and MDG Progress: How Useful Is the Fragility Concept?' European University Institute Working Paper 2010/20. San Domenico di Fiesole (FI), Italy: Robert Schuman Centre For Advanced Studies.

Hellier, J. and S. Lambrecht (2012). 'Inequality, Growth and Welfare: The Main Links'. Society for the Study of Economic Inequality (ECINEQ) Working Paper 258. Verona, Italy: ECINEQ.

Hicks, N. and P. Streeten (1979). 'Indicators of Development: The Search for a Basic Needs Yardstick', *World Development* 7(6): 567–80.

Hills, J. and K. Stewart (2005). *A More Equal Society? New Labour, Poverty, Inequality and Exclusion*, 1st ed. Bristol: Policy Press.

Hirschman, A. (1958). *The Strategy of Economic Development*, New Haven CT: Yale University.

Hirschman, A. (1963). *Journeys Toward Progress*. New York: Twentieth Century Fund.

Hulme, D. (2013). 'Poverty in Development Thought: Symptoms or Causes... Synthesis or Uneasy Compromise?' in B. Currie-Alder, R. Kanbur, D. Malone, and R. Mehora (eds) *International Development: Ideas, Experience, and Prospects*, Oxford: Oxford University Press, 81–97.

Hulme, D. (2015). *Global Poverty*, London: Routledge.

Hulme, D., K. Moore, and A. Shepherd (2001). 'Chronic Poverty: Meanings and Analytical Frameworks'. CPRC Working Paper 2. Chronic Poverty Research Centre. http://www.chronicpoverty.org/pdfs/02Hulme_et_al.pdf (accessed 13 March 2015).

ILO (2015). *World Employment Social Outlook*. ILO: Geneva.

IMF (2011). *Revenue Mobilization in Developing Countries*. Washington DC: IMF.

IMF (2014). *World Economic Outlook (WEO)*. Washington DC: IMF.

Inklaar, R. and D. Rao (2014). 'Cross-Country Income Levels over Time: Did the Developing World suddenly Become much Richer?' Groningen Growth and Development Centre (GGDC) Research Memorandum. The Netherlands: University of Groningen.

International Comparison Program (ICP) (2014a). *Purchasing Power Parities and Real Expenditures of World Economies: Summary of Results and Findings of the 2011 International Comparison Program*, Washington DC: World Bank.

International Comparison Program (ICP) (2014b). *Purchasing Power Parities and the Real Size of World Economies: A Comprehensive Report of the 2011 International Comparison Program*, Washington DC: World Bank.

International Labour Organization (ILO) (1977). *Meeting Basic Needs: Strategies for Eradicating Mass Poverty and Unemployment*, Geneva: ILO.

International Labour Organization (ILO) (1976). *Employment, Growth and Basic Needs: A One-world Problem*, Geneva: ILO.

Ioannou, I. and G. Serafeim (2012). 'What Drives Corporate Social Performance? The Role of Nation-level Institutions', *Journal of International Business Studies*, 43(9): 834–64.

Jerven, M. (2013). *Poor Numbers: How We Are Misled by African Development Statistics and What to Do about It*, Ithaca NY: Cornell University Press.

Jolliffe, D. and E. Prydz (2015). 'Global Poverty Goals and Prices: How Purchasing Power Parity Matters'. World Bank Policy Research Working Paper. Washington DC: World Bank.

Judge, W., S. Fainshmidt, and J. Brown (2014). 'Which Model of Capitalism best Delivers both Wealth and Equality?' *Journal of International Business Studies* 45: 363–86.

Kabeer, N., C. Piza, and L. Taylor (2012). 'What Are the Economic Impacts of Conditional Cash Transfer Programmes? A Systematic Review of the Evidence (Technical Report)'. London: EPPI-Centre, Social Science Research Unit, Institute of Education, University of London.

Kakwani, N. and E. Pernia (2000). 'What Is Pro-Poor Growth?' *Asian Development Review: Studies of Asian and Pacific Economic Issues* 18(1): 1–16.

Kaldor, N. (1955–6). 'Alternative Theories of Distribution', *The Review of Economic Studies* 23(2): 83–100.

Kalwij, A. and A. Verschoor (2007). 'Not by Growth Alone: The Role of the Distribution of Income in Regional Diversity in Poverty Reduction', *European Economic Review* 51(4): 805–29.

Kanbur, R. (1999). 'The Strange Case of the Washington Consensus: A Brief Note on John Williamson's "What Should The Bank Think About The Washington Consensus?"' Mimeo. Ithaca NY: Cornell University.

Kanbur, R. (2005). *Growth, Inequality and Poverty: Some Hard Questions*, New York: Cornell University.

Kanbur, R. (2011). 'Does Kuznets Still Matter?' Mimeo. Ithaca NY: Cornell University.

Kanbur, R. and A. Sumner (2012). 'Poor Countries or Poor People? Development Assistance and the New Geography of Global Poverty', *Journal of International Development* 24(6): 686–95.

Kapur, D., J. P. Lewis, and R. Webb (1997). *The World Bank: Its First Half Century*, Washington DC: Brookings Institution.

Karayalcin, C. and K. McCollister (2005). 'Income Distribution, Sovereign Debt, and Public Investment', *Economics & Politics* 17(3): 351–65.

Karver, J., C. Kenny, and A. Sumner (2012). 'MDGs 2.0: What Goals, Targets, and Timeframe?' Center for Global Development (CGD) Working Paper. Washington DC: CGD.

Kaufmann, D. and A. Kraay (2015). 'World Governance Indicators', http://info.worldbank.org/governance/wgi/index.aspx#home (accessed 1 August 2015).

Kaul, I., I. Grunberg, and M. A. Stern (1999). 'Defining Global Public Goods', in I. Kaul, I. Grunberg, and M. A. Stern (eds) *Global Public Goods: International Cooperation in the 21st Century*, New York: UNDP, 2–9.

Keefer, P. and S. Knack (2002). 'Polarization, Politics and Property Rights: Links between Inequality and Growth', *Public Choice* 111(1–2): 127–54.

Khan, A., Arif Naveed, Emma Samman, Moizza Binat Sarwar, and Chris Hoy (2015). *Progress under Scrutiny: Poverty Reduction in Pakistan*. London: ODI.

Kharas, H. (2010). 'The Emerging Middle Class in Developing Countries'. OECD Development Center Working Paper 285. Washington DC: Brookings Institution.

Kindleberger, C. P. (1967). *Europe's Postwar Growth*, Cambridge MA: Harvard University Press.

Kirkpatrick, C. and A. Barrientos (2004). 'The Lewis Model after 50 Years', *The Manchester School* 72(6): 679–90.

Klasen, S. (2010a). 'Levels and Trends in Absolute Poverty in the World: What We Know and What We Don't'. Paper prepared for the International Association for Research in Income and Wealth, St. Gallen, Switzerland, August 22–28.

Klasen, S. (2010b). 'Measuring and Monitoring Inclusive Growth: Multiple Definitions, Open Questions, and Some Constructive Proposals'. Asian Development Bank (ADB) Sustainable Development 12. Working Paper Series. Manila: ADB.

Knack, S. and P. Keefer (1995). 'Institutions and Economic Performance: Cross-country Tests Using Alternative Institutional Measures', *Economics & Politics* 7(3): 207–27.

Knowles, S. (2005). 'Inequality and Economic Growth: The Empirical Relationship Reconsidered in Light of Comparable Data', *Journal of Development Studies* 41(1): 135–59.

Kojima, M. and D. Koplow (2015). 'Fossil Fuel Subsidies: Approaches and Valuation'. World Bank Working Paper. Washington DC: World Bank.

Kraay, A. (2006). 'When Is Growth Pro-Poor? Evidence from a Panel of Countries', *Journal of Development Economics* 80: 198–227.

Kuznets, S. (1955). 'Economic Growth and Income Inequality', *American Economic Review* 45(1): 1–28.

Kuznets, S. (1963). 'Quantitative Aspects of the Economic Growth of Nations: VIII, Distribution and Income by Size', *Economic Development and Cultural Change* 11(2): 1–80.

Leibenstein, Harvey (1957). *Economic Backwardness and Economic Growth*, New York: John Wiley and Sons.

Lewis, W. A. (1954). 'Economic Development with Unlimited Supplies of Labour', *The Manchester School* 22(2): 139–91.

Lewis, W. A. (1969). *Aspects of Tropical Trade, 1883–1965*, Stockholm: Almqvist and Wicksell.

Lewis, W. A. (1972). 'Reflections on Unlimited Labour', in L. E. diMarco (ed.) *International Economics and Development (Essays in Honour of Raoul Prebisch)*, New York: Academic Press, 75–96.

Lewis, W. A. (1976). 'Development and Distribution', in A. Cairncross and M. Puri (eds) *Employment, Income Distribution and Development Strategy: Essays in Honour of Hans Singer*, London: Macmillan, 26–42.

Lewis, W. A. (1979). 'The Dual Economy Revisited', *The Manchester School*, 47(3): 211–29.

Lewis, O. (1959). *Five Families: Mexican Case Studies in the Culture of Poverty*, New York: Basic Books.

Lewis, O. (1965). *The Children of Sanchez*, Harmondsworth: Penguin.

Li, H. and H.-f. Zou (1998). 'Income Inequality Is not Harmful for Growth: Theory and Evidence', *Review of Development Economics* 2(3): 318–34.

Lindert, P. (2000). 'Three Centuries of Inequality in Britain and America', in A. B. Atinson and F. Bourguignon (eds) *Handbook of Income Distribution*, i, Amsterdam: Elsevier, 167–216.

Lindert, P. and Williamson, J. (2001). Does Globalization Make the World More Unequal? National Bureau of Economic Research (NBER) Working Paper. Cambridge MA: NBER.

List, J. and C. Gallet (1999). 'The Kuznets Curve: What Happens after the Inverted-U?' *Review of Development Economics* 3: 200–6.

Loayza, N. and C. Raddatz (2010). 'The Composition of Growth Matters for Poverty Alleviation', *Journal of Development Economics* 93(1): 137–51.

Lopez, J. (2005). 'Pro-Poor Growth: A Review of What We Know (and What We Don't)'. Mimeo. Washington DC: World Bank.

López-Calva, Luis F. and N. Lustig (2010). 'Explaining the Decline in Inequality in Latin America: Technological Change, Educational Upgrading, and Democracy' in *Declining Inequality in Latin America: A Decade of Progress*, Brookings Institution and UNDP, 1–24.

López-Calva, Luis F. and E. Ortiz-Juarez (2014). 'A Vulnerability Approach to the Definition of the Middle Class', *The Journal of Economic Inequality* 12(1): 23–47.

Lustig, N. (2012). 'Fiscal Policy and Income Redistribution in Latin America: Challenging the Conventional Wisdom'. Tulane University Economics Working Paper 1124. New Orleans: Tulane University.

Lustig, N., L. Lopez-Calva, and E. Ortiz-Juarez (2012). 'Declining Inequality in Latin America in the 2000s: The Cases of Argentina, Brazil, and Mexico', *World Development* 44: 129–41.

Mansuri, G. and V. Rao (2011). 'Localizing Development: Does Participation Work?' World Bank Policy Research Report, draft version. Washington DC: World Bank.

Maskin, E. (2015). 'Why Haven't Global Markets Reduced Inequality in Emerging Economies?' *World Bank Economic Review* 29(supplement 1): S48–S52.

Mavrotas, G. (ed.) (2010). *Foreign Aid for Development: Issues, Challenges, and the New Agenda*, Oxford: Oxford University Press.

Mawdsley, E. (2012). *From Recipients to Donors: Emerging Powers and the Changing Development Landscape*, London: Zed Books.

Mazundar, D. (2012). 'Decreasing Poverty and Increasing Inequality in India', in *Tackling Inequalities in Brazil, China, India and South Africa: The Role of Labour Market and Social Policies*, Paris: OECD Publishing.

McGranahan, D., E. Pizarro, and C. Richard (1985). *Measurement and Analysis of Socio-Economic Development: An Enquiry into International Indicators of Development and Quantitative Interrelations of Social and Economic Components of Development*, Geneva: United Nations Research Institute for Social Development (UNRISD).

McKinley, T. (2010). Inclusive Growth Criteria and Indicators: An Inclusive Growth Index for Diagnosis of Country Progress. ADB: Manila.

Meltzer, A. G. and S. F. Richards (1981). 'A Rational Theory of the Size of Government', *Journal of Political Economy* 89(5): 914–27.

Milanovic, B. (2005). 'Can We Discern the Effect of Globalization on Income Distribution? Evidence from Household Surveys', *World Bank Economic Review* 19(1): 21–44.

Milanovic, B. (2012). 'Global Inequality Recalculated and Updated: The Effect of New PPP Estimates on Global Inequality and 2005 Estimates', *Journal of Economic Inequality* 10(1): 1–18.

Misselhorn, M. and S. Klasen (2006). 'Determinants of the Growth Semi-Elasticity of Poverty Reduction', Proceedings of the German Development Economics Conference, Berlin.

Moore, M. (2001). *Types of Political Systems: A Practical Framework for DFID Staff*, London: DFID.

Moore, M. (2007). 'How Does Taxation Affect the Quality of Governance?' IDS Working Paper 280. Brighton: IDS.

Morris, D. (1979). *Measuring the Condition of the World's Poor: The Physical Quality of Life Index*, London: Cass.

Moser, C. O. N. (1998). 'The Asset Vulnerability Framework: Reassessing Urban Poverty Reduction Strategies', *World Development* 26(1): 1–19.

Mosley, P. (2004). 'Severe Poverty and Growth: A Macro-Micro Analysis'. Chronic Poverty Research Centre (CPRC) Working Paper 51. Manchester: CPRC.

Mosley, P., J. Hudson, and A. Verschoor (2004). 'Aid, Poverty Reduction and the New Conditionality', *Economic Journal* 114: 214–43.

Muinelo-Gallo, L. and O. Roca-Sagales (2011). 'Economic Growth and Inequality: The Role of Fiscal Policies', *Australian Economic Papers* 50: 74–97.

Narayan, D. et al. (1999). *Voices of the Poor: Crying out for Change*. Washington DC: World Bank.

Nel, P. (2006). 'The Return of Inequality', *Third World Quarterly* 27(4): 689–706.

Nel, P. (2008). *The Politics of Economic Inequality in Developing Countries*, New York: Palgrave Macmillan.

Nelson, R. (1956). 'A Theory of the Low-Level Equilibrium Trap in Underdeveloped Economies', *American Economic Review* 46(5): 894–908.

Nissanke, M. and E. Thorbecke (2006). 'Channels and Policy Debate in the Globalization–Inequality–Poverty Nexus', *World Development* 34(8): 1338–60.

North, D. C. (1990). *Institutions, Institutional Change and Economic Performance*. New York: Cambridge University Press.

Nussbaum, M. (2000). *Women and Human Development: The Capabilities Approach*, Cambridge: Cambridge University Press.

Ocampo, J. (2003). *Capital-Account and Countercyclical Prudential Regulation in Developing Countries*. Santiago: CEPAL.

Ocampo, J. and S. Griffith-Jones (2007). 'A Countercyclical Framework for a Development-friendly International Financial Architecture', DESA Working Paper 39, UNDESA.

OECD (2005). 'The Politics of Policy Coherence', in *Fostering Development in a Global Economy: A Whole of Government Perspective*, OECD, Paris: OECD.

OECD (2010). *Resource Flows to Fragile and Conflict Affected States*, Paris: OECD.

OECD (2011). *Latin American Economic Outlook: How Middle Class Is Latin America?* Paris: OECD Development Center.

OECD (2013). *Fragile States 2013: Resource Flows and Trends in a Shifting World*, Paris: OECD.

OECD-DAC (2003). *Harmonising Donor Practices for Effective Aid Delivery*, Paris: OECD.

Ohno, K. (2009). 'Avoiding the Middle Income Trap: Renovating Industrial Policy Formulation in Vietnam', *ASEAN Economic Bulletin* 26(1): 25–43.

Ostry, J., A. Berg, and C. Tsangarides (2014). 'Redistribution, Inequality, and Growth'. International Monetary Fund (IMF) Staff Discussion Note. Washington DC: IMF.

Ottersen, T., A. Kamath, S. Moon, and J.-A. Røttingen (2014). 'Development Assistance for Health: Quantitative Allocation Criteria and Contribution Norms'. Chatham House: Centre On Global Health Security Working Group Papers. London: Chatham House.

Oxford Poverty and Human Development Initiative (OPHI) (2014). *Multidimensional Poverty Data Set*, Oxford: OPHI.

Palma, J. G. (2006). 'Globalizing Inequality: 'Centrifugal' and 'Centripetal' Forces at Work'. DESA Working Paper 35. New York: UN Department of Economic and Social Affairs.

Palma, J. G. (2011). 'Homogeneous Middles vs. Heterogeneous Tails, and the End of the "Inverted-U": The Share of the Rich Is What It's all about', *Development and Change* 42(1): 87–153.

Palma, G. (2013). 'Has the Income Share of the Middle and Upper-Middle Been Stable over Time, or Is its Current Homogeneity across the World the Outcome of a Process of Convergence? The 'Palma Ratio' Revisited'. Cambridge Working Papers in Economics. Cambridge: University of Cambridge.

Palma, G. (2014a). 'Has the Income Share of the Middle and Upper-middle Been Stable around the "50/50 rule", or Has It Converged towards that Level? The "Palma Ratio" Revisited', *Development and Change* 45(6): 1416–48.

Palma, J. G. (2014b). 'Why Is Inequality so Unequal across the World? Could It Be that Every Nation Gets the Inequality It Deserves?' in J. Stiglitz and K. Basu (eds)

Proceedings of IEA Roundtable on Shared Prosperity and Growth. Washington DC: World Bank.

Perraton, P. (2005). 'Review Article: Joseph Stiglitz's *Globalisation and its Discontents*', *Journal of International Development* 16(6): 897–906.

Perotti, R. (1996). 'Growth, Income Distribution and Democracy: What the Data Say', *Journal of Economic Growth* 1(2): 149–87.

Persson, T. and G. Tabellini (1994). 'Is Inequality Harmful for Growth? Theory and Evidence', *American Economic Review* 84: 600–21.

Picciotto, R. (2005). 'The Evaluation of Policy Coherence for Development', *Evaluation* 11(3): 311–30.

Piketty, T. (1995). 'Social Mobility and Redistributive Politics', *Quarterly Journal of Economics* 1103: 551–84.

Piketty T., G. Postel-Vinay, and J. L. Rosenthal (2006). 'Wealth Concentration in a Developing Economy: Paris and France, 1807–1994', *American Economic Review*, 96(1): 236–56.

Piketty, T. and G. Zucman (2013). 'Capital Is Back: Wealth–Income Ratios in Rich Countries 1700–2010', *Quarterly Journal of Economics*, 129(3): 1155–210.

Pogge, T. (2013). 'Poverty, Hunger, and Cosmetic Progress', in M. Langford, A. Sumner, and A. Yamin (eds) *The Millennium Development Goals and Human Rights*, New York: Cambridge University Press, 209–31.

Polanyi, K. (1957). *The Great Transformation: The Political and Economic Origins of Our Time*. Boston, MA: Beacon Press.

Pritchett, P. (2006). 'Who Is Not Poor? Dreaming of a World truly Free of Poverty', *World Bank Res Obs* (Spring) 21(1): 1–23.

Ranieri, R. and R. Ramos (2013). *Inclusive Growth: Building Up A Concept*. Brasilia: International Policy Centre for Inclusive Growth (IPC-IG).

Ranis, G. (2004). 'Human Development and Economic Growth'. Yale University Economic Growth Center Discussion Paper 887. New Haven CT: Yale University.

Ranis, Gustav and Frances Stewart (1999). 'V-Goods and the Role of the Urban Informal Sector in Development', *Economic Development and Cultural Change* 47(2): 259–88.

Rao, R. (2006). 'On "Inequality Traps" and Development Policy'. World Bank Other Operational Studies 9588, Washington DC: World Bank.

Rauniyar, G. and R. Kanbur (2010). *Inclusive Development: Two Papers on Conceptualization, Application, and the ADB Perspective*. Manila: Asian Development Bank (ADB).

Ravallion, M. (1995). 'Growth and Poverty: Evidence for Developing Countries in the 1980s', *Economic Letters* 48: 411–17.

Ravallion, M. (1997). 'Can High-Inequality Developing Countries Escape Absolute Poverty?' *Economic Letters* 56: 51–7.

Ravallion, M. (2001). 'Growth, Inequality and Poverty: Looking behind the Averages', *World Development* 29(11): 1803–15.

Ravallion, M. (2002). 'How Not to Count the Poor? A Reply to Reddy and Pogge'. Mimeo. Washington DC: World Bank.

Ravallion, M. (2004). 'Measuring Pro-Poor Growth: A Primer'. World Bank Working Paper 3242. Washington DC: World Bank.

Ravallion, M. (2005a). 'Inequality Is Bad for the Poor'. World Bank Policy Research Working Paper 3677. Washington DC: World Bank.

Ravallion, M. (2005b). 'Looking beyond Averages in the Trade and Poverty Debate'. World Bank Working Paper 3461. Washington DC: World Bank.

Ravallion, M. (2008). 'A Reply to Reddy and Pogge', in S. Anand, P. Segal, and J. Stiglitz (eds) *Debates on the Measurement of Poverty*, Oxford: Oxford University Press, 86–101.

Ravallion, M. (2009). 'Do Poorer Countries have less Capacity for Redistribution?' Policy Research Working Paper 5046. Washington DC: World Bank.

Ravallion, M. (2010a). 'The Developing World's Bulging (but Vulnerable) "Middle Class"'. Policy Research Working Paper 4816. Washington DC: World Bank.

Ravallion, M. (2010b). 'Price Levels and Economic Growth: Making Sense of the PPP Changes between ICP Rounds'. World Bank Policy Research Working Paper. Washington DC: World Bank.

Ravallion, M. (2013). 'The Idea of Antipoverty Policy'. National Bureau of Economic Research (NBER) Working Paper. Cambridge MA: NBER.

Ravallion, M. (2014a). 'India's Puzzling New PPP'. Center for Global Development (CGD) Blog, 5 August. http://www.cgdev.org/blog/india's-puzzling-new-pp (accessed 3 March 2015).

Ravallion, M. (2014b). 'An Exploration of the International Comparison Program's New Global Economic Landscape'. National Bureau of Economic Research (NBER) Working Paper. Cambridge MA: NBER.

Ravallion, M. and S. Chen (1996). 'Data in Transition: Assessing Rural Living', *China Economic Review* 7: 23–56.

Ravallion, M. and S. Chen (1997). 'What Can New Survey Data Tell Us about Recent Changes in Distribution and Poverty', *World Bank Economic Review* 11(2): 357–82.

Ravallion, M. and S. Chen (2015). 'Rising Food Prices in Poor Countries: A New Clue to Those Puzzling PPP Revisions'. Center for Global Development (CGD) Blog, 27 January. http://www.cgdev.org/blog/rising-food-prices-poor-countries-new-clue-those-puzzling-ppp-revisions (accessed 3 March 2015).

Ravallion, M. and G. Datt (1999). 'When Is Growth Pro-Poor? Evidence from the Diverse Experiences of India's States'. World Bank Working Paper 2263. Washington DC: World Bank.

Ravallion, M. and G. Datt (2002). 'Why Has Economic Growth Been More ProPoor in Some States of India than Others?' Journal of Development Economics 68(2): 381–400.

Ravallion, R., S. Chen, and P. Sangraula (2008). 'Dollar-A-Day Revisited'. World Bank Working Paper. Washington DC: World Bank.

Redding, G. (2005). 'The Thick Description and Comparison of Societal Systems of Capitalism', *Journal of International Business Studies*, 36(2): 123–55.

Reddy, S. and T. Pogge (2002). 'How Not to Count the Poor (Version 3.0)'. Mimeo. New York: Barnard College.

Reddy, S. and T. Pogge (2005). 'How Not to Count the Poor (version 6.2)'. Mimeo. New York: Barnard College.

Rehme, G. (2001). 'Redistribution of Personal Income, Education and Economic Performance across Countries'. Mimeo. Darmstadt, Germany: Technische Universität Darmstadt.

Rodrik, D. (2002). 'After Neoliberalism, What?' Paper presented at 'Alternatives to Neoliberalism', Washington DC, May 23.

Rodrik, D. (2015). 'Premature Deindustrialization'. NBER Working Paper No. 20935. Cambridge, MA: NBER.

Roine, J. and Waldenström, D. (2014). 'Long-run Trends in the Distribution of Income and Wealth'. IZA (Institute for the Study of Labour) Discussion Paper No. 8157. Bonn: IZA.

Rosenstein-Rodan, P. (1943). 'Problems of Industrialisation in Eastern and Southeastern Europe', *The Economic Journal* 53: 202–11.

Rostow, W. (1960). *The Stages of Economic Growth: A Non-Communist Manifesto*, Cambridge: Cambridge University Press.

Ruggeri, C., Ruhi Saith Laderchi, and Frances Stewart (2003). 'Does it Matter that We Don't Agree on the Definition of Poverty? A Comparison of Four Approaches'. Queen Elizabeth House (QEH) Working Paper. Oxford: QEH.

Rutstein, S. and G. Rojas (2006). *Guide to DHS Statistics*, Calverton MD: ORC Macro.

Sachs, J. D. (2005). *The End of Poverty: Economic Possibilities for Our Time*, New York: Penguin.

Sarkar, J. (2005). 'Mortality, Fertility, and Persistent Income Inequality'. 75th Southern Economic Association Conference, Washington DC.

Schröder, M. (2013). Integrating Varieties of Capitalism and Welfare State Research: A Unified Typology of Capitalisms. New York: Palgrave Macmillan.

Schultz, T. W. (1953). *The Economic Organization of Agriculture*, New York: McGraw-Hill.

Seers, D. (1963). 'The Limitations of the Special Case', *Bulletin of the Oxford Institute of Economics and Statistics* 25(2): 77–98; reprinted in K. Martin and J. Knapp (eds) *The Teaching of Development Economics: Its Position in the Present State of Knowledge* (1967), London: Frank Cass, 1–27.

Seers, D. (1969). 'The Meaning of Development', *International Development Review* 11: 2–6.

Seers, D. (1972). 'What Are We Trying to Measure?' *Journal of Development Studies* 8(3): 21–36; reprinted in N. Baster (ed.) *Measuring Development: The Role and Adequacy of Development Indicators* (1972), London: Frank Cass, 21–36.

Sen, A. (1981). *Poverty and Famines: An Essay on Entitlement and Deprivation*, Oxford: Clarendon Press.

Sen, A. (1983). 'Poor, Relatively Speaking', *Oxford Economic Papers*, New Series, 35(2): 153–69.

Sen, A. (1992). *Inequality Reexamined*, Cambridge MA: Harvard University Press.

Sen, A. K. (1999). *Development as Freedom*, Oxford: Oxford University Press.

Sen, A. K. (1997). *On Economic Inequality*, Oxford: Oxford University Press.

Sharkh, M. A. and I. Gough (2009). 'Global Welfare Regimes: A Cluster Analysis'. CDDRL Working papers, no. 91. Stanford CA: CDDRL.

Sharma, M., G. Inchauste, and J. Feng (2011). *Rising Inequality with High Growth and Falling Poverty: An Eye on East Asia and Pacific*, Washington DC: World Bank.

Singh, A. (1977). UK industry and the world economy: A case of de-industrialisation? Cambridge Journal of Economics. 1 (2): 113–36.

Smith, B. and K. Moore (2006). 'Intergenerational Transmission of Poverty in Sub-Saharan Africa'. Chronic Poverty Research Centre (CRPC) Working Paper 59. Manchester/London: CRPC.

Soares, S., R. Guerreiro Osório, F. Veras Soares, M. Medeiros, and E. Zepeda (2009). 'Conditional Cash Transfers in Brazil, Chile and Mexico: Impacts Upon Inequality', *Estudios Económicos* 1: 207–24.

Solt, F. (2014). *The Standardized World Income Inequality Database Version 5.0*. University of Iowa. http://myweb.uiowa.edu/fsolt/swiid/swiid.html (accessed 3 March 2015).

Son, H. and N. Kakwani (2003). 'Poverty Reduction: Do Initial Conditions Matter?' Mimeo. Washington DC: World Bank.

Standard and Poor's (2015). 'Sovereign Ratings', http://www.standardandpoors.com/en_EU/web/guest/home (accessed 1 August 2015).

Standing, G. (2011). *The Precariat: The New Dangerous Class*, London: Bloomsbury Academic.

Stewart, F. (2000). 'Income Distribution and Development'. Queen Elizabeth House (QEH) Working Paper. Oxford University. Oxford: QEH.

Stewart, F., R. Saith, and B. Harriss-White (eds) (2007). *Defining Poverty in the Developing World*, Basingstoke: Palgrave Macmillan.

Stiglitz, J. (1998a). 'More Instruments and Broader Goals: Moving towards the Post-Washington Consensus'. UNU WIDER Annual Lecture, Helsinki, 7 January.

Stiglitz, J. (1998b). 'Towards a New Paradigm for Development: Strategies, Policies and Processes'. Prebisch Lecture at UNCTAD, Geneva, 19 October.

Stiglitz, J. (2005). 'The Post Washington Consensus'. Initiative for Policy Dialogue Working Paper. Columbia NY: Columbia University.

Stiglitz, J. E., A. Sen, and J.-P. Fitoussi (2009). 'Report by the Commission on the Measurement of Economic Performance and Social Progress'. Paris. http://www.insee.fr/fr/publications-et-ser vices/dossiers_web/stiglitz/doc-commission/RAPPORT_anglais.pdf (accessed 1 January 2015).

Streeck, W. and K. Yamamura (2001). *The Origins of Nonliberal Capitalism: Germany and Japan in Comparison*. Ithaca NY: Cornell University Press.

Streeten, P. (1959). 'Unbalanced Growth', *Oxford Economic Papers* 11(2): 167–90.

Streeten, P. (1984). 'Basic Needs: Some Unsettled Questions', *World Development* 12(9): 973–80.

Sumner, A. (2010). 'Global Poverty and the New Bottom Billion: What if Three-Quarters of the World's Poor Live in Middle-Income Countries?' Institute of Development Studies (IDS) Working Paper 349. Brighton: IDS.

Sumner, A. (2012a). 'The New Face of Poverty: How Has the Composition of Poverty in Low Income and Lower Middle-Income Countries (excluding China) Changed since the 1990s?' Institute of Development Studies (IDS) Working Paper 408. Brighton: IDS.

Sumner, A. (2012b). 'Where Do the Poor Live?' *World Development* 40(5): 865–77.

Sumner, A. (2012c). 'Where Do the World's Poor Live? A New Update'. Institute of Development Studies (IDS) Working Paper 393. Brighton: IDS.

Sumner, A. (2012d). 'Poverty, Vulnerability and Class', *Public Administration and Development* 32(4–5): 444–54.

Sumner, A. (2013a). 'Global Poverty, Aid, and Middle-Income Countries: Are the Country Classifications Moribund or Is Global Poverty in the Process of "Nationalizing"?' United Nations University, World Institute of Development Economics Research (UNU-WIDER) Working Paper. Helsinki: UNU-WIDER.

Sumner, A. (2013b). 'Poverty, Politics and Aid: Is a Reframing of Global Poverty Approaching?' *Third World Quarterly* 34(3): 357–77.

Sumner, A. (2013c). 'Who Are the Poor? New Regional Estimates of the Composition of Education and Health "Poverty" by Spatial and Social Inequalities'. Overseas Development Institute (ODI) Working Paper. London: ODI.

Sumner, A. (2013d). 'Why Does National Inequality Matter?'. In *Humanity Divided: Confronting Inequality in Developing Countries*. New York: UNDP.

Sumner, A. (2016). Why are some people poor? European Journal of Development Research 28(2): 130–142.

Sumner, A. and R. Mallet (2012). *The Future of Foreign Aid*. Basingstoke: Palgrave Macmillan.

Sumner, A. and S. Tezanos (2014). 'How Has the Developing World Changed since the 1990s? A Dynamic and Multidimensional Taxonomy of Developing Countries'. Center for Global Development (CGD) Working Paper. Washington DC: CGD.

Sumner, A. and M. Tiwari (2009). *After 2015: International Development Policy at a Crossroads*, Basingstoke: Palgrave Macmillan.

Sumner, A., A. Yusuf, and Y. Suara (2014). 'Prospects for the Poor: A Set of Poverty Measures Based on the Probability of Remaining Poor (or Not) in Indonesia'. Center for Economics and Development Studies Working Paper. Bandung: Center for Economics and Development Studies, Department of Economics,Padjadjaran University, Indonesia.

Suryahadi, Asep, Gracia Hadiwidjaja, and Sudarno Sumarto (2012). 'Economic Growth and Poverty Reduction in Indonesia before and after the Asian Financial Crisis', *Bulletin of Indonesian Economic Studies* 48(2): 209-27.

Svensson, J. (1998). 'Investment, Property Rights and Political Instability: Theory and Evidence', *European Economic Review* 42: 1317-42.

Tezanos, S. and A. Sumner (2013). 'Revisiting the Meaning of Development: A Multidimensional Taxonomy of Developing Countries', *Journal of Development Studies* 49(12): 1728-45.

Thaler, R. and Cass Sunstein (2008). *Nudge: Improving Decisions about Health, Wealth, and Happiness*, New Haven CT: Yale University Press.

Thirtle, C., I. Irz, L. Lin, V. McKenzie-Hill, and S. Wiggins (2001). 'The Relationship between Changes in Agricultural Productivity and the Incidence of Poverty in Developing Countries'. Department for International Development Report No.7946. London: Department for International Development.

Timmer, P. (1997). 'How well Did the Poor Connect to the Growth Process?' Consulting Assistance on Economic Reform II Discussion Paper 17. Harvard: Harvard Institute of International Development.

Tinbergen, J., (1975). *Income Difference: Recent Research*. Amsterdam: North-Holland Publishing Company.

Torche, F. and L. F. López-Calva (2012). 'Stability and Vulnerability of the Latin American Middle Class', UNU-WIDER Working Paper. Helsinki: UNU-WIDER.

Torgler, B. (2005). 'Tax Morale in Latin America', *Public Choice* 122(1/2): 133-57.

Townsend, P. (1979). *Poverty in the United Kingdom*, London: Allen Lane and Penguin Books.

Tribe M., F. Nixson, and A. Sumner (2010). *Economics and Development Studies*, London: Routledge.

United Nations (UN) (1995). *World Summit for Social Development Programme of Action—Chapter 2*. http://www.un.org/esa/socdev/wssd/text-version/agreements/poach2.htm (accessed 3 March 2015).

United Nations (UN) (2014). *The MDGs Report 2014*, New York: UN.

United Nations Children's Fund (UNICEF) (2007). *Working Paper of the Task Force on UNICEF Engagement in Countries with Low Child Mortality*. New York: UNICEF.

United Nations Children's Fund (UNICEF) (2011). *Boys and Girls in the Life Cycle*, New York: UNICEF.

United Nations Development Programme (UNDP) (1990–present). *Human Development Report*, New York: UNDP.

United Nations Development Programme (UNDP) (2010). *Human Development Report*, New York: UNDP.

United Nations Research Institute on Social Development (UNRISD) (1970). *Contents and Measurement of Socioeconomic Development*, Geneva: UNRISD.

Wade, R. (1990). *Governing the Market: Economic Theory and the Role of Government in East Asian Industrialization*. Princeton: Princeton University Press.

Wade, R. (2005). 'Does Inequality Matter?' *Challenge* 48(5): 12–38.

Weber, M. (1978). *Economy and Society: An Outline of Interpretive Sociology*, Berkley CA: University of California Press.

Weimer, J. and J. Pape (1999). 'A Taxonomy of Systems of Corporate Governance', *Corporate Governance: An International Review* 7(2): 152–66.

White, H. and E. Anderson (2001). 'Growth versus Distribution: Does the Pattern of Growth Matter?' *Development Policy Review* 19(3): 267–89.

Whitley, R. (1991). 'The Social Construction of Business Systems in East Asia', *Organization Studies* 12(1): 1–28.

Whitley, R. (1999). *Divergent Capitalisms: The Social Structuring and Change of Business Systems*. Oxford: Oxford University Press.

Williamson, J. (1990). 'What Washington Means by Policy Reform', in J. Williamson (ed.) *Latin American Adjustment: How Much Has Happened?* Washington DC: Institute for International Economics.

Witt, M. A. and G. Redding (2013). 'Asian Business Systems: Institutional Comparison, Clusters, and Implications for Varieties of Capitalism and Business Systems Theory', *Socio-Economic Review* 11(2): 265–300.

Wood, G. and I. Gough (2006). 'A Comparative Welfare Regime Approach to Global Social Policy', *World Development* 34: 1696–1712.

World Bank (1989). *Per Capita Income: Estimating Internationally Comparable Numbers*, Washington DC: World Bank.

World Bank (1990). *World Development Report*, Washington DC: World Bank.

World Bank (1993). *East Asia Miracle: Economic Growth and Public Policy*. Oxford: Oxford University Press.

World Bank (2008). *Commission on Growth and Development*, Washington DC: World Bank.

World Bank (2013a). *Ethiopia Economic Update: Laying the Foundation for Achieving Middle Income Status*, Washington DC: World Bank.

World Bank (2013b). *Harmonized List of Fragile Situations FY13*, Washington DC: World Bank.

World Bank (2014). *World Development Indicators*, Washington DC: World Bank.

World Bank (2015a). *World Development Indicators*, Washington DC: World Bank.

World Bank (2015b). *Country Classification: A Short History*. World Bank. http://data.wor ldbank.org/about/country-and-lending-groups (accessed 3 March 2015).

Wood, G. and I. Gough (2006). 'A Comparative Welfare Regime Approach to Global Social Policy', *World Development* 34(10): 1696–712.

Yamamura, K. and W. Streeck (eds) (2003). *The End of Diversity? Prospects of German and Japanese Capitalism*. Ithaca NY: Cornell University Press.

Yusuf, Arief A., Ahmad Komarulzaman, M. Purnagunawan, and Budy P. Resosudarmo (2013). 'Growth, Poverty, and Labor Market Rigidity in Indonesia: A General Equilibrium Investigation'. Working Paper in Economics and Development Studies 201304. Bandung: Department of Economics, Padjadjaran University.

Yusuf, Arief Anshory, and Budy P. Resosudarmo (2008). 'Mitigating Distributional Impact of Fuel Pricing Reform: The Indonesian Experience', *ASEAN Economic Bulletin* 25(1): 32–47.

■ INDEX

Tables and figures are indicated by an italic *t* and *f* following the page number.